THE GREATEST CENTURY
OF REFORMATION

The Reformation Society
Cape Town
South Africa

THE GREATEST CENTURY OF REFORMATION

by Dr Peter Hammond

Permission is hereby granted to any church, mission, magazine or periodical to reprint, or quote from, any portion of this publication on condition that the passage is quoted in context and that due acknowledgement of source be given.

Please also mail a copy of any article to: Frontline Fellowship
P.O. Box 74, Newlands, 7725 Cape Town, South Africa
or e-mail: admin@frontline.org.za

Scripture quotations taken from the Holy Bible,
King James Version and New King James Version,
Copyright © 1982 by Thomas Nelson, used with permission

Typesetting by Colin Newman
Cover Design by Daniela Hammond
First published 2006.
New Revised and Expanded edition 2017
Updated 2021
Copyright © 2021 by Peter Hammond
ISBN: 978-0-9946971-7-2

The Reformation Society
P O Box 74 Newlands 7725
Cape Town South Africa
Tel: (+27) 21 689 4480
info@ReformationSA.org
ReformationSA.org

Dedication

This book is dedicated to **Dr. R.C. Sproul** of St. Andrews Chapel,
Ligonier Ministries and Reformation Bible College.
His Reformation Trust books have faithfully promoted
the historic Reformed Christian Faith.
The Reformation Study Bible which he edited
has been an invaluable aid in discipling
pastors and missionaries throughout Africa
in returning to the Word of God as our ultimate authority
in all matters of faith and conduct.

The Church worldwide has been enriched, educated, equipped and empowered by the over 50 years of preaching, teaching and writing ministry of Dr. R.C. Sproul.

THE GREATEST CENTURY OF REFORMATION
by Dr Peter Hammond
CONTENTS

Forewords - by Rev. Phillip Kayser, Mike Evans, Dr. Fritz Haus, Dr. Shai Mulder,
Rev. Bill Bathman, Alison Shortridge, Dorothea Scarborough,
Rev. Mike O'Donovan, Pastor Mike Kiley and Dr. Martin Holdt   3
Introduction - Dr. Jay Grimstead   9
Preface   11

CHAPTER

1	A Century of Repression, Revolt and Reformation	13
2	Preparation for Reformation –Waldensians, Wycliffe, Anne of Bohemia, Hus, Gutenberg and Savonarola	35
3	Martin Luther - Captive to the Word of God	67
4	Ulrich Zwingli – The Reformer of Zürich	85
5	William Tyndale and the Battle for the Bible	95
6	Heinrich Bullinger – Consolidating the Reformation	103
7	Martin Bucer – The Reformer of Straßburg	107
8	Thomas Cranmer and the English Reformation	109
9	The Politicians Behind the English Reformation	117
10	Anne Askew – A Daughter of the Reformation	123
11	Bloody Mary and the Martyrs of the English Reformation	127
12	Philipp Melanchthon – The Teacher of Germany	133
13	Guillaume Farel - Fiery Debater and Evangelist	135
14	John Calvin - A Heart Aflame and a Mind Renewed	141
15	John Knox – and the Reformation in Scotland	151
16	Pierre Viret – French Evangelist and Reformer	167
17	Albrecht Dürer – Evangelist and Reformer in Art	169
18	How the Reformation Changed the Church	173
19	How the Reformation Changed the World	183
20	Luther's Practical Programme to Revive Your Prayer Life	199

APPENDIX

1	The People of the Reformation	205
2	Chronology of the Reformation	207
3	Reformation Calendar of Key Events and Dates	213
4	The Popes of Rome	221
5	Libel Against Luther	225
6	Did the Reformers Persecute the Anabaptists?	229
7	Some Roman Catholic Heresies and Inventions	233
8	Is Celebrating the Reformation Anti-Catholic?	237
9	The Challenge of Islam According to the Reformers	239
10	The Five Points of Calvinism	242
11	The Power of Printing	245
12	25 Steps You Can Take for Reformation Today	247
13	Reformation Key Contacts	249
14	Questions for Discussion	251
15	Map of the Reformation	261
16	Reformation Celebration with the Eurochor	262

Bibliography   275

The Greatest Century of Reformation

The Reformation Monument in Worms, Germany.

FOREWORDS

Dr. Peter Hammond's newly revised book *The Greatest Century of Reformation* is a gem. No, it is more than a gem; it is spiritual dynamite. It will be nearly impossible for a Christian to read this book without being stirred up to serve our Lord and Saviour Jesus Christ even more passionately, faithfully and consistently than he, or she, already has. It is not just a fantastic reference; it is a fantastic devotional read.

Like the best of the older historians, Peter does not just present facts; he applies them to God's glory and for the good of the Church. Our Providential History Festival has always been impressed with Peter's grasp of history and his ability to practically apply the lessons of history and he has not disappointed with this new book.

At times I was moved to tears by the testimonies of the past and at times I was moved to action, but the book is a gripping read from beginning to end. We live in a time when the lessons of the Reformation are desperately needed and this book extracts those lessons in powerful ways.

May *The Greatest Century of Reformation* be a book that is read far and wide. A big "Thank You" to Dr. Hammond for serving the Church in this way.

Rev. Phillip G. Kayser, PhD, Biblical Blueprints
President of Providential History Festival
Chairman of the Board of Frontline Fellowship

There has never been a greater need for a book on the Reformation than now. Historical facts have been, at best, ignored or blurred, at worst evacuated! The absolutes of yesterday, *Sola Scriptura, Sola Fide*... no longer hold sway. Instead, the uncertainties of open theology, the vagueries of experimental theology and the insistence on unity have all but cancelled the non-negotiables of the Reformation!

To be reminded of the major battles of yesterday, and the men who paid the supreme sacrifice for the upholding of Truth, is vital if the present generation is not to sell out to the trends and the fads which are culturally inherited and have nothing to do with the Gospel as revealed once and for all to the saints!

Peter Hammond, in his unique non-compromising style, leaves the reader with no alternative...either a return to Biblical revelation or the ongoing pursuit of man-pleasing religion!

Mike Evans, Directeur Général, Évangile 21
Previous Principal of Geneva Bible Institute

Having known Peter Hammond as a young unmarried student of Theology (I was one of his lecturers), the author has, in recent years, surprised me with amazement and respect by his grasp of history, and clear understanding of events and designs of the Eternal Plan of *Heilsgeschichte* (Salvation History).

As one who was born in the land of the Reformation and predestined to grow up among the Lutheran, Reformed and Free Church traditions, I count it a tremendous privilege to have walked many times the streets of Wittenberg, Zurich, Geneva, Saxony, Wartburg and many other Reformation sites.

Dr. Hammond has done a lot of disciplined reading and research to enable him to write these objective, factual and documentary chapters. It's an inspiration for our Faith in Jesus Christ and the Bible. I heartily endorse and recommend this Reformation Book.

Dr. Fritz Haus, Baptist Theologian and Missionary

The Reformation reminds us of ordinary Christians of the past, who stood their ground as brave soldiers of the Cross of Jesus Christ! We as soldiers of Christ's Army are challenged by Luther, Calvin and other war heroes, to stand our ground in the 21st Century, to make a difference and to seek the face of God for Revival. Let us take up the challenges of our day, by facing the music, not running away, taking the bullet from the front and not from the rear. *"Trust in the Lord with all your heart and lean not on your own understanding; in all your ways acknowledge Him and He shall direct your paths."* Proverbs 3:5-6. May God give us Godly wisdom according to James 1:5 and that we soldiers of Jesus Christ will keep our eyes on our Lord and Saviour Jesus Christ (Hebrews 12:2).

Dr F Shai Mulder, Back to the Bible Mission, South Africa

By the beginning of the 16th Century true Christianity was virtually unrecognizable. The Church had moved far from its original message of salvation by grace through faith as the gift of God.

Our Lord Jesus, Who promised to build His Church and not allow the gates of hell, or Rome, to prevail against it, raised up a succession of godly men to bring the ship of Faith back on God's intended course. This book examines the lives and times of these divinely chosen men.

It has been my pleasure and spiritual benefit to hear Dr. Hammond's Reformation lectures at Livingstone House. This book is the fruit of many years of diligent study, searching historical records and personally visiting all the major geographical centres of Reformation activity in Europe. I make no apology in recommending this book as a classic crash-

Forewords

course in understanding how the Protestant Reformation changed forever the history of Western Civilization and quite possibly led to the establishment of the United States of America.

Rev. Bill Bathman, Chairman, Frontline Fellowship

Sometimes we tend to forget how much we owe to the courageous Reformers of five hundred years ago. Our Bibles, our freedom of worship, our educational opportunities, to say nothing of our prosperity and our scientific achievements - all these are directly attributable to the Reformation. Yet these freedoms and benefits we enjoy were won by the blood, sweat and tears of our Christian brothers and sisters of half a millennium ago. It is a sad fact that many of us have forgotten the sacrifices that they made.

Peter Hammond has undertaken a monumental task in producing a book to help inform us of our Christian history and heritage. As he discusses each Reformer, we begin to understand the dynamic quality of these men, who were very ordinary human beings with their normal human failings, but who were driven by a Faith and a vision that puts ours to shame. We are inspired anew as we see what Christ did with these ordinary - and yet extraordinary - individuals, and how His purposes were realized, although it often took many years of suffering and tears before the results came.

Not only does this book help us gain some insight into the Reformation, and those who led it, but it also encourages us to continue their work in our day. Getting back to the truth of God's Word was not easy for those sixteenth-century people, but they persevered - even to the point of laying down their lives - and the generations who followed them reaped the benefits, both spiritual and material. We too need to face the apostasy of our day with courage and determination and lay a foundation on which future generations will be able to build - a foundation of Faith, courage and hard work. As you read *The Greatest Century of Reformation*, may you be inspired to put on the full armour of God and with the sword of the Spirit do battle with the enemy - and prevail. *" 'Not by might, nor by power, but by My Spirit,' saith the LORD of Hosts"* Zechariah 4:6

Alison Shortridge, Co-Director: Theocentric Christian Education

The great events of the Reformation are largely forgotten today. Many Christians are ignorant of the sacrifices that secured their religion and liberty. In the words of the late Bishop Stephen Bradley, *"we are in danger of forgetting truths for which previous generations gave their lives."*

This book is to correct that situation. In bold style it outlines the lives and times of Jan Hus, John Wycliffe, William Tyndale, Martin Luther, Ulrich Zwingli, John Calvin, John Knox and others. It describes their spiritual awakening and commitment to the cause of God. It chronicles their Faith, struggles and sacrifices. All the Reformers were persecuted. Many were burned at the stake. Their Bibles and writings were destroyed. And yet, through them God brought light, truth and freedom to the nations.

When the Bible (being in Latin) was a closed book to most, the Reformers translated and made it available to all. They showed that God is sovereign and His Word the final authority on all things, that Jesus Christ is the only Head of the Church and that man is justified by God's grace alone on the basis of His finished work.

Jesus says: *"Behold, I make all things new."* And so, with the knowledge of the Bible came newness of life to families and nations, a Revival and revitalisation of Christendom. It affected all areas of life: church, government, economics, science and art and laid the foundations for our present freedoms and living standards.

This book makes us proud of our noble Christian heritage. It shows Who God is, what He says, what He has done and how He works. It strengthens faith and raises courage. May the Lord use it to accomplish great things in our time.

Dorothea Scarborough, Founder Gospel Defence League

Dr Peter Hammond's book *"The Greatest Century of Reformation"* is a must-read for any believer who recognizes the cultural decay that has beset the Western world and who longs to see the restoration of a fully authentic and comprehensive Biblical Christianity in our time. The call is upon us to *"contend earnestly for the Faith that was once for all delivered to the saints"* Jude 3.

To be effective in this task of recovery, we need to understand the work of the Holy Spirit in history. We need to see how He accomplished His amazing work of Reformation in previous times of departure from Holy Scripture, wherein we have been given the divine blueprint for the building of Christ's unstoppable Church and the transformation of society in every nation.

The Great Reformation of the sixteenth century was a historical watershed that involved an astounding return to Biblical Faith, that reset the foundations for an ascendant Western civilization, that demonstrated the power of godly order in society. The signature of God that was unmistakable in Western culture must be recovered in our day of declension by means of a new and more comprehensive Reformation wherein we will see the Revival of Biblical Faith to the glory of God. We can and must seek the Living God for an outpouring of the Holy Spirit in a day of power that will drive back the gates of hell and raise the banner for the victory of King Jesus. God has commissioned His people to bring the nations under the sway of the Lord's crown and sceptre through the regenerating power of Christ's glorious world transforming Gospel. The Reformers of yesteryear understood this. May God raise the same spirit of Reformation and Revival in our day, in a tide turning outpouring of His mercy and power that unseats the wickedness and darkness that seeks to dominate our age.

"The Greatest Century of Reformation" will be a vital tool and indeed an effective weapon in the hands of many, as God's covenanted people press forward in this day of challenge and unprecedented opportunity that we face on our watch. May we be found faithful to the charge of the Lord. May His honour be celebrated as we pray and apply His own awe-inspiring Words, *"Our Father in Heaven, hallowed be Thy Name, Thy Kingdom come, Thy will be done on earth as it is in Heaven."*

Rev. Mike O'Donovan, His Heart Beat Ministries

Having known Peter Hammond for many years, as a man who holds the truth as a sacred trust, I urge you to read, *The Greatest Century of Reformation*. Be awakened to courage as you walk in the path of God's messengers during this period of Reformation. Experience a fresh awakening to Faith as you witness God's sovereign power at work when a man or woman places their trust in Him.

Walk in the steps of the Reformers and watch them challenge the impossible, with God behind them. Then consider in this most perilous hour of history, do we dare believe that God will act in that way again in our time?

Luther faced a most destructive antagonism against Biblical Christianity. Once again this antagonism is rampant in modern history. When you lay down this book, dare to call upon the Mighty God, who arms Himself with light and pray for a new Reformation to challenge this pervading darkness. Will you count yourself as one who will stand for God? Together, let us say to the next generation, we gave our best.

Pastor Mike Kiley, Founder of The Home Church

Church history is an amazing and wonderful record of how God has worked in the world in which we live. Tragically, most Christians know all too little about the remarkable movement of the Spirit which took place in Europe centuries ago, the effects of which are still with us today. So many of the things we take for granted, which God gives to mankind by common grace, are legacies of the Reformation. Had it not been for the Reformation, we would still have been in a state of spiritual darkness such as prevailed in our world before this awakening took place and we would have been far worse off than we are now.

The instruments God used to overturn evil and establish truth and righteousness, men like John Calvin, Martin Luther, Ulrich Zwingli and others were eminently godly men who became mighty in the Scriptures and through whose preaching and writing masses of people were brought out of spiritual ignorance into the glorious light of the Gospel. Such was the impact of these men upon society that at all levels life was enhanced for the glory of God.

As a priority, we need to know our Bibles well. By the same token, we ought to be well acquainted with history, because history is His story. The story of the Reformation is the story of Gods mercy towards mankind. It is a story of Gods power to overturn unrighteousness and to establish His truth, in a fallen world, on a large scale. There is so much that we can learn from this chapter in church history.

Reading Peter Hammond's outstanding outline of what happened then will surely stimulate a yearning for a Reformation to come upon the Church of Jesus Christ again. If conditions in Europe were so abysmal before the Reformation, and if that part of history is a demonstration of how mightily God is able to step in and change the course of history, then we ought to take fresh courage from the fact that our God, who does not change, is able to do the same in our day.

We are deeply indebted to Peter Hammond for a fresh and excellent reminder of the facts of history concerning the greatest century of Reformation. This is a book we ought not only to read for ourselves, but we should urge our friends, and especially our children, to read it too. They need to be acquainted with the truth of how God glorifies His Son Jesus Christ when it seems as if all hope is lost. We become the beneficiaries of the work the Holy Spirit does when God raises up men to spread the truth of His Word in such a way that people return to their Maker through the Redeemer Jesus Christ.

What a book, and how sorely needed is this new book!

"Will You not revive us again, that Your people may rejoice in You?"
Psalm 85: 6

Dr. Martin Holdt, Reformed Baptist Association

Introduction

by Dr. Jay Grimstead

It is indeed an honor to write an Introduction to Dr. Peter Hammond's expanded version of *"The Greatest Century of Reformation."* I tell friends and fellow Theologians that Peter's 2006 edition of this book is the most exciting and most inspiring book I have read in the past 25 years! It inspired me the way the books of Dr. Francis Schaeffer, my mentor and personal friend, inspired me in the 1960's, 70's and 80's. It is also an honor to be the personal friend and Co-worker in the Kingdom of God with Peter Hammond whom I consider to be one of my modern-day heroes.

When I first encountered the heroes of the Church's history in seminary in the 1950's, I found the church's history to be fascinating and very inspiring to me personally. As I read and re-read the powerful, world-changing histories of these heroes of the Faith which Dr. Hammond brings before us in this book, my heart kept pumping adrenaline and I continually was re-motivated to pour out my life blood for King Jesus as did these courageous brothers and sisters of earlier generations. I have probably bought and given away more of this one book to young, Christian warriors I know and love than any other book in my library.

I hope to some day teach a class based upon this entire book to young leaders and use the *"Questions for Discussion"* in the back of the book as my discussion guide. There are powerful tools for Reformation work in the back of this book and the 6 pages of the *"Chronology of the Reformation"* (pages 207 to 212) are worth the price of the book.

I suggest that every young, Christian Warrior in the Kingdom of God read, study and teach the character studies and doctrine of this book.

Dr. Jay Grimstead,
Director of the Coalition on Revival
Convenor Global Church Council

The Monument to Reformer Dr. Martin Luther in Dresden.

Preface

The Greatest Century of Reformation is the next in the series begun by our **Greatest Century of Missions** book. The vision is to provide pastors, teachers, parents and students with a series of inspiring history books which will give the broad sweep of memorable characters and momentous events that shaped that century. By incorporating a generous quantity of selected artwork, photographs and maps, focusing on the personalities and activities that God used, it is my prayer that these books will inspire, inform and involve you in a hunger for Revival and vision for Reformation in our own day.

The 16th Century was the greatest century of Reformation.
The 17th Century was the greatest century of the Puritans.
The 18th Century was the greatest century of Revival.
The 19th Century was the greatest century of Missions.
The 20th Century was the greatest century of Persecution.

By focusing on a common theme for each century I pray that these books will enrich, encourage, empower and enlist readers to be more courageous, faithful and effective in fulfilling the Great Commission of our Lord Jesus Christ.

I am eternally grateful to my Theological Professor, Dr. Fritz Haus who taught me to love praying the Psalms and singing Martin Luther's **A Mighty Fortress is Our God**. It was Dr. Haus's enthusiasm for the Reformation doctrines of Dr. Luther that first inspired me to read up on and research the Reformation.

My father-in-law, Rev. Bill Bathman, arranged for my research visit to Wittenberg, after our mission to Poland. I am grateful for all his encouragement and practical support that ensured that this book was thoroughly researched.

I am also grateful to Mike Evans for inviting me to minister at the Geneva Bible Institute and showing me around St. Peter's Church where Calvin ministered and for taking me to the inspiring Reformation Monument.

I also want to thank Alison Shortridge, Dorothea Scarborough, Nicolas Collins and Taryn Lourens for helping with the proof reading; and Colin Newman for all the typesetting and DTP work. My Graphic Design daughter, Daniela, designed the cover and most of the posters at the end of the book.

May God be pleased to use this book to motivate and mobilize us to work for Biblical Reformation and pray for Spiritual Revival. May the examples of the Reformers inspire you to go back to the Bible, love God wholeheartedly and fear God alone. Refuse to be intimidated, distracted or deviated. Seek first God's Kingdom. Expect opposition and criticism as an inevitable price of taking God's Word seriously. Let us get back to the Bible and apply the Lordship of Christ to all areas of life.

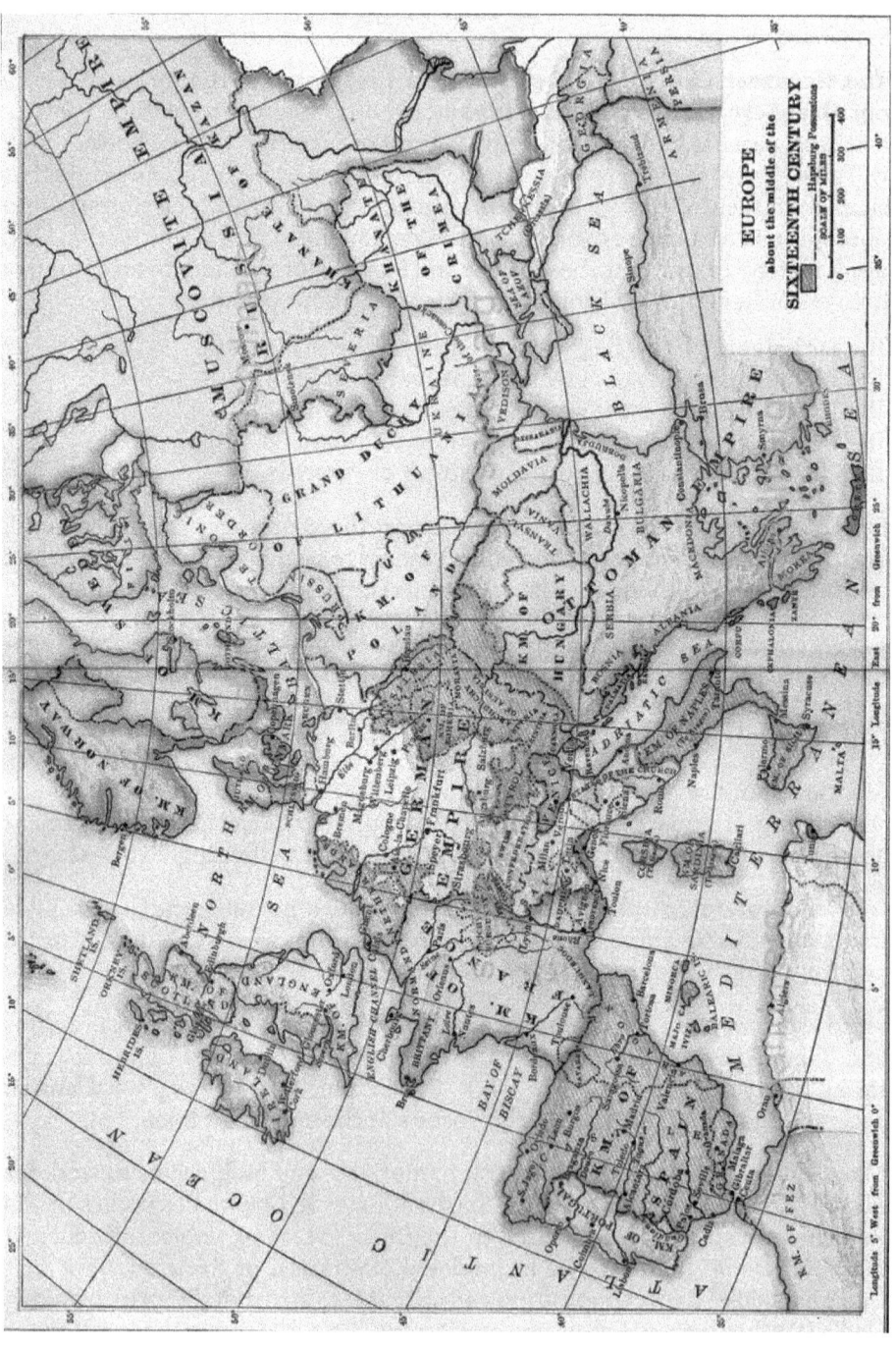

Chapter 1
A Century of Repression, Revolt and Reformation

A Geo-Strategic Overview of the 16th Century

Shortly after Martin Luther was born, the last Muslim stronghold in Spain, Grenada, fell and the liberation of the Iberian Peninsula was complete. Then Christopher Columbus, sailing west across the Atlantic Ocean, discovered the Americas, the New World. While South Western Europe was celebrating its freedom after 8 centuries of oppression and occupation under Islam, South Eastern Europe was facing the relentless onslaughts of invasion by the Turks. Since the fall of the greatest city in the world at that time, Constantinople, to the Turks, in 1453, with the massacre of all the Christians in that city, the Turks had been an ever-present threat to Christendom, as Europe was then known.

The Renaissance

Threatened from the East by a relentless Islamic Jihad, Europe was suffering from the internal corruption of the Renaissance. The Renaissance was a time of material advance and spiritual decline. It led to the rise of absolutism and the loss of the individual rights and representative governments which Christian principles had developed throughout the Middle Ages. Renaissance rulers, epitomised by Machiavelli, rationalized despotism. Machiavelli advised rulers to be careful to maintain public relations through patronage of the arts and conspicuous charities, in order to create popularity and to mask their hold on power.

A Return to Paganism

Although Ancient Rome had practiced human sacrifices, slavery, infanticide, persecuted Christians and fed martyrs to wild beasts, Renaissance scholars began to hail the pagans as wiser and their times as superior to the Christian. This Renaissance trend to turn towards the graves of Rome and Greece was not progress but a regression to a pagan past, a rejection of the Christian Faith. While Renaissance Italians revived the pagan writings and customs of Ancient Greece and Rome and unearthed their statues, paintings and plays, immorality flourished and degeneracy accelerated. Along with the physical and intellectual exhumations, the ancient intellectual and spiritual diseases that had led both Rome and Greece to self-destruction came to infect life in Europe.

Literature became shallow and imitative. Absurd ancient theories about *"Humours"* were resuscitated at the expense of medical research. Everyone's municipal freedoms and individual rights were lost as Humanists extolled the tyrannical Roman laws, which tyrants were quick to adopt.

The impact of glorifying a licentious past was absolutely devastating upon the morals and behaviour of Southern Europe. The despairing conclusion of Renaissance Humanism was that life is meaningless. To escape from this intellectual cul-de-sac, many began to plunge into the blind fortune of astrology and magic. Many people who had lost their belief in sin and rejected the idea of eternal life, desperately sought for earthly fame and fortune.

Paganism deepened as the Renaissance extended. From the 14th to the 16th Centuries, many cities in Southern Europe appointed official astrologers. Universities had official stargazers. Even popes relied on Horoscopes.

The scandalous selling of salvation by papal salesman extraordinaire, Johan Tetzel, prompted Luther's protest.

CORRUPTION CHALLENGED

With almost any position in the Catholic church open to the highest bidder, church positions became dominated by corrupt, money-grabbing Humanists who ruthlessly persecuted genuine believers.

Martin Luther, a brilliant lawyer and Theologian visited Rome in 1510. Luther was shocked at the corruption and degeneracy of Rome: *"Everything is permitted in Rome, except to be an honest man."*

To finance the pope's extravagant living and the construction of St. Peter's Cathedral, the Catholic church was selling *"dispensations"* that allowed purchasers to break Church rules, to eat meat on fast days, to marry a close relative, to commit adultery and so on. In addition, the Catholic church sold *"indulgences,"* which could only be cashed in Heaven - to which they claimed to hold the keys. These Heavenly credits could be balanced against one's sins committed on earth.

These earthly and spiritual pardons were being sold by a Dominican monk, John Tetzel, in Saxony, when Dr. Martin Luther, now a professor at Wittenberg University, wrote *The 95 Theses* in protest. Luther argued that only God can forgive sins, it is better to help the poor than to buy indulgences and truly repentant people do not desire to avoid punishment, but rather seek it.

Luther's challenge was in Latin, but some enterprising printer translated it into German and began to print and sell copies of it. Soon *The 95 Theses* were available in French, Spanish, Flemish, Dutch and Italian. Within weeks Luther's dramatic challenge against the unBiblical corruption of indulgences was being read in the market places and palaces of Europe. Even the pope was handed a copy to read.

31 October 1517 - Martin Luther nailed his 95 Theses on the Wittenberg church door.

MARTIN LUTHER TAKES ON THE HOLY ROMAN EMPIRE

Between 1517 and 1520, more than 300,000 copies of Luther's writings were sold throughout Europe. It was the first time in history that a revolutionary idea had impacted a continent through a mass medium. Translators, printers, journalists and itinerant salesmen worked together to challenge the entire social and ecclesiastical system of the Catholic church and the Holy Roman Empire.

At about the same time that Cortez was entering Mexico and encountering Montezuma and the bloodthirsty Aztec Empire, Luther was challenging the Holy Roman Empire in Europe.

In 1520, the pope issued Luther with a *Bull* – an ultimatum to submit and recant or be excommunicated. Luther's response was to burn the *Papal Bull* in public and then to write three booklets challenging foundational teachings of the pope. Luther's booklets: *"An Appeal To the Christian Nobility"; "The Babylonian Captivity of the Church"* and *"The Freedom of a Christian"* created a sensation. Printing presses ran around the clock, turning out new editions. Luther rejected the right of the Vatican to interfere with the princes. He also recommended a national church and the expulsion of all papal representatives.

10 December 1520 - Martin Luther burns the Papal Bull.

He taught that faith alone and not good works, makes man righteous. Good works follow from faith. *"The tree bears fruit, the fruit does not bear the tree."* Luther taught that not only could we receive forgiveness for our sins, but victory over the power of sin, over our own carnal nature, by God's grace alone. By the end of 1520, Luther was proclaiming the pope *"Anti-Christ."*

Excommunicated by the pope, all that stood between Luther and death at the hands of the Emperor was the protection of the Elector of Saxony. Prince Fredrick was reported to have said: *"There is much in the Bible about Christ, but not much about Rome."*

Prince Fredrick of Saxony was one of the most senior and influential electors in Germany. He had been a serious contender for the position of Emperor of the Holy Roman Empire. Charles V was Emperor of Germany, King of Spain, Sardinia, Sicily and the Netherlands. His ships were sailing around the globe, his vast armies dominated all of Europe. However, Charles V, could not ignore the authority of Prince Fredrick, because Germany was still largely feudal and the Emperor's power was not absolute. The German people still enjoyed many of the rights and powers which the Renaissance had elsewhere swept away. Only recently crowned Emperor and just 21 years old, Charles V had to be seen to respect the authority of the Electors who had only just crowned him. Prince Fredrick extracted a guarantee of safe conduct for Luther from the Emperor.

CONFRONTATION

Summoned to Worms on 18 April 1521, Martin Luther stood firm before the Emperor, 6 Princes, 24 Dukes, 30 Archbishops and Bishops and 7 Ambassadors. The young Emperor sat on a raised dais, surrounded by men in gleaming armour, mitered Archbishops and splendidly dressed nobles.

Luther was denied any opportunity to debate or defend his doctrines. He was asked two questions, first: to confirm that the publications on the table were his and the second: whether he would recant, admit that his writings were all heretical and reject them.

Confirming that the books, booklets and leaflets were his writings, Luther pointed out that they were of different types, including basic Christian doctrine, which were accepted Christian truths – he could not recant Scriptural truth. Other of his works exposed the corrupt living, scandalous abuses and evils of the popes. If he were to reject these writings he would be as a *"cloak that covers evil."* At this, the Emperor leaned forward and shouted: *"No!"* Luther continued that other of his works were against private individuals who had attacked his work and attempted to defend popery. He confessed that, in these, he had written too harshly.

CAPTIVE TO THE WORD OF GOD

The court demanded that Luther recant all his writings. Pressed again, in Latin, if he would recant, Luther answered in German: *"Unless I am convinced by Scripture or clear reasoning that I am in error – for popes and Councils have often erred and contradicted themselves – I cannot recant, for I am subject to the Scriptures I have quoted;* **my conscience is captive to the Word of God**. *It is unsafe and dangerous to do anything against one's conscience. Here I stand. I cannot do otherwise. So help me God. Amen."*

18 April 1521 - Martin Luther stands firm before Emperor Charles V at the Diet of Worms.

Luther's courageous and historic speech before the assembled might and authority of the Holy Roman Empire and the Catholic church shook the world.

A Century of Repression, Revolt and Reformation

OUTLAW

Furious, Charles V wanted Luther burned as a heretic. Prince Fredrick insisted that he honour his guarantee of safe conduct. Luther was allowed to leave, but the Emperor and four Electors, signed a statement declaring Luther an outlaw. Prince Fredrick of Saxony and the Elector of the Palatinate, refused to sign.

KIDNAPPED

While frantic efforts were made to arrest Luther, Prince Fredrick secretly arranged for his kidnapping and spiriting away to be hidden as *Junker Jorg* (Knight George) in the Wartburg Castle.

The Kidnapping of Martin Luther.

THE BIBLE IN GERMAN

There, in disguise, in seclusion, Luther began a Bible translation *Blitzkrieg* and by the next year, 1522, the German New Testament was on sale for only a week's wages, empowering people like never before.

REVOLUTION

Back in Wittenberg, Luther's colleagues, Philipp Melanchthon (a 21 year old professor of Greek) and Andreas Bodenstein Karlstadt (a 30 year old professor of Philosophy and Theology) continued the work of Reformation in Luther's absence. Karlstadt took Luther's intellectual rebellion and turned it into a religious revolution. He whipped up the crowds to destroy statues, shrines and all religious artefacts as idols that needed to be destroyed. When Luther heard of this, he was shocked. Luther taught that people should not take the law into their own hands. Everything should be done decently and in order. And eliminating idolatry in our hearts comes before eradicating images in the churches.

THE PROBLEM WITH IMAGES

Images were a central means of communicating basic Gospel truths in the Middle Ages. As very few of the population could read and write, Bible stories were depicted through stain glass windows, statues and pictures. During the Middle Ages, it began to be accepted that Christians would not only learn the Faith through these visual representations, but should also express the faith through reverencing these. An entire

19

devotional system was developed and an industry involving carpenters, painters, goldsmiths, silversmiths and other artisans built their livelihoods around providing images for the church. The Reformation, with its rejection of such idolatry, posed an economic threat to many of these businesses.

THE REFORMATION SPREADS

Luther was far and away the most popular author in Europe. His writings outsold all others in Spain, France, Italy, the Netherlands, Switzerland, England and Germany.

Priests and nuns poured from the church and rushed towards marriage. Princes were converted to the Reformation. The new pope, Adrian VI, elected in 1521 upon the death of Leo X, demanded Luther's arrest. The Prince of Saxony refused to co-operate.

THE PEASANTS REVOLT

Radical opportunists, such as Thomas Munzer, used this intellectual and spiritual upheaval to try to launch a political revolution. By the end of 1524, over 30,000 armed peasants had risen up and began looting castles and monasteries, pillaging churches, kidnapping nobles, demanding ransoms and committing widespread arson and mass murder.

Horrified, Luther issued a pamphlet in 1524: *"Against The Robbing and Murdering Hordes of Peasants."* He not only disassociated from these bandits and revolutionaries, but he applied Biblical principles as to the duty of the princes to use the sword to protect the law abiding and to punish the lawbreakers. The princes responded decisively against this anarchy and lawlessness. Munzer and 5,000 of his followers were wiped out by the knights. Another 20,000 rebellious peasants were killed in Alsace.

The greatest loss of life during this peasant's rebellion occurred in Austria. Charles V's younger brother, Ferdinand, crushed the rebellion - with 130,000 peasants being killed in battle, or by execution. The peasant's revolt had been disastrous. Hundreds of castles and monasteries had been ruined. Hundreds of towns were depopulated and impoverished. Over 50,000 homeless wandered across the countryside, or hid in the forests. There were many widows and orphans. Because many of the rebels had destroyed the charters that recorded the municipal rights and feudal dues, new charters, many far more demanding, were drawn up. Censorship laws were enforced all over Europe.

TURKISH INVASION

Then, in 1526, the Muslim Turks attacked Hungary. Suleiman, the Magnificent, overwhelmed the small Hungarian army of 30,000 with his 300,000 invading Turks. King Louis II of Hungary was killed and the capital, Buda (what is today Budapest) was captured and looted by the Turks. The Turkish invaders drove off over 200,000 Hungarian Christians into Islamic slavery.

ROME IS SACKED

The next year, 1527, Emperor Charles V led his army to capture Rome, the richest city in Europe. The corruption and meddling of the pope had outraged even ardent Catholic Charles V. Now his army sacked Rome itself. The pope was held for an immense ransom. Throughout Europe this was seen as the Judgment of God upon a debauched city and a corrupt church.

REPRESSION IN THE NETHERLANDS

The Catholic Inquisition in the Netherlands demanded that all hold to and believe the doctrines of the Holy Roman Catholic church. "Men and women who disobey this command shall be punished as disturbers of public order. Women who have fallen into heresy shall be burned alive. Men, if they recant, shall lose their heads. If they continue obstinate, they shall be burned at the stake. The Inquisition is to enquire into the private opinions of every person, of whatever degree. Law officers of all kinds shall assist the Inquisition at their peril. Those who know where heretics are concealed, shall denounce them, or they shall suffer as heretics themselves." Under this edict, in the Netherlands alone, over 50,000 Protestants were killed.

Inquisition burning Protestants for "heresy."

ZWINGLI'S REFORMATION

In Switzerland, Ulrich Zwingli had launched a parallel Reformation starting with the expository preaching of the Gospel of Matthew, 1 January 1519, in *Grossmünster* in Zürich. The City Council supported Zwingli's Reforms. All Zürich clergymen were ordered to preach only from the Scripture. The Bible became the basis for all law. The Council abolished the mass. All religious images, statues, relics and ornaments were removed from churches. Monks, nuns and priests were permitted to marry. Soon other Swiss cantons were embracing the Reformation.

1 January 1519 - Ulrich Zwingli preaching in Grossmünster.

In 1529, a Protestant missionary from Zürich was burned at the stake for preaching the Gospel in the Catholic canton of Schwyz. Zürich stopped all trade with Schwyz in protest. The Catholic Cantons declared war. At the Battle of Kappel, October 1531, 8,000 Catholic soldiers overwhelmed the 1,500 Protestants. Zürich Reformer, Ulrich Zwingli, was severely injured in this battle and was killed by a Catholic captain when he refused to call upon the Virgin Mary.

REPRESSION IN FRANCE

At the beginning of the 16th Century, France was the largest and richest nation in Europe. France had a population of 16 million at a time when Spain had 7 million and England 3 million. Paris was the largest city in Europe with a population of 300,000.

Luther's books poured into France. French Reformer, Jacques le Fevre, published a French translation of the New Testament in 1523 and the next year the Psalms. He was denounced as a *"heretic."*

King Francis I ordered vigorous persecution to stamp out the Protestant Faith in his realm. Protestants were branded, their hands and noses amputated, red-hot irons were applied to the head. Many were burned alive.

At the same time that Francis I was ordering mutilations and tortures on Protestants, his sister, Marguerite, was herself praying with Reformer Farel and protecting Protestants.

The Outlaw John Calvin

Brilliant young law student, John Calvin, was converted to the Protestant Faith and started to call for a purified Christianity, stressing salvation through grace. He wrote a treatise on life after death and another on Christian Doctrine. Calvin was arrested twice and after a number of life-threatening escapes, Calvin was declared an outlaw and he was on the run from the authorities.

By 1536, he had produced *"The Institutes of the Christian Religion"* a Theological masterpiece, systematically expounding the Biblical Faith, conduct and devotion of the Protestant Faith.

Farel Wins Geneva to the Reformation

When French Protestant preacher, Guillaume Farel, first came to Geneva it was a very immoral city. Geneva had a prostitute's quarter, priests living with concubines and a corrupt bishop. Farel first came to Geneva in October 1532. Farel was a missionary from Bern, the strongest Protestant canton in Switzerland. Farel had played a leading role in bringing about the triumph of the Reformation in Bern, Neuchatel and several other towns. He had also won over the Waldenses to embrace the principles of the Reformation. Farel's fiery preaching and unbeatable logic in debate with the Catholics won the city. As hundreds of Genevans were won to Christ, Farel seized the Cathedral of St. Peter and on 21 May 1536, the General Assembly of citizens voted in favour of the Reformation and made the Protestant Faith the official religion of Geneva.

1536 - Farel preaching in the marketplace of Geneva.

CALVIN'S CALL TO GENEVA

With Geneva in revolt against its bishop and against the Duke of Savoy, Farel knew that his eloquence and evangelistic zeal was not sufficient to disciple this distracted city. It was at that opportune time that a local war compelled Calvin to divert through Geneva. He had planned to spend only one night in Geneva. When Farel heard that this famous French scholar and author was passing through, he hurried to recruit him. Calvin's mind was set on his studies, but Farel would have none of that. He threatened that God would curse his studies if he refused to aid the church in Geneva at this critical time. Visibly shaken and struck with terror, Calvin reluctantly agreed to serve in Geneva. Calvin began his ministry in the Church of St. Peter by preaching through the Epistles of St. Paul.

TURBULENT TIMES

King Francis I of France shocked all of Christendom by making an alliance with the Turks in his war against Charles V. His political and military gamble failed, he was defeated and died bankrupt and disgraced, in 1547. The deaths of both France I and Henry VIII in the same year, 1547, emphasized the turbulence of that time when Luther, Zwingli, Farel and Tyndale contended with the popes and Charles V, Henry VIII and Francis I for the heart, mind and soul of Christendom.

The Protestant Faith swept across Europe flourishing in Switzerland, Scandinavia, Germany, Holland, England and Scotland.

The martyrdom of George Wishart.

SCOTLAND

Scottish Reformer, George Wishart, was burned at the stake in Scotland. The Archbishop responsible for his execution, Cardinal David Beaton, was brutally assassinated in revenge. Protestants captured the Castle of St. Andrews. They were joined by John Knox, besieged by a French fleet, captured and condemned to the galleys.

REFORMATION IN ENGLAND

When King Henry VIII of England died, his 9 year old son, a dedicated Protestant, Edward VI, became king. Archbishop Thomas Cranmer initiated sweeping Reforms. All paintings and images were removed from churches. The mass was abolished and replaced with communion. The English language replaced Latin in worship services. The English *"Book of Common Prayer"* was introduced. Priests received permission to marry. Stone altars were demolished and replaced by tables. Protestant books and pamphlets flooded England.

CALVIN'S GENEVA

Guided by John Calvin's Biblical preaching and systematic teaching, Geneva became the hub of the Reformation. Refugees fleeing persecution found sanctuary in Geneva. Calvin's writings produced the greatest concentration of printers and publishing firms in the world. Calvin established an Academy that taught Greek, Hebrew, Latin and Theology. Graduates of Geneva's Academy carried the Reformed teachings into France, Holland, England and Scotland.

FIRST PROTESTANT KING OF ENGLAND

King Edward VI of England intervened to secure the release of the Protestants of St. Andrews, including John Knox, from the galleys of France, in a prisoner exchange. Knox was appointed a royal chaplain and helped Archbishop Cranmer in producing *"The Book of Common Prayer."* Then the young Protestant King Edward became seriously ill. Rumours that he had been poisoned by a Catholic assassin abounded.

LADY JANE GREY

Fears for the future of the Reformation in England at the imminent death of King Edward VI caused the Regent, the Duke of Northumberland, to persuade the King to alter the Laws of Succession to bypass his Catholic sister, Mary and crown Lady Jane Grey as Queen. In the end Edward's death came swiftly, as the Catholic forces mustered to place Mary Tudor on the throne of England. Jane was Queen for only 9 days when the forces of Mary arrested and imprisoned her in the Tower of London. Pressured by her cousin, Mary, to renounce her Protestant Faith and embrace Catholicism, 16 year old Queen Jane courageously remained steadfast and was beheaded as a result.

Lady Jane Grey

BLOODY MARY

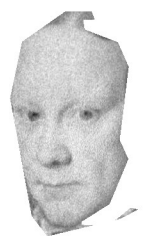

Queen Mary married the heir to the Holy Roman Empire, Prince Philip of Spain. Philip arrived with a huge fleet of ships and a vast Spanish entourage to dominate the English court. Cardinal Reginald Pole was appointed Archbishop of Canterbury. England was formally returned to Catholicism and the most prominent Protestant bishops, including Hooper, Ridley, Latimer and (the previous Archbishop) Thomas Cranmer, were burned at the stake, followed by hundreds of other prominent Protestant leaders. With every execution resistance to Catholicism spread and commitment to the Reformation doctrines deepened.

THE END OF CHARLES V

As Charles V abdicated in 1556, Mary's husband Philip became King Philip II. Soon English troops and Cavalry were being sent to the Netherlands to help crush the widespread Protestant revolt. From the perspective of the Holy Roman Empire, the year 1558 was disastrous. Charles V, (the Emperor who Martin Luther had defied with his *"my conscience is captive to the Word of God...Here I stand..."* speech), died in agony, 21 September 1558. Charles V had condemned over 30,000 Protestants to torturous executions during his reign.

Burning of Bishops Latimer and Ridley in Oxford.

REVERSAL OF FORTUNES

Shortly after that, on 17 November 1558, *"Blood Mary"* died of fever. Twelve hours later her Cardinal Pole, Archbishop of Canterbury, died of the same fever in Lambeth Palace. 1559 began with the Protestants on the march and with the Catholic cause in defeat and retreat. Emperor Charles V was now dead. His sister, Mary, the former Regent of the Netherlands had also died. Mary of Lorraine, Regent of Scotland, was out of power and on the run. *"Bloody Mary's"* Counter Reformation in England had been counterproductive, instead of returning England to Catholicism, she had only succeeded in entrenching the vast majority of Englishmen in their commitment to the Reformation. On 15 January 1559, Protestant Elizabeth Tudor was crowned Queen of England.

1559 - John Knox's sermons reverberated throughout Scotland.

KNOX TAKES SCOTLAND BY STORM
On 2 May 1559, John Knox returned from exile to Scotland. His fiery sermon against idolatry galvanized the Scottish into immediate action. Altars were demolished. Images, statutes and crucifixes were removed from churches. The Scottish Lords of the Congregation worked together with the English to force all French troops to leave Scottish soil. The Scottish Parliament instructed Knox to draw up a Confession of Faith, which was adopted into law.

GENEVA BIBLE
In 1560, the Geneva Bible was published. Before it was replaced by the King James Version (1611) over 140 editions of the Geneva Bible were published.

MARY QUEEN OF SCOTS
The attempt to return Scotland to Catholicism by the return of Mary Stuart, Queen of Scots, in 1561, put the Reformation in jeopardy. Mary Stuart was heir to England's throne if Elizabeth died. Numerous Catholic assassination attempts and intrigues to replace Elizabeth I with Mary Queen of Scots underlined the peril to the cause of Reformation and freedom in England itself.

Mary Queen of Scots' immorality and intrigues outraged the population of Scotland. John Knox's courageous confrontations of Mary and the scandal caused by her complicity in the murder of her husband and

The Duke of Alva terrorised Holland.

marrying of his murderer, finally led to her being forced to abdicate in 1567. Her infant son was crowned James VI of Scotland (he later became James I of England). Knox preached at James VI's coronation.

CATHOLIC CRUELTY IN HOLLAND

Meanwhile, while the Reformation was triumphing in Britain, it was under relentless attack on the continent of Europe. Charles V's son, Philip II, was determined to crush the flourishing Protestant Faith in Holland. In 1566, Philip issued a proclamation requiring all his subjects to accept the decrees made by the Council of Trent. All who would not comply with these demands were to be delivered to the Inquisitors.

In 1567, Philip sent in his Spanish troops, led by the cruel Duke of Alva. Alva set up the Council of Blood which had 8,000 Dutch Protestants executed. Another 30,000 had their property confiscated. In 1568, the Inquisition condemned all the inhabitants of the Netherlands – 3 million men, women and children – to death as *"heretics."*

WILLIAM PRINCE OF ORANGE

William the Silent, Prince of Orange, became the leader of the persecuted Dutch Protestants. William and his Dutch soldiers fought valiantly, despite overwhelming odds. Their greatest strength was their skilled navy, which, although they were vastly outnumbered and outgunned by the Spanish, triumphed over the Spanish time and again. In 1579, the 7 Northern provinces joined to form the United Provinces of the Netherlands. In 1581, the United Provinces declared the Netherlands to be independent of Spain. In 1584, the Dutch suffered a severe blow when a Spanish agent assassinated Prince William – the Father of Dutch Liberties. The Dutch Protestants continued to fight for their freedom until 1648 when their independence from Spain was finally secured.

William, Prince of Orange.

A Century of Repression, Revolt and Reformation

THE MUSLIM THREAT

Muslim pirates enslaved Christian Europeans.

It was not as though Europe's only threat was from treacherous tyrants. Just the year before the St. Bartholomew's Day Massacre in France, Europe faced a most desperate attack from the Muslim Turks. In 1571, the Turkish Empire stretched from the Ukraine to Hungary to Egypt and Persia, from North Africa to the Caspian Sea. Turkish warships attacked Christian shipping from all along North Africa. Turkish pirates pillaged and looted the coasts of Europe capturing Christians as slaves as far afield as England and Ireland.

THE FALL OF CYPRUS

In 1571, Cyprus fell to the Turks. 5,000 Greek and Italian Christians killed 30,000 Turkish attackers in their fierce resistance. Only after all supplies were exhausted and guarantees of safe conduct were offered, did the garrison finally surrender. But the Turks treacherously had all the Venetian prisoners executed and the rest of the Christians shipped to Constantinople as slaves. The courageous Christian General, Bragadino, had his nose and ears cut off, his teeth broken and was whipped daily until 17 August, when he was flayed alive in the city square. The Turks laid waste to the island of Corfu and massed their fleets to attack Europe.

THE BATTLE OF LEPANTO

The European forces were led by Don John of Austria, half-brother of Philip II. The Battle of Lepanto on 7 October 1571 was one of the most critical naval battles in history. The Christian forces, with 208 warships were outnumbered by the larger Turkish fleet of 230. The Christian forces closed in for the fight in hand to hand combat with the enemy.

7 October 1571 - Christian forces overwelm Ottoman Turks at the Battle of Lepanto.

Spanish and German infantry flowed onto the Turkish vessels and, in ferocious hand-to-hand combat, overwhelmed the Turks. The Turkish losses were estimated at over 30,000 dead and wounded and 15,000 prisoners. On their side, the Christians had lost 10 galleys, 8,000 men killed and 21,000 wounded. Lepanto was one of the great turning points in history. It ended the fear of the Turks that had threatened to overwhelm all of Europe. It stopped the Turkish advance. Church bells tolled throughout Europe as many prayers of thanksgiving were offered by millions of grateful Europeans. As historian, Otto Scott, observed: *"Only God could have saved so divided a Europe against so determined and savage, rich and heavily armed a foe. After Lepanto the Turk remained a menace, but not an unconquerable one."*

MASSACRES IN FRANCE

The St. Bartholomew's Day Massacre horrified Protestants worldwide and entrenched the conviction that the Catholic church was treacherous and that any guarantees given by them or treaties signed would not be honoured. Up to 30,000 Protestants were massacred throughout France, including the leader of the French Huguenots, Admiral Gaspard de Coligny. The massacre was ordered by King Charles IX under the influence of his mother Catherine de Medici.

24 August 1572 - St. Bartholomew's Day Massacre throughout France.

THE ST. BARTHOLOMEW'S DAY MASSACRE

The St. Bartholomew's Day Massacre, 24 August 1572, began at 3 in the morning. The first to be murdered was the aristocratic Admiral Coligny. Henry of Guise supervised the attack. His men burst into Coligny's home, stabbed the Admiral and threw him out of the window. As Coligny landed at Guise's feet, Henry of Guise spat on the body and then told his men to spread the word that the king commanded the death of all Huguenots: *"Kill them all! Kill them all!"*

Horrible slaughter and mutilations followed. Approximately 5,000 Protestants were murdered in Paris alone. The Spanish Ambassador wrote: *"As I write, they are killing them all, they are stripping them naked...sparing not even the children. Blessed be God!"* Similar massacres occurred in Lyon, Dijon, Tours, Rouen, Troyes and Toulouse. A total of 30,000 Protestants were murdered on St. Bartholomew's Day throughout France.

When the news reached Rome, the Cardinal of Lorraine gave the bearer of this news a thousand crowns. Gregory XIII and his Cardinals attended a solemn high mass of thanksgiving. The pope ordered a special medal to be struck commemorating the massacre with the words *"Pontifex Colbni Necent Probat"* (The pope approves the killing of Coligny).

Catherine de Medici views the aftermath of the St. Bartholomew's Day Massacre, 1572.

RESISTANCE STIFFENS

The St. Bartholomew's Day Massacre permanently altered Protestant thinking. Calvinists turned from previously accepting the divine right of kings to questioning the entire institution of the monarchy. The Catholic cause, already stained by *"Bloody Mary's"* persecutions in England and the Duke of Alva's slaughter in the Netherlands, was now indelibly identified with the most bestial persecutions, tyranny and treachery.

Two months later, the Calvinists launched an offensive that lasted nearly a year. At its conclusion, Charles IX was forced to sign another treaty guaranteeing freedom of worship in France. English gold and practical support boosted the Protestant resistance in the Netherlands and Scotland.

Jesuit assassins and conspirators arrived in England to arrange for the overthrow of Elizabeth I and her replacement with Mary Stuart. An army bearing papal banners invaded Ireland. In 1583, a Catholic plot involving English noblemen and a Spanish plan for invasion was uncovered. The Spanish Ambassador was expelled from England. As long as Mary Stuart remained alive she presented a clear and present danger to the life of Elizabeth and the survival of the Protestant Faith and freedom in England. Mary Stuart represented Spain, the vast Catholic international and the Guises of France. Parliament placed Mary Stuart on trial at Fotheringay Castle. Despite attempts by Elizabeth to stop the proceedings, Mary Stuart was sentenced to death and executed 12 May 1587.

CIVIL WAR IN FRANCE

Philip II, who had recently conquered Portugal, now began to prepare for an invasion of England. This was while France was torn by civil war with three armies in the field, one led by the giggling transvestite with a whitened face, Henry III, the other by Henry Duke of Guise and the third by Henry of Navarre, a Protestant.

THE SPANISH ARMADA

King Philip of Spain then launched what the Spaniards called, the *"Invincible Armada."* The world had never before seen such a powerful fleet. Having recently defeated the Turkish fleet, the tiny English Navy was not perceived to be any significant obstacle to the Spanish invasion and conquest of England. Philip looked forward to the destruction of the Protestants and the restoration of Catholicism in England. With the English support severed, it would be easy for him to finally crush the rebellion in the Netherlands.

GOD BLEW AND THEY WERE SCATTERED

However, while churches throughout England held extraordinary prayer meetings, a storm wrecked the Spanish plans. The Duke of Parma's invasion barges from Holland were not able to be used and the English tactic of setting fire ships amongst the huge Spanish galleons, created confusion. Courageous action by English seamen and continuing storms decimated and broke up the Spanish Armada. Dutch support also helped the English defeat the Spanish Armada. Most of what was left of Philip's fleet was devastated by more storms on the coast of Scotland and Ireland. Only a miserable remnant of the once proud Armada limped back into the ports of Spain. 51 Spanish ships and 20,000 men had been lost. The English Navy had not even lost one ship!

1588 - By God's grace the English Navy defeats the Spanish Armada.

A GREAT WATERSHED

The greatest superpower of Europe at that time had suffered a crippling blow. The defeat of the Spanish Armada in 1588 marked a great watershed in history. It signalled the decline of Spain and the rise of England. Commemorative medals were struck with the inscriptions: *"God blew and they were scattered!"* and *"Man proposes, God disposes."*

THE RISE OF PROTESTANT NAVAL POWERS

Before 1588, the world powers were Spain and Portugal. These Roman Catholic empires dominated the seas and the overseas possessions of

Europe. Only after the English defeated the Spanish Armada did the possibility arise of Protestant missionaries crossing the seas. As the Dutch and British grew in military and naval strength, they were able to challenge the Catholic dominance of the seas and the new continents. Foreign missions now became a distinct possibility.

THE DEFEAT OF SPAIN & TRIUMPH OF THE REFORMATION
Had the Armada succeeded, recent history would be unrecognisable. In the 16th Century, Spain led the Catholic cause; England the Protestant. All of Europe feared Spain. It had defeated all its adversaries, even the Turk. The Catholic nations of Europe had every expectation that Spain would succeed in crushing Protestantism by conquering England and Holland. When the Armada failed, the mystique of Spanish invincibility was destroyed. With the defeat of Catholic Spain the Vatican cause floundered. If *"Bloody Mary"* had undermined the Catholic credibility, the defeat of the Spanish Armada eradicated every hope that the Reformation in England could be reversed.

The extraordinary energies that had been released by the rediscovery of the Bible in the common tongue, had led to the most extraordinary spiritual Revival in history, freed the Christians of Northern Europe from the decadence of Renaissance paganism and led to the greatest birth of freedom and scientific discoveries in history.

The 16th Century was the Greatest Century of Reformation.

"Stand fast therefore in the liberty by which Christ has made us free, and do not be entangled again with a yoke of bondage." Galatians 5:1

The Reformation Monument in Geneva to: Farel, Calvin, Beza and Knox.

Chapter 2
Preparation for Reformation

"Those from among you shall build the old waste places; You shall raise up the foundations of many generations; And you shall be called the Repairer of the Breach, The Restorer of Streets to Dwell In." Isaiah 58:12

The Reformation in Europe during the 16th Century was one of the most important epochs in the history of the world. The Reformation gave us the Bible – now freely available in our own languages. The now almost universally acknowledged principles of religious freedom, liberty of conscience, the rule of law, separation of powers and constitutionally limited republics were unthinkable before the Reformation. The Reformers fought for the principles that Scripture alone is our final authority, Christ alone is the Head of the Church and Justification is by God's grace, on the basis of the finished work of Christ, received by faith alone.

Some influential developments which preceded the Reformation:

- **"The Black Death."** The Bubonic plague, spread by lice on rats from China, wiped out over one third of Europe's population.

- The **invasion of Muslim Turks** who swept over the Balkans and even reached the gates of Vienna.

- There was also **a massive influx of pagan Greek humanistic writings** (as a result of the fall of Constantinople and the Byzantine Empire). This led to a renaissance of pagan humanistic thinking.

- There was **widespread corruption** of the Roman Catholic system with superstitions and un-Biblical doctrines taught and with positions in the church for sale – open to the highest bidder.

- People were also encouraged to *"purchase salvation"* with the sale of **Papal Indulgences.**

- The invention of the **printing press** and the printing of the first book (**a Bible**) in **1456**, by Johan Gutenberg, was one very positive development, which made possible the rapid dissemination of Reformation doctrines.

The Waldensians

Firm and Faithful Alpine Fighters for the Faith

Statue of Peter Waldo in Worms.

Peter Waldo was a wealthy merchant, well respected and a man of influence, in the community of Lyons. One evening, while entertaining friends at his home, one of them suffered a sudden seizure and died. This incident so shook Waldo that he began to seriously think of his soul and eternity beyond the grave. He began to regularly attend church services, but was not satisfied with the superficial rituals in Latin.

Studying the Scriptures

He employed two priests to come to his house to translate the Gospels of Christ into French. Waldo was most excited as he read, meditated on and carefully studied the Words of Christ. Yet, instead of comfort and peace, he found conviction and challenge. He saw himself as the foolish rich man who was laying up treasures on earth, but was spiritually poor towards God. Again and again he read the Words of Christ: *"Take heed and beware of covetousness, for the abundance of a man's life consisteth not in those things which he possesseth"* Luke 12:15.

A Determination to Follow Christ

He determined to obey the command of Christ to the rich man recorded in Mark 10:22: *"If you wish to be perfect, sell what you have and follow Me."* This Waldo saw as the Gospel resolution to his personal crisis. He determined to follow this exhortation of Christ literally. He gave all of his possessions to the poor in his community as restitution for his former business practices. He denied himself and followed Christ as a poor man.

As Waldo's friends, family and neighbours thought him insane, he replied to them: *"My friends and fellow citizens, I am not out of my mind as some of you think. I have avenged myself on these my enemies, who kept me in such slavery, that I cared more for money than for God and served more willingly the creature rather than the Creator."*

After Waldo had finished distributing all of his property and possessions, he found many of the poor standing by his side, not content with mere existence, but desiring to live as true Christians, even as Waldo was demonstrating and proclaiming.

The Bible was placed on The Index of Forbidden Books, 1229.

After receiving a call from the pope's representative to clarify his position and the intentions of his new movement, Waldo declared: *"We have decided to live by the Words of the Gospel, especially that of the sermon on the Mount and the Commandments, that is, to live in poverty, without concern for tomorrow. But we hold that also those who continue to live their lives in the world doing good will be saved."*

Waldo did not intend to separate from the Catholic Church, but rather to work for its reformation from within. It also was not his intention to start a new church. From the beginning the Waldensians described themselves only as: *"The poor."* Vows of poverty in the Middle Ages were not unusual. There were numerous monastic movements, which had done that, such as The Franciscans of Francis of Assisi. However, Waldo remained a layman and his followers did not call themselves *"brothers"* as the monks did, but as *"co-members"* of the *"society."* They took these terms from the business world and avoided describing themselves in religious terms. They wanted only to be a group of lay persons who were working together for the living and preaching of the Gospel. Their purpose was to live the Christian Faith according to the teachings of Jesus Christ, as found in the Gospels.

A BIBLE STUDY MOVEMENT

For this purpose they emphasised the importance of hearing and understanding the Word of God, the Bible. It was from the Scriptures that men and women could know Christ as the focus of their Faith. They chose to live in voluntary poverty and sought to be faithful in proclaiming the Gospel in public. This greatly offended the religious leaders of their time and brought the wrath of the Catholic church upon them.

Pressure Begins to Build

The archbishop of Lyons attempted to stop Waldo from preaching. Public preaching, according to the Catholic theologians, was reserved for the clergy alone. According to Catholic belief and practice at that time, Waldo, the merchant, not being ordained, had no right to preach. This Waldo challenged: *"Who are the real successors of the Apostles? Not necessarily those who are ordained, but rather those who respond to the Lord's call and live like the Apostles of old. What makes one a true heir to the Apostles is not ecclesiastical ordination, but faithfulness to the Word of God. The authority to preach God's Word does not come through any church organisation, but from Christ Himself."* Waldo asserted that God's Word and His Spirit do surely act within the church, but they are not solely administered by it.

A Decisive Challenge

As a result, Waldo was severely threatened by the archbishop of Lyon. The archbishop ordered him to cease his preaching. To this Waldo responded: **"It is better to obey God than man."** For this bold defiance, quoting the words of the Apostle Peter in Acts 4:19, his followers began to call him Peter Waldo.

Persecution Unleashed

The archbishop excommunicated Waldo and had him banished from the city. With great zeal, Peter Waldo and his followers scattered the Gospel seed throughout Northern Italy, Southern France, Switzerland, Austria and Germany. The Council of Verona pronounced fearsome anathemas upon *the poor men of Lyons* who presumed to preach the Gospel without ordination and to dare to translate the Scriptures from Latin into the vernacular. As a result, the Waldensians were hunted down by agents of the Inquisition and many thousands were imprisoned, tortured and put to death.

Resistance Grows

At first the Waldensians were pacifists, rejecting any form of violence, even in self-defense. They also refused to take oaths. However, in time, other generations of Waldensians grew to be resourceful soldiers, tenacious fighters and innovative military strategists, defeating Catholic armies and securing religious freedom for their beleaguered families in the Alps of Piedmont.

Some of the Waldensian **precepts for living in the world** included:
1. We must not love the world.
2. We must, if possible, live at peace with men.

3. We must shun evil company.
4. We must not avenge ourselves.
5. We must love our enemies.
6. We must possess our souls in patience.
7. We must not be unequally yoked with unbelievers.

Some of the Waldensian **precepts for personal holiness** included:
1. We shall not serve the lusts of the flesh.
2. We shall govern worldly thoughts.
3. We shall mortify our members.
4. We shall shun idleness.
5. We shall practice works of mercy.
6. We shall live in faith and morality.
7. We shall fight against lusts.
8. We shall speak to one another of the Will of God.
9. We shall diligently examine our consciences.
10. We shall purify, improve and compose the spirit and mind.

Resilience Under Fire and Sword
Despite centuries of relentless and vicious, persecution and harsh oppression, the Waldensians not only managed to survive, but to expand, always attracting new followers and managing to proclaim the Gospel in new areas.

Reformation Revelations
Peter Waldo grasped the great Reformation principles of the supreme authority of Holy Scripture and salvation by grace through faith. He lifted up the principle that Christ's Law must be supreme. He recognised that the churches had become unfaithful to God's Law and to the Gospel of Christ. In their worldly quest for temporal riches and power, the church had long since abandoned the humility of Christ and the poverty of the Apostles. By compromising with the world it had lost its spiritual power.

Thousands of Waldensians were murdered by the papacy.

EVANGELISTS
But the Waldensians did not seek to be separatists, but to purify the church from within. From the very beginning of this movement, the Waldensians have always been known as distributors of the Scriptures and Christian literature. As a result, their followers were found as far afield as the Danube River in Austria, in Northern Germany and in Bohemia where their teachings and example helped inspire the great Bohemian professor and Reformer Jan Hus.

TRAVELING SALESMEN
Some of the most effective Waldensian evangelists were salesmen, merchants who travelled from town to town selling fabrics, clothing, jewelry, artifacts and alluding to more precious goods in their possession – to jewels of inestimable value, even The Pearl of Great Price – the Gospel of Jesus.

GOSPEL SIMPLICITY
In German, the Waldensians were called: *"Apostles."* The Polish described them as: *"Men who tell the truth."* The Waldensians became known as those who proclaimed the Bible as the only rule for faith and conduct. They rejected the papacy, purgatory, indulgences, the mass and other forms of superstition, as unBiblical. They rejected religious formalism in favour of Gospel simplicity. They promoted Christ-centred worship, Bible reading, faithful prayer and Scriptural preaching as the responsibility of all believers.

TRIBULATION

The Council of Valencia (1229) forbid men who were not priests to read the Bible, whether in Latin, or in the vernacular. The Bible itself was placed on *The Index of Forbidden Books*. A savage wave of persecution rose up against the Waldensians. The Inquisition resorted to a murderous campaign which tortured and slaughtered thousands of these faithful Bible believers.

PROTESTANT ALLIES

Early in the Reformation, French Reformer, Guillaume Farel, travelled across the Alps and recruited the Waldensians into the mainstream of the Reformation. The persecution of the Waldensians intensified in the 17th Century and in 1655,

OLIVER CROMWELL
1599
1658

Oliver Cromwell, Lord Protector of England, declared a Solemn Fast on behalf of the suffering Waldensian believers. The Protector threatened to send the English Navy to the Mediterranean to strike a blow on behalf of the Protestant cause and threatened military intervention unless the persecution ceased. Oliver Cromwell's secretary, John Milton, wrote a famous sonnet on the Massacres at Piedmont and Cromwell himself headed a campaign to raise support for the Waldensians with a personal gift of 2,000 pounds. He urged their cause so whole-heartedly that over half a million pounds was donated for the suffering Waldensians.

Cromwell's vigorous intercession and threat of mobilising English naval and military action, brought the persecution of the Waldensians to a close. The Waldensians survive to this day, the oldest Evangelical church, with a heritage of over 800 years of faithful proclamation of the Gospel and firm resistance against tyranny.

"To him who overcomes, I will give the right to eat from the Tree of Life." Revelation 2:7

JOHN WYCLIFFE (1320 - 1384)

THE MORNING STAR OF THE REFORMATION

In the 14th Century, Oxford was the most outstanding university in the world and John Wycliffe was its leading Theologian and philosopher.

The Black Death (the Bubonic Plague), which killed a third of the population of Europe, led Wycliffe to search the Scriptures and find salvation in Christ.

THE KING'S CHAMPION

As a professor at Oxford University, Wycliffe represented England in a controversy with the pope. Wycliffe championed the independence of England from Papal control. He supported King Edward III's refusal to pay taxes to the pope. (It was only one step away from denying the political supremacy of the pope over nations to questioning his spiritual supremacy over churches). The royal favour which Wycliffe earned from this confrontation protected him later in life.

Wycliffe's patron and protector was John of Gaunt. This English prince was the most powerful political figure in late 14th Century England. Gaunt, known in his day as the Duke of Lancaster, was effectively the Prime Minister of England during the last years of the 50-year reign of his then senile father, King Edward III. Gaunt was *"a wise diplomat, a bold soldier, the epitome of chivalry, hard on his enemies and always faithful to what he believed was best for England."* In 1399 Gaunt's son ascended the throne as King Henry IV.

ALL AUTHORITY IS UNDER GOD

In Wycliffe's book *Civil Dominion*, he maintains that the ungodly have no right to rule. All authority is granted by God, but God does not grant any authority to those who are in rebellion against Him. Those who rule unjustly are in breach of the terms under which God delegates authority. So wicked rulers have forfeited their right to rule. In fact, all of those who lead blatantly sinful lives forfeit their rights in this world.

CORRUPTION DISQUALIFIES LEADERS

Wycliffe also taught that the clergy of his time were so corrupt that the secular authorities had the right to confiscate their properties. The Roman church at that time owned about one third of all land in England and claimed exemption from taxation, yet the pope claimed the right to tax the English – to finance his own wars!

Wycliffe translated the Bible into English.

Wycliffe maintained that the English government had the God-given responsibility to correct the abuses of the church within its realm and to remove from office those churchmen who persisted in their corruption and immorality.

SERVANT LEADERSHIP AND SACRIFICE

Wycliffe taught that our personal relationship with God is everything. Character is the fundamental basis of any leadership. He emphasised apostolic poverty, insisting that those who claimed to sit on Saint Peter's chair should, like the Apostle, be without silver or gold. To Wycliffe, those who claimed to follow the Apostles should live poor and humble lives spent in the service of the Church, setting an example of holiness. Therefore the pope of Rome should be a shepherd of the flock and a preacher who brings men to Christ. Wycliffe denounced the worldliness and luxury of the popes and the spiritual bankruptcy of the office of pope. The papacy had departed from the simple Faith and practice of Christ and His disciples. Wycliffe wrote: *"Christ is truth, the pope is the principle of falsehood. Christ lived in poverty, the pope labours for worldly magnificence. Christ refused temporal dominion, the pope seeks it."*

CHRIST ALONE IS THE HEAD OF THE CHURCH

In his book *"The Power of the papacy"* published in 1379, Wycliffe argues that the papacy is an office instituted by man, not God. No pope's authority could extend to secular government. The only authority that any pope might have would depend upon him having the moral character of the

Apostle Peter. Any pope who does not follow Jesus Christ is anti-Christ. Wycliffe proclaimed that *"Christ alone is the Head of the Church."*

UNBIBLICAL PRACTICES CONDEMNED

The Church on earth Wycliffe defined as the whole company of the elect, those chosen by God. The Church is the body of Christ, a unity that knows nothing of popes, hierarchies, monks, friars, priests or nuns. Nor can the salvation of the elect be effected by masses, indulgences, penance, or any other devices of priestcraft. There is nothing in the Bible about transubstantiation, pardons, absolutions, worship of images, the adoration of saints, the treasury of merits laid up at the reserve of the pope, the distinction between venial and mortal sins, or confession to a priest. Compulsory confession Wycliffe considered *"the bondage of anti-Christ."* Wycliffe declared that **the reading and preaching of God's Word** *"is of more value than the administration of any sacrament."*

GOD'S LAW IS SUPREME

In a letter written by Wycliffe to pope Urban VI he maintained: *"The Gospel of Christ is the body of the Law of God, Christ is true God and true man... the Roman pontiff is most bound to this Law of the Gospel...Christ's disciples*

Professor Wycliffe commissioned the Lollards to proclaim the Gospel throughout the land.

are judged...according to their imitation of Christ in their moral life...Christ was the poorest of men during the time of His pilgrimage...He eschewed all worldly dominion...never should any of the faithful imitate the pope himself, nor any of the saints except in so far as he may have imitated the Lord Jesus Christ...the pope should leave temporal dominion to the secular arm...God... has always taught me to obey God rather than men." In this letter Wycliffe also refers to the *"deceitful counsel...malicious counsel...anything contrary to the Law of the Lord"* as *"anti-Christ."*

SCRIPTURE ALONE IS OUR AUTHORITY

In 1378 Wycliffe completed the book *"The Truth of Holy Scripture."* In it he wrote: *"Holy Scripture is the pre-eminent authority for every Christian and the rule of faith and of all human perfection...it is necessary for all men, not for priests alone...Christ and His Apostles taught the people in the language best known to them...therefore the doctrine should not only be in Latin, but in the vernacular...the more these are known the better...believers should have the Scriptures in a language which they fully understand."* Wycliffe taught that Scripture contains everything that is necessary for our salvation. All other authorities must be tested by the Scripture. *"Christ's Law is best and enough and other laws men should not take, but as branches of God's Law."*

TRANSLATING THE SCRIPTURES

Therefore Wycliffe supervised a handful of scholars at Oxford in the translation of the Latin Bible into the English language. This was the very first translation of the entire Bible into the English language. The only source that Wycliffe's translators had to work with was a Latin hand-written manuscript of a translation made 1000 years previously. Wycliffe is called *"the father of English prose"* because of the clarity and effectiveness of his writings and sermons which did much to unify and shape the English language.

THE LOLLARDS EVANGELISE ENGLAND

From Oxford, Wycliffe trained and sent out *"poor priests"* (*the Lollards*) into the fields, villages and churches, to preach in the marketplaces, to read and sing the Scriptures in English and to win people for Christ. These itinerant evangelists became a tremendous power in the land as they spread the knowledge of the Scriptures throughout England.

PERSECUTION FROM PAPAL PHARISEES

As a result of these activities and teachings, one pope issued five bulls against John Wycliffe for *"heresy."* The Catholic Church tried him three times and two popes summoned him to Rome. However, Wycliffe wisely refused each summons and the political protection of the Duke of Lancaster and Queen Anne kept Wycliffe alive and free. He was never imprisoned. However, his followers were hunted down, expelled from Oxford and mercilessly persecuted.

The Lollards were the Field Workers of the Reformation sowing Gospel seed in the marketplaces of England.

HATRED FOR THE BIBLE IN THE COMMON LANGUAGE
To get an idea of the scandal and controversy engendered by Wycliffe's Reformation, we should note what was written by Henry Knighton, a Catholic chronicler: *"Christ gave His Gospel to the clergy...but this master John Wycliffe translated the Gospel from Latin into the English...common to all and more open to the laity and even to women...and so the pearl of the Gospel is thrown before swine and trodden under foot...the jewel of the clergy has been turned into the jest of the laity...has become common."* The Archbishop of Canterbury, Arundel, said: *"that pestilent and most wretched John Wycliffe, of damnable memory, a child of the old devil and himself a child or pupil of anti-Christ...crowned his wickedness by translating the Scriptures into the mother tongue!"*

THE BIBLE IN ENGLISH – BANNED
A synod of clergy in 1408 decreed: *"It is dangerous...to translate the text of Holy Scripture...we decree and ordain that no-one shall in future*

translate on his authority any text of Scripture into the English tongue or into any other tongue, by way of book, booklet or treatise. Nor shall any man read, in public or in private, this kind of book, booklet or treatise, now recently composed in the time of the said John Wycliffe...on the penalty of the greater excommunication."

Catholic bishops condemned the writings of Professor Wycliffe to be burned.

EARTHQUAKE INTERRUPTS ANATHEMAS
In 1382, at a church council called by Archbishop Courtenay, 24 of Wycliffe's teachings were condemned. During that council there was an earthquake. Wycliffe and the Lollards interpreted the earthquake as a sign of God's displeasure with the corrupt and un-Biblical Roman clergy.

ROME VS. JERUSALEM
Wycliffe scorned the idea that because Peter died in Rome therefore every Bishop of Rome is to be set above all of Christendom. By the same reasoning, he noted, the Muslim Turk might conclude that because they controlled Jerusalem, where Christ died, their Mullah has power over the pope!

WHO CAN FORGIVE SINS?
Wycliffe attacked the corruptions, superstitions and abuses of the friars and monks. He exposed their supposed powers to forgive sins as fraudulent. *"Who can forgive sins?"* Wycliffe taught: *"God alone!"* **Christ alone is the Head of the Church and God alone can forgive sins.**

FIELD WORKERS OF THE REFORMATION
Wycliffe's field workers (*the Lollards*) helped to prepare the way for the English Reformation (in the 16th Century) by reading, preaching and singing the Scriptures in English in marketplaces, fields and homes throughout the land.

TURNING THE TABLES
Summoned to appear before a church, council Wycliffe rebuked the bishops for being *"priests of Baal, selling blasphemy and idolatry in*

the mass and indulgences." He then walked out of the assembly and refused a summons from the pope. When Wycliffe was excluded from teaching in Oxford, he withdrew to the congregation at Lutterworth, in Leicestershire, where he devoted himself to writing during his few remaining years.

John Wycliffe on trial - defended by John of Gaunt, the Duke of Lancaster.

Wycliffe's Ashes and Doctrine

In 1428, 44 years after Wycliffe's death, by order of the pope, the bones of Wycliffe were dug up and burned. As one historian commented: *"They burned his bones to ashes and cast them into the Swift, a neighbouring brook running close by. Thus the brook conveyed his ashes to the Avon, the Avon into the Severn, the Severn into the narrow seas and they into the main ocean. And so the ashes of Wycliffe are symbolic of his doctrine, which is now spread throughout the world."* Wycliffe was the father of the Reformation – its morning star. Wycliffe's writings and example inspired John Hus and Martin Luther.

"The fear of the Lord is the beginning of wisdom and the knowledge of the Holy One is understanding." Proverbs 9:10

ANNE OF BOHEMIA (1366 - 1394)

Anne became Queen of England.

THE REFORMERS FRIEND
Anne of Bohemia, was the eldest daughter of Emperor Charles IV of the Holy Roman Empire. Her brother was King Wenceslaus of Bohemia (who was named after the subject of a famous Christmas carol).

A GREAT LOVE FOR THE SCRIPTURES
Anne was taught the truths of the Scripture from her youth. There were a number of faithful Gospel preachers in Bohemia at that time including Conrad Strichna, Johan Melice and Matthias Janovius. Anne asked many probing questions concerning Scriptural truths.

AN INQUIRING MIND
Anne was described as a godly, intelligent young girl with an inquiring mind. She was renowned for her love of reading and for her possession of the Scriptures in three languages. Her favourite books of the Bible were the four Gospels, which she constantly studied.

A HUNGER FOR REFORMATION
Anne came to recognise the many errors prevailing in the Roman church and she persisted in praying for a return to Biblical faithfulness, to the Doctrine of the Apostles and to the purity of the early Church.

CRECY CHANGES BOHEMIA'S ALLEGIANCE
The traditional alliance of Bohemia with France was shattered by their joint defeat at the hands of the English King Edward III and his son, The Black Prince, at the Battle of Crecy in 1346. Richard II's Father, Edward, was called the Black Prince because of his dark coloured armour. Then the Papal Schism further divided the Bohemians from their traditional allies, the French. As France supported pope Clement VII of Avignon, King Wenceslaus chose to support pope Urban VI in Rome. As the English also allied against the French pope, the Bohemians came into alliance with the English.

A New Alliance with England

The Battle of Crecy - 1346.

As King Richard II's father, The Black Prince, died in 1376 and his grandfather, King Edward III, the following year, Richard II became King of England at age 10. Negotiations began to solidify the alliance between Bohemia and England by the marriage of Princess Anne to King Richard.

A Courageous Young King

At age 14, King Richard II showed remarkable courage during the Peasants Revolt of 1381. At Smithfield, at great personal risk, Richard II rode out to meet the violent mob and calmed them into ending the revolt.

Marriage at Westminster

In January 1383, when Richard II was 15 years old and Anne was 16 years old, they were married in St. Stephens Chapel, at Westminster. Although their marriage had been arranged by diplomats, it appears to have been a good, loving and positive partnership. Anne was undoubtedly an excellent influence on Richard during their 12 years together.

A Friend of the Reformation

Reportedly Anne had been persuaded to accept the proposal because of positive reports that she had received of the Reformation work of Professor John Wycliffe of Oxford University.

The Archbishop of York, Arundel, one of the most vitriolic enemies of Wycliffe's Reformation work, was horrified to hear that the Queen owned copies of the Gospels, which she avidly studied.

Professor John Wycliffe was delighted to learn of Anne's love for the Scriptures and he publically compared her to the Biblical Mary who sat at Jesus' feet listening to what the Master had to say.

Protecting the Professor

For her part, Queen Anne protected Wycliffe from his many enemies and intervened on numerous occasions to protect him from prosecution and to save his life.

STUDENTS OF REFORMATION
At the encouragement of Queen Anne, Bohemian students came to Oxford to study under John Wycliffe. Many of these students carried back the Reformation writings and teachings of Wycliffe to Prague, Bohemia and throughout central Europe. Students sponsored by Queen Anne were soon taking the Reformation writings and teachings as far afield as Lithuania.

EVANGELISTIC
Many of Queen Anne's friends and servants became dedicated Christian believers.

GENEROSITY
The common people of England came to love the Queen. Her kindness and generosity to the poor was legendary. It is said that as many as six thousand people were fed daily through her benevolence.

DEEPLY MOURNED
Tragically, this bright and shining light was cut short on the 7 June 1394 as Anne died at age 27 from the plague. Her husband, King Richard II, was devastated and the people of England deeply mourned her.

THE REFORMATION COMES TO BOHEMIA
Many of her Christian friends and servants returned to Bohemia with the translations of the Gospels and writings of John Wycliffe that had been so highly treasured by Queen Anne. These led to the conversion of Professor Jan Hus of Bohemia, the Hussite movement and later the Moravians. From them missionaries went out, literally, to the ends of the earth.

"These things command and teach. Let no one despise your youth, but be an example to the believers in word, in conduct, in love, in spirit, in faith, in purity. Till I come, give attention to reading, to exhortation, to doctrine. Do not neglect the gift that is in you, which was given to you by prophecy with the laying on of the hands of the eldership. Meditate on these things; give yourself entirely to them, that your progress may be evident to all. Take heed to yourself and to the doctrine. Continue in them, for in doing this you will save both yourself and those who hear you." 1 Timothy 4:11-16

Jan Hus (1372 - 1415)

The Reformer of Prague

The Reformation movement launched by Wycliffe and his Lollards in England was intensely opposed and fiercely persecuted by the Roman church. The Reformation movement was largely driven underground in the British Isles. But Wycliffe's teachings spread to Bohemia where they resulted in a dynamic revival. The two nations of England and Bohemia were linked in 1383 by the marriage of Anne of Bohemia to King Richard II of England. Prague students went to Oxford and English students went to Prague.

Preparation for Reformation

Scripture translations from the persecuted Waldensian refugees had begun entering Bohemia in the 13th Century. When Anne of Bohemia married King Richard II she sent copies of Wycliffe's writings back to her homeland. Queen Anne's love for the Bible was shared by many of her countrymen. Soon, Conrad Stickna was preaching the Gospel in the open air to large crowds. Matthew of Janov travelled throughout Bohemia preaching against the abuses of the church. His followers were imprisoned and burned at the stake. John Milic, Archdeacon of the cathedral in Prague, preached fearlessly against the abuses of the church and wrote *"Anti-Christ Has Come"* over a cardinal's doorway. He was imprisoned.

Courageous Czech Confronts Corruption

Born in the village of Husinec, Jan Hus studied for the priesthood and received a Master's degree in 1396. In 1402 he was appointed preacher in Bethlehem Chapel. Jan Hus, when appointed Rector of Prague University at age 34, also began to preach Reformation principles (in the common Language) in the Chapel of Bethlehem in Prague. Hus translated Wycliffe's works into German, exposed the superstitions, fraudulent *"miracles"* and the sale of indulgences. In 1405, Hus denounced

Hus teaching Biblical principles.

the alleged appearances of *"Christ's blood"* on communion wafers as an elaborate hoax. He condemned the sins of the clergy as *"fornicators"*, *"parasites"*, *"money misers"*, *"fat swine"*, *"drunks"* and *"gluttons."* He condemned the practice of simony (buying spiritual offices) and the taking of multiple paid positions without faithfully serving any. He described churches that sold indulgences as *"brothels."*

The Reformer of Prague, Professor Jan Hus.

Hus adopted Wycliffe's view of the Church as an elect community with Christ – not the pope – as its true Head. Hus's fiery sermons in the Bohemian language received widespread enthusiastic support. Hus believed pastors should be examples of God-fearing integrity. He preached vivid, accessible sermons, which captured the people's imaginations. Hus was described by his supporters as *"a passionate Reformer."*

Hus teaching in Bethlehem Chapel, Prague.

On the walls of the Chapel of Bethlehem were paintings contrasting the behaviour of the popes and Christ. The pope rode a horse; Christ walked bare-foot. Jesus washed the disciples' feet; the pope preferred having his feet kissed. Hus insisted that no human institution – including the church - can be ultimate in authority. Only God has ultimate authority.

In 1410 the Archbishop obtained from the pope a ban on teaching in chapels, including specifically the Bethlehem Chapel. This ban Hus refused to obey. In that same year the Archbishop burned over 200 volumes of Wycliffe's works. Hus responded: *"Fire does not consume truth. It is always the mark of a little mind that it vents its anger on inanimate objects."* Hus defended Wycliffe's orthodoxy. Hus was summoned to Rome, but wisely refused to go.

THE PAPACY STRIKES BACK

Archbishop Zbynek excommunicated Hus. (Hus was actually excommunicated 5 times) Hus was described as *"radical"* and *"dangerous."* Hus then openly attacked the pope's sale of indulgences in support of his war against Naples. The pope thereupon placed the City of Prague under a papal interdict. This meant that the entire city was placed under an ecclesiastical ban (all churches were closed, no masses were allowed, no confessions received, no marriages or burials permitted). Until this time Hus had been protected by the king, university and nobility from the wrath of the pope. But with the entire city in turmoil, the Reformer chose to go into exile. During this time Hus wrote: *"On the Church."* And he preached in the villages and countryside.

TREACHERY AT CONSTANCE

Hus lived during The Great Schism when Europe was divided between two and then three rival popes who bitterly anathematized one another. A General Church Council was called at Constance in 1415 to heal 'The Great Schism' (that had raged from 1378). It was this Council of Constance, which aimed to bring the Schism to an end, that summoned Hus. The Emperor Sigismund guaranteed Hus safe conduct in both directions, whatever the outcome of the case against him might be.

However, upon arriving, Hus was imprisoned on orders of pope John XXII. Despite the Imperial guarantee of safe conduct, Hus was taken through a mockery of a trial in which he was allowed no defence. Hus had hoped to present his views to the assembled authorities, but instead he found himself a victim of a cruel Inquisition, which condemned him for heresies, which he had neither believed nor taught (including that he had claimed to be the fourth member of the Trinity!) Hus prayed aloud that Christ might forgive his judges and accusers.

STEADFAST TO THE END

Under pressure to recant Hus declared: *"I would not, for a chapel full of gold, recede from the truth...the truth stands and is mighty forever."* Hus stated that he would prefer to be burned in public than to be silenced in private *"in order that all Christendom might know what I said in the end."*

Jan Hus on trial at Constance, 1415.

Despite the emperor's safe conduct guarantee, Professor Hus was burned at Constance.

On 6 July 1415 Hus was condemned to death and taken to the outskirts of the city of Constance to be burned. Hus prayed: *"O most holy Christ… strengthen my spirit…give me a fearless heart, a right faith, a firm hope, a perfect love, that for Thy sake I may lay down my life with patience and joy."*

On arriving at the execution ground, Hus knelt and prayed: *"God is my witness that the evidence against me is false. I have never thought nor preached except with the one intention of winning men, if possible, from their sins.* **In the truth of the Gospel I have written, taught and preached; today I will gladly die."** Hus died singing *"Jesus, Son of the Living God, have mercy on me."* He was 43 years old.

RESISTANCE TO ROME SPREADS

After Hus's martyrdom his followers organised military resistance to the Holy Roman Empire. Remarkably, these vastly outnumbered Hussites repelled six crusades against them. These Hussites fought under Hus's motto: **"Truth conquers."** They proved that you could take on the Holy Roman Empire – and survive!

A Spiritual Heritage

His followers, *The Unity of the Brotherhood*, survived as an independent church, co-operating with the Waldensians and later with the Lutherans and the Calvinists. The Hussites became known as the Moravians. Under Count Nicholas Van Zinzendorf the Moravians started a prayer chain that lasted 150 years! During that extended prayer meeting, 2,400 Moravian missionaries were sent throughout the world. Moravians were instrumental in the conversion of John Wesley.

"Truth cannot be burned."

The Goose and the Swan

One interesting anecdote is that Hus is accredited with making a prophecy at his death. *"My goose is cooked!"* he said. (Hus is the Bohemian word for goose!) *"But a hundred years from now a swan will arise whose voice you will not be able to silence."* Many saw Martin Luther as that voice, hence the prevalence of swans in Lutheran art and architecture.

Monument to Reformer and Professor Jan Hus in Prague.

JOHANNES GUTENBERG (1400 - 1468)
THE INVENTOR OF THE PRINTING PRESS

MAN OF THE MILLENNIUM

At the end of the 20th Century, numerous publications discussed who they believed were the most important people of the millennium. Johannes Gutenberg, the inventor of the Printing Press, was in everybody's top 10 and many voted him as The Most Important Man of the Millennium!

AN INSATIABLE APPETITE FOR KNOWLEDGE

Johannes Gutenberg was born in the city of Mainz near the shores of the Rhine River. His father, Friel Gensfleisch, married Else Von Gutenberg, who gave her name to her second son, Johannes. As a young boy, Johannes developed an insatiable appetite for knowledge, reading every book he came across.

AN ITINERANT STUDENT

During his teen years, Johannes and his family were forced into exile twice due to political in-fighting and conflicts. Johannes travelled from town to town, studying monuments and visiting men who were renowned for their knowledge in science, art, or the trades. He travelled alone, on foot, carrying a knapsack with his precious books and clothes. As an itinerant student, he travelled throughout Italy, Switzerland, Germany and Holland.

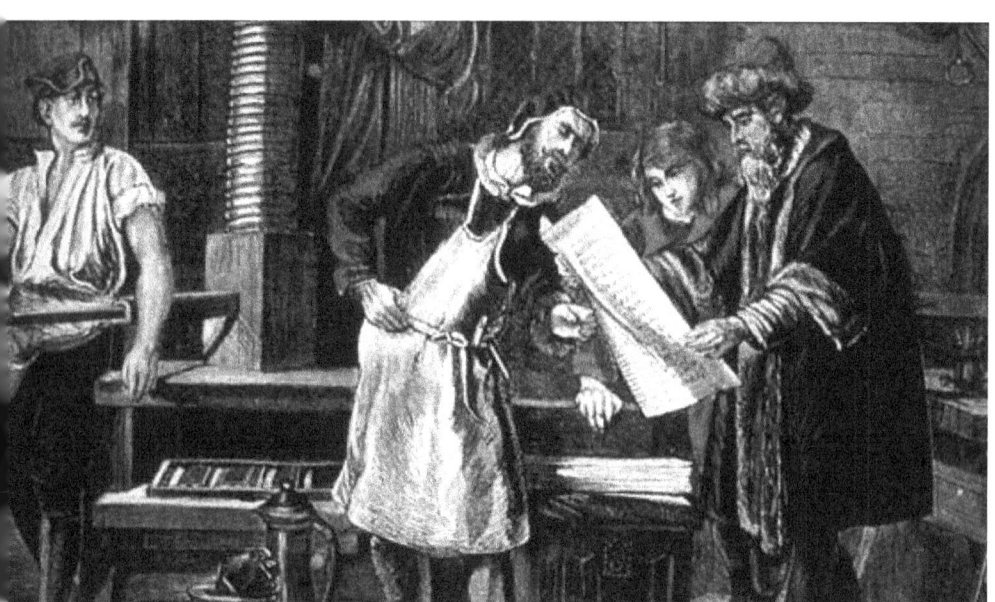

The Printing Press - The Reformer's friend, the tyrants foe.
Gutenberg's printing press provided the technology to advance the Gospel.

A Deepening Love and Growing Vision

His love for God grew and deepened the more he read and studied. The further he travelled, the greater his vision developed of spreading the Word of God to all people.

Inspiration

One day, in Haarlem, his friend, Lawrence Koster, handed him a piece of wood that had letters carved on it, wrapped in a piece of parchment. Some of the sap from the greenwood had hardened into the relief shape of the letters on the parchment. As Johannes saw this simple plaque of wood an inspiration flashed into his heart and mind with the force of lightening. The possibility of producing a machine that could print the Word of God welled up inside him. Gutenberg travelled up the Rhine to Straßburg and closeted himself in his workroom.

Tools and Testing

He fashioned his own tools, developed plans, tested and tried, reorganized and attempted again and again to produce an effective printing machine. Starting with moveable wooden types, he bored through the side of each a small hole to string together the letters of the alphabet cut in relief on one side.

An Immense Vision

Johannes Gutenberg seemed to understand something of the immense importance of this invention upon industry, society and civilisation itself. When he contracted a skilful craftsman, Conrad Saspach, to create a full size version of his scale model, the craftsman responded: *"But it is just a simple press you are asking from me Master Hans."*

"Yes," replied Gutenberg, *"It is a press, certainly, but a press from which shall soon flow in inexhaustible streams the most abundant and most marvellous liquor that has ever flowed to relieve the thirst of man! Through it God will spread His Word. A spring of pure truth shall flow from it! Like a new star, it shall scatter the darkness of ignorance and cause a light heretofore unknown to shine among men."*

LIMITATIONS AND SECRECY

Despite his great vision, Johannes was acutely aware of his limitations. He was just one man, with very limited resources. He was concerned about his work being discovered and possibly pirated for lesser goals. He worked on the mechanics of printing secretly, moving his workshop into the ruins of an old deserted monastery.

DEDICATION AND DISCIPLINE

He spent sleepless nights wearing himself out in pursuit of his invention. He engraved his movable types in wood and projected casting them in metal. He studied hard to find the means of enclosing them in forms, whether of wood or of iron, to make the types into words, phrases, lines and to leave spaces on the paper. He invented coloured mediums, oily and yet able to dry, to reproduce the characters, brushes and dabbers that spread the ink on the letters, boards to hold them and screws and weights to compress them. He invested months and years and his entire fortune in these experiments. There were many disappointments, failures and frustrations before he developed a model press, which combined all elements for an efficient printing press.

THE FIRST BOOK EVER PRINTED

The first book to be printed had to be the Holy Bible; the second was the *Psalter* (the first book to ever bear a date: 1457). The Gutenberg Bible, completed in 1455, was the first book ever published with movable type. Fewer than 200 copies were originally printed and only 48 have survived to this day. Today, the original Gutenberg Bible is considered one of the finest works of art. In 1978 a two-volume edition of the Gutenberg Bible was sold for over $2 million. In 1987 a Gutenberg Bible was sold for $4,9 million, the highest price paid for a book to that date.

OVERCOMING OPPOSITION

At first the Roman Catholic church opposed the Printing Press. For political reasons and for the survival of his invention, Gutenberg wrote a dedication to pope Paul II on behalf of the Printing Press: *"Among the number of blessings which we ought to praise God is this invention, which enables the poorest to procure libraries at a*

low price. Is it not a great glory that volumes that used to cost 100 pieces of gold, are now to be bought for four, or even less and that the fruits of genius… multiply over all the earth!"

Hijacked

Soon Gutenberg could not sustain the demand for printing in his small workshop. He was forced to develop partnerships with moneylender Johann Fust, who unfortunately did not have the integrity of the inventor. Fust hijacked his invention and stole everything from Gutenberg. Despite these trials and betrayals, Gutenberg maintained his integrity and honour, maintaining a faithful Christian witness to the end.

One of the Greatest Inventions in History

Gutenberg's invention of the Printing Press is rightly classified as one of the greatest events in the history of the world. The Printing Press prepared the way for the Reformation and the progress of modern science and literature. The Printing Press became an indispensable tool in the fulfilment of the Great Commission and the development of universal education. Gutenberg's invention enabled multiplied millions to discover for themselves great literature and, most importantly, the Word of God.

The Reformer's Friend, the Tyrant's Foe

This one invention made possible the greatest Revival of Faith and freedom ever experienced. The inventing of the Printing Press played a key role in mobilising the Reformation. Without printing, it is questionable whether there would have been a Protestant Reformation. A century before Luther, Wycliffe and Hus had inspired dedicated movements for Bible study and Reform, but the absence of adequate printing technology severely limited the distribution of their writings. As a result their ideas did not spread as rapidly, or as far, as they could have done. By God's grace, the Printing Press provided the Reformers, Martin Luther, Ulrich Zwingli, William Tyndale, John Calvin and others, with the spiritual weapons they needed to make the Reformation succeed. **"Making disciples of all the nations, teaching obedience to all things…"** Matthew 28:19

GIROLAMO SAVONAROLA (1452 – 1498)
ITALIAN REFORMER AND MARTYR

SERIOUS AND INTELLIGENT
Born of Italian nobility in the city of Ferrara in 1452, Savonarola was described as a serious and intelligent boy who, at an early age, gravitated to the writings of some of the most learned men in history. He received instruction in philosophy, logic and medicine from his father and grandfather. From studying the writings of Plato and Dante, he came to develop a deep spiritual hunger. The pictorial illustrations of hell in Dante's *Inferno* tormented him.

THE CENTRE OF THE RENAISSANCE
In 1475, he decided to become a monk and joined the Dominicans. After an intense time of study, he was sent to the city of Florence. In the 15th Century, the centre of the Renaissance was Florence, Italy. From this centre of science and art, masters such as Michelangelo, Leonardo Da Vinci and Raphael produced exquisite and timeless art.

FEARLESS PREACHING
In studying the writings of Augustine of Hippo, Savonarola came to see how far the church had fallen from its Apostolic calling. Girolamo Savonarola began fearlessly to preach Christ amidst the moral decay, irreligious lifestyles, superstitious beliefs and unbiblical practices of the clergy and community. He was 38 years old when he began his work of Reformation in Florence.

CONFRONTING CORRUPTION
Vast crowds gathered to hear his denunciations of the prevalent corruption and immorality. The majestic cathedral was filled to overflowing by citizens of Florence eager to hear this celebrated orator expose the corruptions of the ruling Medici family and the idolatry and corruptions of the Roman church. Savonarola preached repentance from sin with a growing earnestness. Many hardened sinners surrendered their lives to Christ and forsook their evil ways of life.

INCORRUPTIBLE

The ruler of Florence, Lorenzo Medici, tried to silence the Reformer with gifts and attempted bribes. However, Savonarola was relentless and incorruptible. When Lorenzo was dying, at age 44, he sent for Savonarola, but when the Reformer found that Lorenzo had no intention of repenting of his sins, he refused him the blessing which was customary to grant to the dying.

REFORMATION IN FLORENCE

The people ousted Lorenzo's son and unanimously chose Savonarola as ruler of Florence. For three years Savonarola governed Florence with justice and efficiency. Savonarola intended the city to become an example of a Christian commonwealth in which God is the Ruler and His Gospel the Sovereign Law. Dens of iniquity and vice were closed down. Gambling was outlawed; licentious books and pictures were destroyed in a *"bonfire of vanities."*

PAPAL POWER PLAY

Some people began to resent the strictness of the new rule. Pope Alexander was one of the most notoriously immoral popes with five illegitimate children whom he openly promoted to high office. This pope engaged in the most unscrupulous conduct, including bribery and murder. Pope Alexander VI took the lead in attacking the Reformer of Florence. Firstly, Alexander VI tried to make Savonarola a cardinal and offered him great bribes. Savonarola rejected all these declaring: *"I do not desire any other crown than the crown of a martyr."*

EXCOMMUNICATION AND TORTURE

Thereafter the pope attempted to spread slander to undermine the authority of Savonarola. Then the pope excommunicated and imprisoned him. People who had previously acclaimed and supported Savonarola now allowed him to be tortured and joined in a chorus of condemnation of the courageous Reformer.

STEADFAST

However, Savonarola remained steadfast. He refused to be shaken in his convictions even after the most unbearable tortures. On 23 May 1498, Savonarola was burned to death in the great square in the city of Florence. Before a huge crowd, a bishop declared to the condemned Savonarola: *"I separate thee from the church militant and triumphant."* Savonarola responded: *"Militant, not triumphant, for you have no power to separate me from the Church triumphant – to which I go."* Savonarola died at age 45.

REGENERATION

"We must regenerate the church," taught Savonarola. *"None are saved by their own works. No man can boast of himself; and if, in the presence of God, we could ask all these justified of sins – have you been saved by your own strength? All would reply as with one voice: 'Not unto us O Lord! Not unto us; but to Him be the glory!'"*

SCRIPTURE ALONE

Savonarola gave special emphasis to the authority of the Bible. *"I preach the regeneration of the church, taking the Scriptures as my sole guide."*

CHRIST ALONE

As Savonarola was being severely tortured on the rack, he prayed: *"O Lord... I do not rely on my own justification, but on Thy mercy."* In between his tortures, he wrote meditations on Psalm 32 and 51, which Martin Luther later published, describing them as: *"a piece of Evangelical testimony and Christian truth."*

COURAGE AND FAITH

Savonarola met his martyrdom with courage and faith, declaring: *"Should I not willingly die for His sake Who willingly died for me, a sinful man?"*

Preparation for Reformation

"Do not be afraid of those who kill the body and after that have no more that they can do." Luke 12:14

The monument to Reformer Savonarola in Florence, Italy.

The Reformation Monument in Worms, Germany.

Chapter 3
Martin Luther
Captive to the Word of God

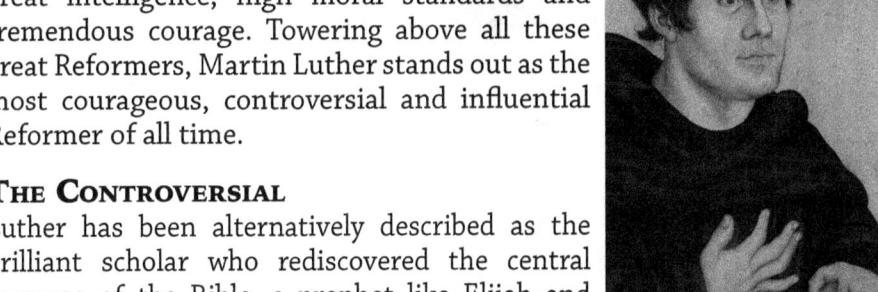

The Reformation was one of the most momentous turning points in world history. It was led by men of strong faith, deep convictions, great intelligence, high moral standards and tremendous courage. Towering above all these great Reformers, Martin Luther stands out as the most courageous, controversial and influential Reformer of all time.

The Controversial
Luther has been alternatively described as the brilliant scholar who rediscovered the central message of the Bible, a prophet like Elijah and John the Baptist to reform God's people, the liberator who arose to free his people from the oppression of Rome, the last medieval man and the first modern man. Zwingli described him as: *"the Hercules who defeated the tyranny of Rome."* Pope Leo X called Luther: *"A wild boar, ravaging his vineyard."* Emperor Charles V described him as: *"A demon in the habit of a monk!"*

The Son
Martin Luther was born 10 November 1483 in Eisleben, Saxony. His father, Hans Luder, had worked hard to climb the *"social ladder"* from his humble peasant origins to become a successful copper mining entrepreneur. Hans married Margaretha Lindemann, the daughter of a prosperous and gifted family that included doctors, lawyers, university professors and politicians. Hans Luder owned several mines and smelters and he became a member of the City Council in Mansfield, where Martin was raised, under the strict discipline typical of that time.

The Student
From age 7, Martin began studying Latin at school. Hans intended his son to become a lawyer, so he was sent on to the University of Erfurt before his 14th birthday. Martin proved to be extraordinarily intelligent and he earned his BA and MA degrees in the shortest time allowed by the statutes of the University. Martin proved so effective in debating that he earned the nickname: *"the philosopher."*

67

THE STORM

As Martin excelled in his studies, he began to be concerned about the state of his soul and the suitability of the career his father had set before him. While travelling on foot, near the town of Stotternhein, a violent thunderstorm brought Martin to his knees. With lightning striking all around him, Luther cried out for protection to the patron saint of miners: *"St. Anne, help me, I will become a monk!"* The storm around him matched the conflict raging within his soul.

THE MONK

Although his parents were pious people, they were shocked when he abandoned his legal studies at Erfurt and entered the Augustinian monastery. Martin was 21 years old when, in July 1505, he gave away all his possessions – including his lute, his many books and clothing – and entered the Black Cloister of the Augustinians. Luther quickly adapted to monastic life, throwing himself wholeheartedly into the manual labour, spiritual disciplines and studies required. He went way beyond the fasts, prayers and ascetic practices required and forced himself to sleep on the cold stone floor without a blanket, whipped himself and seriously damaged his health. He was described as: *"devout, earnest, relentlessly self-disciplined, unsparingly self-critical, intelligent..."* and *"impeccable."* Luther rigorously pursued the monastic ideal and devoted himself to study, prayer and the sacraments. He wearied his priest with his confessions and with his punishments of himself with fasting, sleepless nights and flagellation (whipping).

Luther found peace with God while studying the Book of Romans.

THE PROFESSOR

Luther's wise and godly superior, Johannes von Staupitz, recognised Martin's great intellectual talents and to channel his energies away from excessive introspection ordered him to undertake further studies, including Hebrew, Greek and the Scriptures, to become a university lecturer for the order. Luther was ordained a priest in 1507 and studied and taught at the Universities of Wittenberg and Erfurt (1508 – 1511). In 1512, Martin Luther received his doctoral degree and took the traditional vow on becoming a professor at Wittenberg University to teach and defend the Scriptures faithfully. This vow would be a tremendous source of encouragement to him later. Luther never viewed himself as a rebel, but rather as a Theologian seeking to be faithful to the vow required of him to teach and defend Holy Scripture. Luther committed most of the New Testament, much of the Old Testament and all of the Psalms to memory.

WITTENBERG

The University of Wittenberg had been founded by Prince Frederick of Saxony in 1502. Luther's friend from his university days in Erfurt, George Spalatin, was now chaplain and secretary to the Prince and closely involved in the Prince's pet project of his new university. Wittenberg at this time was a small river town with only about 2,000 residents. Prince Frederick wanted to build it up into his new capital of Saxony.

STUDIES THAT SHOOK THE WORLD

From 1513 to 1517, Luther lectured at the University on the Psalms, Romans and Galatians. Being a university professor would have been a full-time job; however, Luther had other responsibilities as well. He was the supervisor for 11 Augustinian monasteries, including the one at Wittenberg. Luther was also responsible for preaching regularly at the monastery chapel, the town church and the castle church. It was a combination of Luther's theological and pastoral concerns that led him to take the actions that sparked the Reformation.

Luther receiving his Doctorate.

SEEKING PEACE WITH GOD

Luther had long been troubled spiritually with the righteousness of God. God demanded absolute righteousness: *"Be perfect, even as your Father in Heaven is perfect." "Be holy, as I am Holy."* We are obligated to love God whole-heartedly and our neighbours as ourselves. It was because of his great concern for his eternal salvation that Luther had sought to flee the world. In spite of the bitter grief and anger of his father, he had buried himself in the cloister and devoted himself to a life of the strictest asceticism. Yet, despite devoting himself to earning salvation by good works, cheerfully performing the humblest tasks, praying, fasting, chastising himself even beyond the strictest monastic rules, he was still oppressed with a terrible sense of his utter sinfulness and lost condition.

"THE JUST SHALL LIVE BY FAITH"

Then Luther found some comfort in the devotional writings of Bernard of Clairvaux, who stressed the free grace of Christ for salvation. The writings of Augustine provided further light. Then, as he begun to study the Scriptures, in the original Hebrew and Greek, joy unspeakable flooded his heart. It was 1512, as he began to study Paul's Epistle to the Romans, that the verse **"For in the Gospel a righteousness from God is revealed, a righteousness that is by faith from first to last, just as it is written: the righteous will live by faith"** Romans 1:17

BORN AGAIN

Luther later testified that as he began to understand that this righteousness of God is a free gift by God's grace through which we may live by faith, *"I felt entirely born again and was led through open gates into Paradise itself. Suddenly the whole of Scripture had a different appearance for me. I recounted the passages which I had memorised and realised that other passages, too, showed that the work of God is what God works in us… thus St. Paul's words that* **the just shall live by faith**, *did indeed become to me the gateway to Paradise."* The burden of his sin rolled away. Up until then, Luther had tried to earn salvation by his good works, although he never felt that he had been able to do enough. Now, God had spoken to him through the Scripture. Man is not saved by works, but by faith alone.

A TURNING POINT

As a doctor, Luther had taken an oath to serve the Church faithfully by the study and teaching of Holy Scripture. At the university, he was responsible to prepare pastors. Now, having experienced God's grace in Christ, studying God's Word, Luther began to see the emptiness, self-absorption, pious pretence and superstitious unbelief of his previous religious devotion. Nor could Luther fail to recognise the same pious fraud and pharisaic futility all around him. In 1510, before being made a professor at Wittenberg, Luther had been sent to Rome for his monastic order. What he had seen there had shocked and disillusioned him. Rome was the pre-eminent symbol of ancient civilisation and *"the residence of Christ's Vicar on earth"* the pope. Luther was horrified by the blatant immorality and degeneracy prevalent in Rome.

UNDERSTANDING CATHOLICISM

The centre of medieval Roman Catholic church life was the Mass, the Sacrament of the altar. The Roman Catholic institution placed much emphasis on the punishment of sin in Purgatory, as a place of

During Luther's visit to Rome he was shocked and deeply disillusioned by the prevalent immorality.

cleansing by fire before the faithful were deemed fit to enter Heaven. They taught that there were four sacraments that dealt with the forgiveness and the removal of sin and the cancellation of its punishment: Baptism, The Mass, Penance and Extreme Unction. The heart of Penance was the priestly act of Absolution whereby the priest pardoned the sins and released the penitent from eternal punishment. Upon the words of Absolution, pronounced by the priest, the penitent sinner received the forgiveness of sins, release from eternal punishment and restoration to a state of grace. This would require the sinner making some satisfaction, by saying a prescribed number of prayers, by fasting, by giving alms, by going on a pilgrimage, or by taking part in a crusade.

INDULGENCES

In time, the medieval church had come to allow the penitent to substitute the payment of a sum of money for other forms of penalty or satisfaction. The priest could then issue an official statement, an indulgence, declaring the release from other penalties through the payment of money. In time, the Catholic church came to allow indulgences to be bought, not only for oneself, but also for relatives and friends who had died and passed into Purgatory. They claimed that these indulgences would shorten the time that would otherwise have to be spent suffering in Purgatory. This practice of granting indulgences was based upon the Catholic doctrine of *Works of Supererogation*. This unbiblical doctrine claimed that works done beyond the demands of God's Law earned a reward. As Christ and the saints had *"perfected Holiness"* and *"laid up a rich treasury of merits"* in Heaven, the Roman church claimed that it could draw upon this treasury of *"extra merits"* to provide satisfaction for those who paid a specified sum to the church.

THE INDULGENCE INDUSTRY

This system of indulgences was very popular with the masses of people who preferred to pay a sum of money to saying many prayers and partaking in many masses to shorten the suffering in Purgatory of either themselves or a loved one. The industry of indulgences had also become a tremendous source of income for the papacy. In order to fund the building of the magnificent St. Peter's Cathedral in Rome, pope Leo X had authorised a plenary, or total indulgence. And so it was on this papal fundraising campaign to complete the construction of St. Peters *Basilica* that the Dominican monk and indulgence salesman extraordinary, John Tetzel, arrived in Saxony. The shameless and scandalous manner in which Tetzel hawked the indulgences outraged Martin Luther. Sales jingles such as: *"As soon as the coin clinks in the chest, a soul flies up to Heavenly rest"* were deceiving gullible people about their eternal souls.

DISTRATION AND DECEPTION

Dr. Luther's study of the Scripture had convinced him that salvation came by the grace of God alone, based upon the Atonement of Christ on the Cross alone, received by faith alone. Indulgences could not remove any guilt and could only induce a false sense of security. People were being deceived for eternity.

THE 95 THESES

Concerns that had been growing since his visit to Rome in 1510 led Professor Luther now to make a formal objection to the abuses of indulgences. On All Saint's Day (1 November), people would be coming from far and wide in order to view the more than 5,000 relics exhibited in the *Schlosskirche*, which had been built specifically for the purpose of housing this massive collection. So, on 31 October 1517, Martin Luther nailed his 95 Theses against indulgences on to the door of the castle church. He also posted a copy to the Archbishop of Mainz.

A SENSATIONAL CALL TO REPENTANCE

These Theses created such a sensation that within 2 weeks, they had been printed and read throughout Germany. Within the month, translations were being printed and sold all over Europe. The 95 Theses begin with the words: *"Since our Lord and Master, Jesus Christ says: 'Repent, for the Kingdom of Heaven is near' (Matthew 4:17), He wants the whole life of a believer to be a life of Repentance."*

Luther maintained that no sacrament can take away our responsibility to respond to Christ's command by an inner repentance evidenced by an outward change, a transformation and renewal of our entire life. Luther emphasised that it is God alone who can forgive sins and that indulgences are a fraud. It would be far better to give to the poor, than to waste one's money on indulgences. If the pope really had power over the souls suffering in Purgatory, why would he not release them out of pure Christian charity?

THE EMPIRE STRIKES BACK

Luther's *95 Theses* radically undermined Tetzel's business, almost bringing the sale of indulgences to a standstill. Tetzel, Mazzolini and John Eck published attacks on Luther, defending the sale of indulgences. When none of Luther's friends rose to his defence, Luther felt deserted. Many of his closest friends believed that he had been too rash in his criticism of this established church practice. With the pope's power challenged and papal profits eroded, church officials mobilised their forces to bring this rebellious professor into line. First the Augustinians at their regular meeting in Heidelberg sought to silence Luther. Then he underwent three excruciating interviews with Cardinal Cajetan in Augsburg. Then, in June 1519, Johann Eck debated Luther in Leipzig.

RESEARCH AND RESISTANCE

Some close friends of Luther tried to persuade him to settle things peacefully by giving in, but to Luther this was now a matter of principle.

Scriptural truth and eternal souls were at stake. In preparation of the Leipzig debate, Luther had plunged into the study of church history and canon law. His studies convinced Luther that many of the decretals, such as the Donation of Constantine, were forgeries.

4 July 1519 - Professor Luther debated Johann Eck in Leipzig.

THE LEIPZIG DEBATE

On 4 July 1519, Eck and Luther faced one another in Leipzig. The issue being debated was the supremacy of the pope. Luther pointed out that the Eastern Greek Church was part of the Church of Christ, even though it had never acknowledged the supremacy of the Bishop in Rome. The great Church Councils of Nicea, Chalcedon and Ephesus knew nothing of papal supremacy. But Eck maneuvered Luther into a corner and provoked him to defend some of the teachings of (condemned *heretic*) Jan Hus. By making Luther openly take a stand on the side of a man official condemned by the church as a heretic, Eck was convinced that he had won the debate. However, Luther greatly strengthened his cause amongst his followers, winning many new supporters, including Martin Bucer, (who became a crucial leader of the Reformation, even helping to disciple John Calvin). Luther published an account of the Leipzig debate and followed this up with an abundance of teaching pamphlets. *"On Good Works"* had a far-reaching effect teaching that man is saved by faith alone. *"The noblest of all good works is to believe in Jesus Christ."* Luther maintained: that shoemakers, housekeepers, farmers and businessmen, if they do their work to the glory of God, are more pleasing to God than monks and nuns.

EXCOMMUNICATION

Bulla contra Erro
res Martini Lutheri
et sequacium.

The Papal Bull excommunicating Luther.

On 15 June 1520, pope Leo X signed the Bull excommunicating Luther. Describing Luther's teaching as: *"heretical," "scandalous," "false," "offensive"* and *"seducing,"* the Bull called upon all Christians to burn Luther's books and forbade Luther to preach. All towns or districts that sheltered him would be placed under an interdict. In response, Luther wrote: *"Against the Execrable Bull of AntiChrist."* On 10 December 1520, surrounded by a large crowd of students and lecturers, he burned the papal bull, along with books of canon law, outside the walls of Wittenberg. Having exhausted all ecclesiastical means to bring Luther to heel, pope Leo now appealed to the Emperor to deal with Luther.

SUMMONED TO WORMS

Previously, in 1518, when the pope had summoned Luther to Rome, Prince Frederick had brought all his influence to have this papal summons cancelled. When Luther had been summoned to Augsburg and Leipzig, Prince Fredrick had arranged for safe conduct guarantees. But now that Emperor Maximilian had died, Charles V of Spain had been elected Emperor of the Holy Roman Empire. Prince Frederick himself had been a serious contender for this position and still held tremendous influence. So he prevailed upon Charles V to guarantee safe conduct for Luther as he was summoned to Worms for a Council of German rulers.

THE STATE

In the year before his summons to the Diet of Worms, Luther published some of his most powerful and influential treatises. In the *Address to the German Nobility* (August 1520) he called on the Princes to correct the abuses within the church and to free the German church from the exploitation of Rome.

THE CHURCH

In *The Babylonian Captivity of the Church* (October 1520), Luther argued that Rome's sacramental system held Christians captive. He attacked the papacy for depriving individual Christians of their freedom to approach God directly by faith – without the mediation of unbiblical priests and sacraments. To be valid, a sacrament had to be instituted by Christ and

Luther burning the Papal Bull outside the gates of Wittenberg.

be exclusively Christian. By these tests, he could find no justification for five of the Roman Catholic sacraments. Luther retained only Baptism and The Lord's Supper and placed these within the community of believers, rather than in the hands of a church hierarchy. Indeed, Luther dismissed the traditional view of the church as the sacred hierarchy headed by the pope and presented the Biblical view of the Church as a community of the regenerate in which all believers are priests, having direct access to God through Christ.

THE CHRISTIAN LIFE

In *The Liberty of a Christian Man* (November 1520), Luther presented the essentials of Christian belief and behaviour. Luther removed the necessity of monasticism by stressing that the essence of Christian living lies in serving God in our calling, whether secular or ecclesiastical. In promoting this Protestant Work Ethic, Luther laid the foundation for free enterprise and the tremendous productivity it has inspired. He taught that good works do not make a man good, but a good man does good works. Fruit does not produce a tree, but a tree does produce fruit. We are not saved by doing good works, but by grace alone. However, once saved, we should expect good works to flow as the fruit of true faith.

FACING CERTAIN DEATH

Summoned to Worms, Luther believed that he was going to his death. He insisted that his co-worker, Philipp Melanchthon, remain in Wittenberg. *"My dear brother, if I do not come back, if my enemies put me to death, you will go on teaching and standing fast in the truth; if you live, my death will matter little."* Luther at Worms was 37 years old. He had been excommunicated by the pope. Luther would have remembered that the Martyr, Professor Jan Hus, a century before had travelled to Constance with an imperial safe conduct, which was not honoured. Luther declared: *"Though Hus was burned, the truth was not burned and Christ still lives... I shall go to Worms, though there be as many devils there as tiles on the roofs."* Luther's journey to Worms was like a victory parade. Crowds lined the roads cheering the man who had dared to stand up for Germany against the pope.

BEFORE THE EMPEROR

At 4 o' clock on Wednesday 17 April, Luther stood before the rulers of the Holy Roman Empire. Charles V, Emperor of the Holy Roman Empire, ruled all the Austrian domains, Spain, Netherlands, a large part of Italy and the Americas. At 21 years old, Charles V ruled over a territory larger than any man since Charlemagne. Amidst the pomp and splendour of this imperial gathering stood the throne of the Emperor on a raised platform. It was flanked by knights in gleaming armour, 6 Princes, 24 Dukes, 30 Archbishops and Bishops and 7 Ambassadors.

PRESSURED TO RECANT

Luther was asked to identify whether the books on the table were his writings. Upon Luther's confirmation that they were, an official asked Luther: *"Do you wish to retract them, or do you adhere to them and continue to assert them?"* Luther had come expecting an opportunity to debate the issues, but it was made clear to him that no debate was to be tolerated. The Imperial Diet was ordering him to recant all his writings. Luther requested more time, so that he might answer the question without injury to the Word of God and without peril to his soul. The Emperor granted him 24 hours.

CONFRONTATION

The next day, Thursday 18 April, as the sun was setting and torches were being lit, Martin Luther was ushered into the august assembly. He was asked again whether he would recant what he had written. Luther responded that some of his books taught established Christian doctrine on faith and good works. He could not deny accepted Christian doctrines. Other of his books attacked the papacy and to retract these would be to encourage tyranny and cover up evil. In the third category of books, he had responded to individuals who were defending popery and in these Luther admitted he had written too harshly. The examiner was not satisfied: *"You must give a simple, clear and proper answer... will you recant or not?"*

"HERE I STAND"

Dr. Luther's response, first given in Latin and then repeated in German, shook the world: ***"Unless I am convinced by Scripture or by clear reasoning that I am in error – for popes and councils have often erred and contradicted themselves – I cannot recant, for I am subject to the Scriptures I have quoted; my conscience is captive to the Word of God. It is unsafe and dangerous to do anything against one's conscience. Here I stand. I cannot do otherwise. So help me God. Amen."***

"Here I stand, I can do no other" - Luther before the Emperor Charles V at Worms.

After the shocked silence, cheers rang out for this courageous man who had stood up to the Emperor and the pope. Luther turned and left the tribunal. Numerous German nobles formed a circle around Luther and escorted him safely back to his lodgings.

CONDEMNED

The Emperor was furious. However, Prince Frederick insisted that Charles V honour the guarantee of safe conduct for Luther. Charles V raged against *"this devil in the habit of a monk"* and issued the edict of Worms, which declared Luther an outlaw, ordering his arrest and death as a *"heretic."*

KIDNAPPED

As Luther travelled back to Wittenberg, preaching at towns along the route, armed horsemen plunged out of the forest, snatched Luther from his wagon and dragged him off to Wartburg Castle. This kidnapping had been arranged by Prince Frederick amidst great secrecy in order to preserve Luther's life. Despite the Emperor's decree that anyone helping Luther was subject to the loss of life and property, Frederick risked his throne and life to protect his pastor and professor.

WARTBURG CASTLE

For the 10 months that Luther was hidden at Wartburg Castle, as Knight George (*Junker Jorg*), he translated The New Testament into German and wrote such booklets as: *"On Confession Whether the pope Has the Authority to Require It; On the Abolition of Private Masses"* and *"Monastic Vows."* By 1522, The New Testament in German was on sale for just a week's wages.

REVOLUTION REBUKED

In Luther's absence, Professor Andreas Karlstadt instituted revolutionary changes, which led to growing social unrest. In March 1522, Luther returned to Wittenberg

Luther translating the New Testament.

and in 8 days of intensive preaching, renounced many of Karlstadt's innovations, declaring that he was placing too much emphasis on external reforms and introducing a new legalism that threatened to overshadow justification by faith and the spirituality of the Gospel. Luther feared that the new legalism being introduced would undermine the Reformed movement from within.

THE PEASANTS' REVOLT

When the Peasants' Revolt erupted, Luther was horrified at the anarchy, chaos and bloodshed. He repudiated the revolutionaries and wrote *"Against the Robbing and Murdering Hordes of Peasants."* Aghast at the devastation and massacres caused by the Peasants' Revolt, Luther taught that the princes had the duty to restore social order and crush the insurrection.

Katherine von Bora.

MARRIAGE

Also in 1525, on 13 June, Luther married Katherine von Bora, a former nun from a noble family. Luther called home life: *"the school of character"* and he stressed the importance of the family as the basic building block of society. Luther and Katie were blessed with 6 children.

THE BONDAGE OF THE WILL

Also in 1525, Luther wrote one of his most important books: *"On the Bondage of the Will."* This was in response to Desiderius Erasmus's book on *The Freedom of The Will*, published in 1524. Luther responded scathingly to Erasmus' theories on free will, arguing that man's will is so utterly in bondage to sin, that only God's action could save. Luther articulated the Augustinian view of predestination and declared that he much preferred that his salvation be in God's Hands, rather than in his own. As a result of the exchange between Luther and Erasmus, many Renaissance Humanist scholars ceased to support Luther.

Dr. Martin Luther preaching in Wartburg Castle, 1522.

A Time of Change

The Reformation not only brought about sweeping changes in the church, but dramatic changes in all of society. First of all the Reformation focused on bringing doctrines, forms of church government and of worship and daily life into conformity with the Word of God. This, of course, had tremendous implications for political, economic, social and cultural life as well.

God's Word Above All Things

Luther revised the Latin liturgy and translated it into German. Now the laity received the Communion in both bread and wine, as the Hussites had taught a Century earlier. The whole emphasis in church services changed from the sacramental celebration of the Mass as a sacrifice to the preaching and teaching of God's Word. Luther maintained that every person has the right and duty to read and study the Bible in his own language. This became the foundation of the Reformation: a careful study of the Bible as the source of all truth and as the only legitimate authority, for all questions of faith and conduct.

Scripture Alone is our authority.

The True Church

The Church is a community of believers, not a hierarchy of officials. The Church is an organism rather than an organisation, a living body of which each believer is a member. Luther stressed the priesthood of all believers. We do not gain salvation through the church, but we become members of the Church when we become believers.

REFORMATION BASIC PRINCIPLES

Martin Luther dealt with many primary issues, including:

1. **Authority** – the Bible alone is our ultimate authority and not the councils or leaders of the Church. *The Bible is above tradition.*
2. **Salvation** – is by the grace of God alone, accomplished by the Atonement of Christ alone, received by faith alone. *Grace comes before sacraments.*
3. **The Church** – the true Church is composed of the elect, those regenerated by God's Holy Spirit. *Regenerate Church membership.*
4. **The Priesthood** – consists of all true believers. *The priesthood of all believers.*

THE BATTLE CRIES OF THE REFORMATION

The Protestant Reformation mobilised by Martin Luther rallied around these great battle cries:
Solus Christus – Christ alone is the Head of the Church.
Sola Scriptura – Scripture alone is our ultimate authority.
Sola Gratia – Salvation is by the grace of God alone.
Sola Fide – Justification is received by faith alone.
Soli Deo Gloria – Everything is to be done for the glory of God alone.

SURVIVING AS AN OUTLAW

Despite Luther being declared an outlaw by the Emperor, he survived to minister and write for 25 more years and died, possibly of poison, 18 February 1546.

Wartburg Castle - where Dr. Luther translated the New Testament into German.

TRANSLATOR, AUTHOR AND MUSICIAN

In spite of many illnesses, Luther remained very active and productive as an advisor to princes, theologians and pastors, publishing major commentaries and producing great quantities of books and pamphlets. He completed the translation of the Old Testament into German by 1534. Luther continued preaching and teaching to the end of his life. He frequently entertained students and guests in his home and he produced beautiful poems and hymns, including one hymn that will live forever: *"Ein Feste Burg Ist Unser Gott"* (A Mighty Fortress is Our God).

TEACHER

Luther also did a great deal to promote education. He laboured tirelessly for the establishment of schools everywhere. Luther wrote his *Shorter Catechism* in order to train up children in the essential doctrines of the Faith.

AN EXCEPTIONAL PROFESSOR

It has been common to portray Luther as *"a simple and obscure monk,"* who challenged the pope and emperor. Actually Luther was anything but simple or obscure. He was learned, experienced and accomplished far beyond most men of his age. He had lived in Magdeburg and Eisenach and was one of the most distinguished graduates of the University of Erfurt. Luther travelled to Cologne, to Leipzig and he had crossed the Alps and travelled to Rome. Luther was a great student, with a tremendous breadth of reading, who had excelled in his studies and achieved a Master of Arts and Doctorate in Theology in record time. He was an accomplished best selling author, one of the greatest preachers of all time, a highly respected Theological professor and one of the first professors to lecture in the German language, instead of in Latin.

PRODUCTIVE AND INFLUENTIAL

Far from being a simple monk, Luther was the Prior of his monastery and the district Vicar over 11 other monasteries. Luther was a monk, a priest, a preacher, a professor, a writer and a Reformer. He was one of most courageous and influential people in all of history. The Lutheran Faith was adopted not only in Northern Germany, but also throughout Denmark, Norway, Sweden, Finland and Iceland.

LUTHER CHANGED THE WORLD

Dr. Martin Luther was a controversial figure in his day and has continued to be considered controversial to this very day. There is no doubt that

The Greatest Century of Reformation

Luther's search for peace with God changed the whole course of human history. He challenged the power of Rome over the Christian Church, smashed the chains of superstition and tyranny and restored the Christian liberty to worship God in spirit and in truth.

"For I am not ashamed of the Gospel of Christ, for it is the power of God to salvation for everyone who believes ...For in it the righteousness of God is revealed from faith to faith; as it is written, the just shall live by faith." Romans 1:16-23

Eisleben, Saxony - where Martin Luther was born.

Chapter 4
Ulrich Zwingli
The Reformer of Zürich

1 January marks the birthday of Swiss Reformer Ulrich Zwingli and of the launch of the Reformation in Switzerland. It was on 1 January 1519 that Ulrich Zwingli began expositionary preaching in Zürich, starting with the Gospel of Matthew, Chapter 1. Ulrich Zwingli was the father of the Reformation in Switzerland. Born and raised in the Alps, Zwingli was one of the most colourful and audacious characters in Swiss history. A devout student of Scripture, Zwingli was transformed and shaped by the Word of God. He has been described as *"an amazing combination of intellect, passion and wit."*

Zwingli's home in Wildhaus.

Man of the Mountains
Born at an altitude of 3,600 feet (1,100 metres), the son of the Mayor of Wildhaus, Zwingli studied in Bern, Basel and Vienna. In 1506, he received his MA degree. As a pastor in Glarus, Zwingli served as a chaplain with Swiss mercenary soldiers in Italy. The Swiss regularly hired out their men to fight for foreign powers. At that time, the Swiss generally believed that their national economy depended on this war industry.

"Selling Blood for Gold"
During the Italian campaign, Zwingli saw 6,000 Swiss youth die, in the service of the pope, at Marignon. He returned home convinced that *"selling blood for gold"* not only was a waste of young manhood through senseless violence, but also it was corrupting the men's souls through avarice,

"Selling blood for gold" 6000 Swiss youths died at Marignon in the service of the pope.

85

pride and greed. He observed that the entire country was deteriorating spiritually and morally under the lure of gold from foreign princes. Zwingli spoke out boldly: *"The situation is very serious, we are already contaminated. Religion is in danger of ceasing amongst us. We despise God..."* Zwingli's outspoken preaching against this lucrative profession cost him his pulpit in Glarus. Forced out of Glarus, he was able to secure a pastoral position at Einsiedeln - where he continued to preach against mercenary service.

WON BY THE WORD

When Erasmus's New Testament in Greek appeared in 1516, Zwingli immediately purchased a copy. Zwingli taught himself Hebrew and Greek and wrote out and memorized Paul's Epistles in the Greek New Testament. He carried around his little pocket edition with him, memorizing much of the New Testament. Zwingli was shocked to find that there was a world of difference between the teachings of the Bible and the teachings and practices of the Roman Catholic Church.

Ulrich Zwingli

LAUNCHING A REFORMATION

When Zwingli was appointed pastor at *Grossmünster*, (the Great Cathedral) in Zürich, he began his duties, on 1 January 1519, by preaching through the Gospel of Matthew. This bold action of replacing the mass with the preaching of the Word as the central focus of church services marked the beginning of expository preaching.

FACING DEATH

Shortly after he became pastor in Zürich, the city was hit by the plague. Zwingli showed his courage by giving no thought to his own safety, but staying in Zürich and ministering selflessly to the highly contagious victims. He himself was soon struck down with the plague and nearly died. While in the grip of this debilitating illness, Zwingli wrote *"The Song of the Plague"* in which he shows a vibrant faith in the all sufficiency of God's grace in Christ Jesus:

"Help me, O Lord, my strength and rock; lo at the door I hear death's knock.
Uplift Thine arm once pierced for me; that conquered death and set me free.
Yet if Thy voice in life's midday, Recalls my soul, then I obey.
In faith and hope earth I resign, secure of Heaven, for I am Thine.
My pains increase; haste to console; for fear and woe seize body and soul.

Death is at hand, my senses fail, my tongue is dumb; Now, Christ, prevail.
Lo! satan strains to snatch his prey; I feel his grasp; must I give way?
He harms me not, I feel no loss, for here I lie beneath Thy Cross.
My God! My Lord! Here by Thy hand, upon the earth once more I stand.
Let sin no more rule over me; my mouth shall sing alone to Thee."

REVIVAL SWEEPS ZÜRICH

Zwingli recovered from this ordeal, his faith deepened and matured, his mind resolute. He called the people to return to the Bible as the sole standard of Faith and practice, to recognise Christ as the only true Head of the Church. Zwingli attacked one Roman doctrine after another. He attacked unbelief, superstition and hypocrisy. Eagerly he strove after repentance, applying Christ's Lordship to all areas of life, in Christian love and faith. He emphasized the need to care for and protect widows and orphans, to maintain law and uphold justice. Zwingli was concerned that our personal Christian faith and love also result in justice established by the laws of the community. At the heart of the Swiss Reformation was a dynamic sense of Christian community. The Church is a genuine community, one in body and spirit, having the grace of Christ in common and bearing the fruit of the Spirit, the fruit of Christ and the Spirit of God. This unity must extend beyond matters of the spirit to social concern for the entire community, taught Zwingli.

Removal of all statues, images and relics from *Grossmünster*.

ZÜRICH TRANSFORMED

The debate between Ulrich Zwingli and four delegates from the Bishop of Constance.

As Zwingli systematically preached through the New Testament, he laid the foundations for the Reformation in Switzerland. In 1523, the City Council of Zürich voted to become Protestant.

At the **First Zürich Disputation**, in 1523, the City Council and 600 citizens, convened in the City Hall to observe the debate between Ulrich Zwingli and four delegates from the Bishop of Constance. At this gathering the city formally adopted the Reformation and encouraged Zwingli to continue with his Reforms.

In Zwingli's **67 Theses**, which he made public at The First Zürich Disputation (29 January 1523), he stated: *"3. Christ is the only way to salvation for all who ever were, are and shall be."*

"19. Christ is the only Mediator between God and ourselves.

"42. But if ministers are unfaithful and transgress the Laws of Christ, they may be deposed in accordance with God's Will.

"56. Whoever remits any sin only for the sake of money is the companion of Simon (Magus) and Balaam and a real messenger of the devil."

Diethelm Roist, the Mayor of Zürich from 1524 to 1544, became the chief supporter of Zwingli's Reformation in Zürich. Without Roist's support and protection, it was unlikely that Zwingli's Reformation would have succeeded.

Zwingli was a patriotic Swiss Republican. He was able to pioneer an entirely new Switzerland without any compromise with old unbiblical customs and free from all foreign bondage and interference.

With the support of the City Council, Zwingli launched a comprehensive programme of Reform. The City Council of Zürich put an end to mercenary service. All images, statues and relics were removed from the church buildings. The mass was abolished. Altars, processions and other trappings and superstitions were discarded. The school system was reformed. Monastery buildings were turned into hospitals and orphanages. The Bible became the basis for all law. All Zürich clergymen were ordered to preach only from Scripture. Priests, monks and nuns were permitted to marry.

WORK ETHIC RESTORED

Zwingli worked hard to shift the Swiss economy from dependence on mercenary service to agriculture and trade. He urged the people to productive labour: *"You are a tool in the Hands of God. He demands your service... how fortunate you are that He lets you take part in His work."*

FROM DEATH TO LIFE

Zwingli compared the moral sickness and spiritual death of sin to the plague, which had killed one out of every three people in Zürich and he compared their physical recovery to health to the need for spiritual Reformation of church and society.

Diethelm Roist, Mayor of Zürich.

THE BIBLE TRANSLATED

Zwingli began to translate the Scriptures into Schweizer-Deutsch (*Swiss-German*). His lively and dynamic translation reflects his upbringing amidst the towering mountains and lush valleys of Switzerland's Alps. For example in Psalm 23 he translated: *"In schoner Alp weidet Er mich"*(*In the beautiful Alps He tends me*).

THE WORD OF GOD IS INVINCIBLE

Zwingli compared the Word of God to the mighty Rhine River that flowed out of the Alps: *"For God's sake, do not put yourself at odds with the Word of God. For truly, it will persist as surely as the Rhine follows its course. One can possibly dam it up for a while, but it is impossible to stop it."*

A SOLEMN DUTY

Zwingli took his pastoral duties most seriously, writing that they *"inspired in me more fear than joy, because I knew and I remain convinced, that I would give an account of the blood of the sheep which would perish as a consequence of my carelessness."*

MARRIAGE

Earlier, on behalf of 11 other priests, Zwingli had written to the Bishop of Constance seeking permission for priests to marry. This the Bishop had refused. Now, after 2 years of secret marriage, Ulrich married Anna Reinhart, a young widow with 3 children. Ulrich and Anna Zwingli were blessed with another 3 children in their marriage.

EVANGELISING IN THE MARKET PLACE

Zwingli preached in the market place on Fridays that the crowds from surrounding villages might hear the Word of God. He proclaimed the sufficiency of faith in Christ, the deficiency of superstition and indulgences and the necessity of true repentance and holy living. He also emphasized the importance of caring for the poor and needy, the widow and the orphan. Grace cannot be bought or sold. Zwingli confessed his own sins publicly, including an affair with a nun while a priest in Einsiedeln and declared Christ's saving grace to be sufficient for the salvation of all who truly repent. Zürich's freedom-loving city, known for its efficient army and love of political independence, found itself drawn to this dynamic preacher and Reformer.

Zwingli's pulpit and Bible in *Grossmünster*.

THE DISASTER OF DISUNITY

It is unfortunate that attempts to bring about a unity between the Swiss and the German Reformations failed. Prince Philip of Hesse, in his attempt to bring about a political alliance of Protestant states, sponsored the Marburg Colloquy between Martin Luther and Ulrich Zwingli. This historic meeting was held at Prince Philip's castle at Marburg. Although Zwingli and Luther agreed quickly on 14 Articles of Faith, there was sharp disagreement on the 15th Article - concerning the Lord's Supper.

Luther and Zwingli came from very different backgrounds and perspectives and at several points the debate was harsh and acrimonious. At other points the parties appeared to seek each other's forgiveness for name-calling and for the break down in charity. Ultimately, however, their attempt to forge a theological union, that could be the basis of a political and military alliance failed.

As Reformers, Zwingli and Luther had so much in common. They both rejected the authority of the pope and held to the authority of Scripture alone. They both agreed to the principle of justification by faith alone and rejected the concept of the mass as a sacrifice.

Zwingli had been very complimentary of Luther, describing him in classical allusions *"that one Hercules... who slew the Roman boar."* Zwingli also attributed Biblical titles to Luther: *"Here indeed you were the only faithful David anointed hereto by the Lord and furnished likewise with arms."* But Zwingli did not think that Luther's Reformation went far enough. While Luther taught that whatever is not condemned in Scripture is permitted, Zwingli taught that whatever is not specifically commanded in Scripture should be prohibited.

Luther regarded Zwingli as a *Schwarmer* (a fanatic). Luther insisted that they had to take the Lord's Word's **"This is My body"** literally. Zwingli maintained that this has to be understood as a metaphor (as in **"I am the Vine"** and **"I am the Bread of Life"**). After the Resurrection, Christ ascended bodily into Heaven and sits at the right hand of God. Christ is omnipresent only in His Divinity, not in His humanity. **"The Spirit gives life, the flesh is of no avail."**

THE LORD'S SUPPER

To Zwingli, the chief significance of the Lord's Supper was that it was a meal eaten in celebration, in remembrance and in thanksgiving, for what God has done in Christ, but also to exhibit the transformed fellowship of believers. Zwingli had limited the number of Eucharistic services to 4 times a year, while Luther's Eucharist services were held every Sunday. Zwingli maintained: *"I believe that the real Body of Christ is eaten in the Lord's Supper, sacramentally and spiritually by the religious, faithful and pure mind, as also St. Chrysostom held."*

WHILE THE ENEMY MOBILISED

It was one of Zwingli's greatest regrets that he and Luther could not come to any point of agreement on this 15th doctrinal point. Zwingli urged toleration for the different views. Luther regarded Zwingli's plea for toleration as an indication that the Zürich pastor did not take his own views seriously enough. With the forces of Charles V of the Holy Roman Empire mobilising against them,

Meeting of Luther and Zwingli at Prince Philip's castle in Marburg.

Philip of Hesse was frustrated in his attempts to bring about a union between the Protestants in Switzerland and Germany.

THE BATTLE OF KAPPEL

From the time that Zwingli began his expository preaching on the Gospel of Matthew, 1 January 1519, he only had 12 years to establish the Reformation in Switzerland. He died in 1531 in battle, fighting to defend Zürich from attack. In 1529, a Protestant missionary from Zürich was burned at the stake for preaching the Gospel in the Catholic Canton of Schwyz. Zürich stopped trading with Schwyz in protest. The Catholic Cantons declared war. In October 1531, 8,000 Catholic soldiers met 1,500 Protestant soldiers in battle at Kappel. Historian Myconius described Zwingli's death at the Battle of Kappel: *"Three times Zwingli was thrown to the ground by the advancing forces, but in each case he stood up again. On the fourth occasion, a spear reached his chin and he fell to his knees saying:* **'They can kill the body, but they cannot kill the soul'."**

STEADFAST TO THE LAST

Zwingli's successor, Heinrich Bullinger, added these details: *"While the Catholic forces were looting the bodies of the dead and dying, they found Zwingli still alive, lying on his back, with his hands together as if he was praying and his eyes looking upward to Heaven… He was stricken with a mortal wound, so they asked whether a priest should be fetched to hear his*

The death of Zwingli at the Battle of Kappel, October 1531.

confession. At this, Zwingli shook his head... They encouraged him to call upon Mary, the Mother of God and upon the Saints." When Zwingli again shook his head, the Catholics cursed him and said that he was one of the *"obstinate, cantankerous heretics"* and should get what he deserved. One of the Catholic captains then drew his sword and thrust Zwingli through. When his body was identified, there were tremendous shouts of joy throughout the Catholic camp. It was decided to quarter his body and burn the portions, throwing into the fire the entrails of some pigs and mixing the pig offal with Zwingli's ashes, scattering it to prevent a burial of the great Reformer.

An Enduring Legacy

Although Ulrich Zwingli's career had been cut short at the Battle of Kappel, he laid firm foundations, which were later built upon by Heinrich Bullinger and John Calvin.

Zwingli succeeded in establishing a thoroughly Reformed Church in Zürich, which served as a model for the Swiss National Protestant Church. Zwingli's model of Reform was adopted in Bern, Basel, Schaffhausen, Zürich and later Geneva. His courageous preaching was successful in putting an end to the Swiss custom of selling its soldiers for mercenary service to the French and to the papacy.

The deep internal divisions between the various Protestant cantons were healed shortly after Zwingli's death by a military alliance (The Christian Civic Union), which succeeded in securing the independence of Switzerland. Zwingli's dream of establishing a European-wide alliance against the Hapsburgs was not fully realized, but Bern did make an alliance with Hesse, Straßburg and Constance. Without Bern's military support, Geneva could never have become the international centre of Protestantism, which it achieved under the leadership of John Calvin.

Zwingli's successes and sacrifices were effectively built upon by his successor Heinrich Bullinger, who from 1531 to 1575 served as pastor in *Grossmünster*. Until the founding of the Geneva Academy by Calvin in 1559, the Carolinum in Zürich was the only Theological College in Europe where students could study Reformed Theology. The Academy in Geneva and universities of Heidelburg and Holland, built upon the good foundations laid in Zürich.

The English Prayer Book, The 39 Articles and the Puritan emphasis on Head and Heart, Doctrine and Devotion, as well as the Reformed Episcopacy, adopted by the Church of England, were all built upon the teachings of Ulrich Zwingli and Heinrich Bullinger - which English exiles learned during their time in Zürich. Bullinger, Farel, Viret, Calvin and Beza all consolidated and continued the Reformation begun by Ulrich Zwingli.

"For to me, to live is Christ and to die is gain." Philippians 1:21

"The can kill the body but they cannot kill the soul!"

CHAPTER 5
WILLIAM TYNDALE
AND THE BATTLE FOR THE BIBLE

Bishop Stephen Bradley observed: *"We are in danger of forgetting truths for which previous generations gave their lives."*

That our churches are in danger of forgetting the great Reformation truths, for which previous generations of martyrs willingly laid down their lives, was forcefully impressed upon me during a mission to Europe. I had the opportunity to visit Oxford and see the Martyrs Memorial. It drew my attention to an event that occurred over 450 years before.

Martyr's memorial in Oxford.

THE OXFORD MARTYRS

On 16 October 1555, just outside the walls of Balliol College, Oxford, a stout stake had been driven into the ground with faggots of firewood piled high at its base. Two men were led out and fastened to the stake by a single chain bound around both their waists. The older man was Hugh Latimer, the Bishop of Worcester, one of the most powerful preachers of his day and the other Nicolas Ridley, the Bishop of London, respected as one of the finest Theologians in England.

More wood was carried and piled up around their feet. Then it was set alight. As the wood kindled and the flames began to rise, Bishop Latimer encouraged his companion: *"Be of good cheer, Master*

Hugh Latimer   Nicolas Ridley

Ridley and play the man! We shall this day light such a candle, by God's grace, in England, as I trust shall never be put out." Hundreds in the crowd watching the burning of these bishops wept openly.

The place of their execution is marked today by a small stone cross set in the ground in Broad Street, while nearby in St. Giles stands the imposing Martyrs Memorial, erected 300 years later in memory of these two men and of Thomas Cranmer, the Archbishop of Canterbury, who 4 months after their execution suffered the same torturous death by burning, in the same place and for the same reason.

In his trial, Bishop Ridley was urged to reject the Protestant Faith. His reply: *"As for the doctrine which I have taught, my conscience assureth me that it is sound and according to God's Word...**in confirmation thereof I seal the same with my blood."***

After much further pressure and torment, Bishop Ridley responded: *"So long as the breath is in my body, I will never deny my Lord Christ and His known truth: **God's will be done in me!"***

Bishop Latimer declared: *"I thank God most heartily, that He hath prolonged my life to this end, that I may in this case glorify God by this kind of death."*

FAITH AND FREEDOM

On one day, in 1519, seven men and women in Coventry were burned alive for teaching their children the Lord's Prayer, the Ten Commandments and the Apostles Creed – in English!

THE ILLEGAL ENGLISH BIBLE

It may surprise most English-speaking Christians that the first Bible printed in English was illegal and that the Bible translator was burned alive for the crime of translating God's Word into English.

William Tyndale is known as the father of the English Bible, because he produced the first English translation from the original Hebrew and Greek Scriptures. 150 Years earlier Wycliffe had overseen a hand written translation of the Bible, but this had been translated from the Latin Vulgate. Because of the persecution and determined campaign

Nicolas Ridley and Hugh Latimer at the stake.

to uncover and burn these Bibles, few copies remain. It would take an average of 8 months to produce a single copy of the Wycliffe Bible, as they had to be written out by hand. William Tyndale's translation was the first copy of the Scriptures to be printed in the English language.

The official Roman Catholic and Holy Roman Empire abhorrence for Bibles translated into the vernacular can be seen from these historic quotes: The Archbishop of Canterbury Arundel declared: *"That pestilent and most wretched John Wycliffe, of damnable memory, a child of the old devil and himself a child and pupil of the anti-Christ...crowned his wickedness by translating the Scriptures into the mother tongue."*

William Tyndale translating the Scriptures.

Catholic historian Henry Knighton wrote: *"John Wycliffe translated the Gospel from Latin into the English...made it the property of the masses and common to all and...even to women...and so the pearl of the Gospel is thrown before swine and trodden under foot and what is meant to be the jewel of the clergy has been turned into the jest of the laity...has become common..."*

A synod of clergy in 1408 decreed: *"It is dangerous...to translate the text of Holy Scripture from one language into another...we decree and ordain that no-one shall in future translate on his authority any text of Scripture into the English tongue or into any other tongue, by way of book, booklet or treatise. Nor shall any man read, in public or in private, this kind of book, booklet or treatise, now recently composed in the time of the said John Wycliffe...under penalty of the greater excommunication."*

GOD'S OUTLAW

William Tyndale was a gifted scholar, a graduate of both Oxford and Cambridge Universities. It was at Cambridge that Tyndale was introduced to the writings of Luther and Zwingli. Tyndale earned his M.A. at Oxford, then he was ordained into the ministry, served as a chaplain and tutor and dedicated his life to the translation of the Scriptures from the original Hebrew and Greek languages.

Tyndale was shocked by the ignorance of the Bible prevalent amongst the clergy. To one such cleric he declared: **"I defy the pope and all his laws. If God spares my life, before many years pass I will make it possible for the boy who drives the plough to know more of the Scriptures than you do."**

Failing to obtain any ecclesiastical approval for his proposed translation, Tyndale went into exile to Germany. As he described it *"not only was there no room in my lord of London's palace to translate the New Testament, but also that there was no place to do it in all England."*

Supported by some London merchants, Tyndale sailed in 1524 for Germany, never to return to his homeland. In Hamburg he worked on the New Testament, which was ready for printing by the following year. As the pages began to roll off the press in Cologne, soldiers of the Holy Roman Empire raided the printing press. Tyndale fled with as many of the pages as had so far been printed. Only one incomplete copy of this Cologne New Testament edition survives.

Tyndale moved to Worms where the complete New Testament was published the following year (1526). Of the 6000 copies printed, only three of this edition have survived.

Not only did the first printed edition of the English New Testament need to be produced in Germany, but they had to be smuggled into England. There the bishops did all they could to seek them out and destroy them. The Bishop of London, Cuthbert Tunstall, preached against the translation of the New Testament into English and had copies of Tyndale's New Testaments ceremonially burned at St. Paul's.

Printing the English Bible.

The Archbishop of Canterbury began a campaign of buying up these contraband copies of the New Testament in order to burn them. As Tyndale remarked, his purchases helped provide the finance for the new improved editions.

In 1530 Tyndale's translation of the first five books of the Bible, the Pentateuch (the books of Moses), were printed in Antwerp, Holland. Tyndale continually worked on further revisions and editions of the New Testament. He also wrote *The Parable of Wicked Mammon* and *The Obedience of a Christian Man*.

This book, *The Obedience of a Christian Man*, was studied by Queen Anne Boleyn and even found its way to King Henry VIII who was most impressed: *"This book is for me and all kings to read!"* King Henry VIII sent out his agents to offer Tyndale a high position in his court, a safe return to England and a great salary to oversee his communications.

However, Tyndale was not willing to surrender his work as a Bible translator, Theologian and preacher merely to become a propagandist for the king! In his book *The Practice of Prelates* Tyndale argued against divorce and specifically dared to assert that the king should remain faithful to his first wife! Tyndale maintained that Christians always have the duty to obey civil authority, except where loyalty to God is concerned. Henry's initial enthusiasm for Tyndale turned to rage and so now Tyndale was an outlaw both to the Roman Catholic Church and its Holy Roman Empire and to the English kingdom.

Tyndale also carried out a literary battle with Sir Thomas More, who attacked him in print with *Dialogue Concerning Heresies* in 1529. Tyndale responded with *Answer to More*. More responded with *Confutation* in 1533 and so on.

BETRAYAL AND BURNING

In 1535 Tyndale was betrayed by a fellow Englishman, Henry Phillips, who gained his confidence only to arrange treacherously for his arrest. Tyndale was taken to the state prison in the castle of Vilvorde, near Brussels. For 500 days, Tyndale suffered in a cold, dark and damp dungeon and then on

Tyndale betrayed by fellow Englishman, Henry Phillips.

6 October, 1536, he was taken to a stake where he was garrotted and burned. His last reported words were: *"Lord, open the king of England's eyes."*

TYNDALE'S DYING PRAYER ANSWERED

Tyndale suffered for 500 days in a cold dark dungeon.

The Lord did indeed answer the dying prayer of Tyndale in the most remarkable way. By this time there was an Archbishop of Canterbury (Thomas Cranmer) and a Vicar General (Thomas Cromwell) both of whom were committed to the Protestant cause. They persuaded King Henry to approve the publication of the Coverdale translation. By 1539 every parish church in England was required to make a copy of this English Bible available to all of its parishioners.

Miles Coverdale was a friend of Tyndale's, a fellow Cambridge graduate and Reformer. His edition was the first complete translation of the Bible in English. It consisted mainly of Tyndale's work supplemented with those portions of the Old Testament which Tyndale had not been able to translate before his death.

Then, a year after Tyndale's death, the Matthews Bible appeared. This was the work of another friend and fellow English Reformer, John Rogers. Because of the danger of producing Bible translations, he used the pen-name Thomas Matthews, which was an inversion of William Tyndale's initials (WT), 'TM'. In fact at the end of the Old Testament he had William Tyndale's initials 'WT' printed big and bold.

6 October 1536, Tyndale's dying prayer changed history.

At Archbishop Thomas Cranmer's request, Henry VIII authorised that this Bible be further revised by Coverdale and be called The Great Bible.

And so in this way Tyndale's dying prayer was spectacularly answered. The sudden, unprecedented countrywide access to the Scriptures created widespread excitement. Just in the lifetime of William Shakespeare, 2 million Bibles were sold throughout the British Isles. About 90% of Tyndale's wording passed on into the King James Version of the Bible.

THE MOST INFLUENTIAL ENGLISHMAN
William Tyndale can be described not only as the father of the English Bible, but in a real sense the foremost influence on the shaping of the English language itself. Because Tyndale's translation was the very first from the original Hebrew and Greek into the English language, he had no previous translations to help in his choice of language. While Latin is noun-rich, Greek and Hebrew are verb-rich. At that time the English language had been heavily influenced by French and Latin. Tyndale went back to the original Saxon and found that Saxon English was more compatible with Greek and Hebrew than with Latin and French.

"I defy the pope and all his laws. If God spares my life, before many years pass I will make it possible for the boy who drives the plough to know more of the Scriptures..."

The clarity, simplicity and poetic beauty which Tyndale brought to the English language through his Bible translation served as a linguistic rallying point for the development of the English language. At the time of his translation there were many variations and dialects of English and in many sections of the country the English language was being swamped with French words and Latin concepts. Tyndale's translation rescued English from these Latin trends and established English as an extension of the Biblical Hebrew and Greek worldview.

Thus, every person in the world who writes, speaks, or even thinks, in English, is to a large extent indebted to William Tyndale. It is also extraordinary that while English was one of the minor languages of Europe in the early 16th Century, today it has become a truly worldwide language with over 2 billion people communicating in English.

PIONEERS FOR FREEDOM

The Reformation in the 16th Century was one of the most important epochs in the history of the world. The Reformation gave us the Bible – now freely available in our own languages. The now almost universally acknowledged principles of religious freedom, liberty of conscience, the rule of law, the separation of powers and constitutionally limited republics were unthinkable before the Reformation. The Reformers fought for the principles that Scripture alone is our final authority, that Christ alone is the Head of the Church, that salvation is by the grace of God alone, received by faith alone on the basis of the finished work of Christ alone.

THE POWER OF THE GOSPEL

The Gospel of Christ is life-changing, culture-shaping, history-making and nation-transforming. If it does not change your life and the lives of those around you, then it is not the Biblical Gospel.

"All Scripture is given by inspiration of God and is profitable for doctrine, for reproof, for correction, for instruction in righteousness, that the man of God may be complete, thoroughly equipped for every good work." 2 Timothy 3:16-17

By order of King Henry VIII a Bible in English was to be placed in every parish church in the kingdom - to be accessible to everyone who could read.

CHAPTER 6

HEINRICH BULLINGER
CONSOLIDATING THE REFORMATION

Heinrich Bullinger was Ulrich Zwingli's successor. For 44 years he pastored Grossmünster in Zürich. Considering the important role he played and the prodigious quantity of his writings, it is remarkable that Bullinger is one of the least known of the Reformers.

CONVERSION
Born 18 July 1504, the fifth son of the priest, Henry Bullinger, Heinrich was sent to study at the prestigious Emmerich Seminary on the Rhine, at aged 12. At 15 years old, he enrolled at the University in Cologne, earning his Bachelor of Arts the next year. It was at this time that he was converted to the Reformed Faith through studying the Latin and Greek fathers of the Church.

Heinrich Bullinger - the pastor of pastors and elder statesman of the Reformation in Switzerland.

MARRIAGE
In 1523, Bullinger was called to teach at the Cistercian Monastery of Kappel, near Zürich. Here he taught on the Epistles of Paul and proposed to Anna Adlischweiler, a nun, who remained in a de-consecrated convent. Bullinger's proposal in writing is still preserved: *"Do you want to share with me sorrow and joy and, under my protection, live in love according to God's Order?"* Her *"Yes"* was uttered at Grossmünster, where Ulrich Zwingli was the pastor.

CALL
After the death of Reformer Ulrich Zwingli at the Battle of Kappel in 1531, Bullinger was chosen to become his successor as Pastor of Grossmünster. Appointed the First Minister (the equivalent of a Reformed Bishop) Bullinger and his family moved into the house of Zwingli and he took responsibility for caring for the widow and two dependent children of the Reformer who had been killed in battle. Heinrich Bullinger's marriage to Anna was long and loving and produced 11 children. All of their sons became Protestant ministers.

103

CONSOLIDATION

For the next 44 years, Bullinger presided over the destinies of the church in Zürich, consolidating the Reformation begun by Zwingli. Bullinger was a prolific writer and his widely published work included *Decades of Sermons* (50 sermons on Christian doctrine), *The History of The Reformation* and *The Diary*. Because of his growing authority as a respected Theologian, his conciliatory spirit and his diplomatic gifts, he became the friend of Calvin and Beza and the recognised head of the Reformed churches of Switzerland.

CORRESPONDENCE

He maintained an important correspondence with political and religious leaders throughout the whole of Europe (more than 12,000 of his letters are preserved at the Zentral Bibliotek in Zürich. Through his sermons and publications, including Bible commentaries, he exercised a lasting influence on the Reformed movement worldwide. His *Decades* were many times republished and translated into French and English. Bullinger's correspondents included Henry VIII and Edward VI of England. When, in 1570, Queen Elizabeth needed to prepare a response to the papacy, she turned to Bullinger to draft her reply.

CONFESSIONS

Bullinger's contributions to systematizing the doctrines of Zwingli and organising the churches of Reformed Switzerland, were decisive. In 1537, he wrote *The First Helvetic Confession*, which was adopted by the churches of Zürich, Berne, Basle, Schaffhausen, Saint-Gall, Muehlhauser and Bienne. In 1549, he, along with John Calvin, wrote *The Zürich Agreement* (*Consensus Tigurinus*) on the Lord's Supper. In 1566, Bullinger's *Brief Exposition of The Faith* became the basis for *The Second Helvetic Confession*, which remained for centuries

Grossmünster in Zürich.

the basis for the Reformed Churches of the Swiss Confederation. The Helvetic Confessions were widely known and respected amongst the Reformed communities of France, England, Scotland, Poland, Hungary and Bohemia. They also left an imprint on the Presbyterian Churches in the USA. One historian commented about The Helvetic Confession *"This Confession is the most natural and simplest of all...it says in the clearest way what it means."*

THE STUDENT

Zwingli wrote concerning Bullinger: *"This young man is very learned... he compares everything, he reconciles everything."*

John Calvin praised Bullinger in these words: *"After Melancthon came Bullinger, who has rightly earned great praise: because with doctrine he had an ease which made him most easy to read."*

THE PREACHER

Berthold Haller of Berne wrote: *"God gave you the gift of explaining simply, of lifting the bushel and letting the light of the Holy Word shine."*

Conrad Pellician of Basle wrote: *"A Bishop in his youth, pious, loyal, educated, true and devoted, an incomparable preacher, the words of whom act within as the pen of Christendom...a man of God."*

The Archbishop of Canterbury, in 1586, instructed ministers that they should read a chapter of the Bible each day and one of Bullinger's sermons each week. The Foreword to the English translation of *The Decades* stated: *"These sermons are comparable to a gold mine, the deeper you delve, the richer they are. They abstruseness of Calvin is here replaced with an extraordinary clarity of expression."*

The successor of Calvin, Theodore Beza, had been won to the Reformed Faith at the age of 16, by a tract written by Bullinger. Beza wrote: *"We are used to being strengthened by you"* Beza referred to Bullinger as *"our rudder"* and as his *"father"* in the Faith.

Zürich, the city of Zwingli and Bullinger, a sanctuary for persecuted Protestants.

THE PASTOR

Bullinger was a devoted pastor whose home was constantly open to the hungry, the lost, the persecuted and the spiritual seeker. Although his salary was meagre, he gave many gifts, giving of his own small income to hospitals and institutions of mercy. Bullinger's preaching was powerful and his pen seldom rested. For 44 years, he maintained an average of preaching 7 times a week. His pastoral heart produced one of the first Protestant books on comforting the sick and the dying.

THE REFORMER

Bullinger built upon the solid foundations laid by Ulrich Zwingli and provided an ecclesiastical and Theological order that was thoroughly Reformed.

"Therefore, My beloved brethren, be steadfast, immovable, always abounding in the work of the Lord, knowing that your labour is not in vain in the Lord." 1 Corinthians 15:58

CHAPTER 7

MARTIN BUCER
THE REFORMER OF STRAßBURG

Martin Bucer, the Reformer of Straßburg and mentor of John Calvin.

Martin Bucer (1491 - 1551) was converted to the Protestant Faith when he heard Martin Luther's arguments at the Leipzig debate with Johann Eck, in 1519. Bucer became the leader of the Reformation in Straßburg.

RECONCILER
Bucer tried hard to reconcile the differences between the Swiss Reformer, Ulrich Zwingli and German Reformer, Martin Luther, on their different interpretations of the Lord's Supper. Bucer's tolerance of the doctrinal differences earned Luther's scorn. Luther declared: *"It is better for you to have your enemies, than to set up a fictitious fellowship."* However, although Bucer failed to reconcile Zwingli and Luther, he continued trying throughout his life to unite the Lutheran and Reformed branches of the Protestant Faith.

CALVIN'S MENTOR
When John Calvin was exiled from Geneva, Bucer welcomed him to Straßburg. Calvin pastored the French speaking congregation in Straßburg and developed a firm friendship with Martin Bucer. In some ways, Bucer was Calvin's mentor. During the formative years, between 1538 and 1541, Calvin benefited from Bucer's teaching and organizational skills.

HEARTACHE
In 1541, after playing a key role in the Regensburg Colloquy, Martin Bucer saw four of his five sons and his wife die in the plague.

REFORMATION IN ENGLAND
When Bucer was exiled from Straßburg in 1548 (this was a key condition of a peace treaty dictated by Emperor Charles V), he travelled to England

to assist Archbishop Cranmer with the Reformation in England. Bucer was appointed Regius Professor at Cambridge University and assisted in the production of the 1549 edition of *The Book of Common Prayer*.

"For God is not unjust to forget your work and labour of love which you have shown toward His Name, in that you have ministered to the saints and do minister." Hebrews 6:10

Martin Bucer attempting to mediate between Martin Luther and Ulrich Zwingli.

CHAPTER 8
THOMAS CRANMER AND THE ENGLISH REFORMATION

The Reformation in England was quite different to the Reformations in Europe. There was no one dominant individual to give direction to the Reformation in England. Germany had Martin Luther. Switzerland had Ulrich Zwingli. The French-speaking world had John Calvin. But England's Reformation was very different.

In the 14th Century, Professor John Wycliffe had been the Morning Star of the Reformation. William Tyndale sacrificed his life to provide the first Bible translated from the original Hebrew and Greek and printed into English. But whereas the Reformations in Europe were inspired and directed by religious leaders, the Reformation in England was primarily controlled by political leaders: King Henry VIII, King Edward VI, Queen Elizabeth I and Chancellors such as Thomas Cromwell.

THE CAUTIOUS REFORMER
However, amongst the many notable Reformers who contributed to the English Reformation, the Archbishop of Canterbury, Thomas Cranmer, played a key role. In many ways, Thomas Cranmer was the most cautious, even indecisive of the Reformers – until his final hour.

In the tumultuous political and religious climate of the day, Cranmer was a cautious clergyman who mastered the art of political realities, determining how best to forward the Gospel without losing his livelihood and life, or soul. Cranmer mastered the intrigues of the palace, survived two kings and was martyred under queen Mary Tudor.

Thomas Cranmer, Archbishop of Canterbury, author of the Book of Common Prayer and Martyr.

109

Born 2 July 1489, in Nottinghamshire, Thomas Cranmer studied for the priesthood at Cambridge University. When he married, he lost his fellowship in the College of Jesus, but when his wife, Joan, died at childbirth within a year of their wedding, Jesus College at Cambridge restored Cranmer to the Fellowship. He was ordained as a priest and threw himself into his further studies, becoming an outstanding Theologian.

In 1520, he joined some scholars who met regularly to discuss Luther's Theological movement on the continent. This group was dubbed *"Little Germany."* William Tyndale, who would later give his life translating the Bible into English, was also part of this Theological discussion group, along with Thomas Cranmer. By 1525, Cranmer was praying for the abolition of papal power in England.

THE KING'S MAN

When King Henry VIII heard that this prominent Theologian believed that the king had the right to divorce Catherine and that the king should be the Head of the Church in England, Henry summoned Cranmer and commanded him to write a treatise backing up the king's case. This Cranmer did, using arguments from Scripture, the Church fathers and Church councils. The king appointed Cranmer to his embassy to Rome and then to Germany to communicate with the Lutheran princes.

King Henry VIII

It was in Germany that Cranmer met and married Margaret, the niece of Lutheran Reformer, Andreas Osiander. At that stage in the Church in England priests were not allowed to marry. So Cranmer kept this marriage a secret for his first 14 years as Archbishop. He was convinced that marriage for ministers was Biblical, but he recognised that the time was not ripe for him to make either his marriage, or his Theology, public.

In March 1533, Cranmer was consecrated as the Archbishop of

Canterbury. This required him to take the still Obligatory Oath to be subject to the pope, as the Church in England had not yet separated from Rome. However, the day before, Cranmer signed a statement qualifying this oath that he was not binding himself to *"do or attempt anything which will, or may seem to be, contrary to God's Law, or against his Majesty, the King of England."*

In May, Cranmer convened his court and declared the king's marriage, to Catherine of Aragon, void from the beginning. He then pronounced the king's marriage to Anne Boleyn (which had secretly taken place in January) valid. Cranmer sincerely believed in royal absolutism. He believed that his primary duty was to obey the king, as God's chosen to lead both nation and church.

In 1536, on the instruction of the king, he invalidated the king's marriage to Anne and ruled that Henry's proposed marriage to Anne of Cleves was lawful. Then, 6 months later, Cranmer approved Henry's divorce on the grounds that the original marriage was unlawful!

COURAGE AND COMPROMISE

Although Cranmer received much criticism for appearing to be the lackey of the king, Cranmer was apparently convinced of the Divine right of kings. However, Cranmer did show extraordinary courage. Time and again, alone of all Henry's advisors, he pleaded for the lives of people who had fallen out of royal favour. For example, he pleaded with great courage for the lives of Thomas More, Anne Boleyn and Thomas Cromwell - when the king wanted them beheaded.

While Cranmer articulated the case for Protestant doctrines, he enforced the decisions of the king, such as arresting priests who had wives, even while he himself was secretly married. To most Protestants, Cranmer had compromised the Reformation.

THE SURVIVOR

Cranmer's many enemies hatched several plots to destroy him. But each time, they were foiled by Henry. While Henry lay dying, Cranmer's enemies in the Privy Council (The Cabinet of the King) attempted to arrest Cranmer for treason and send him to the Tower of London for execution. However, the king gave Cranmer his signet ring, which Cranmer produced at a key moment, throwing the Council into confusion. As the king lay dying, it was Cranmer whom Henry called for to pray with him as he died.

THE TIME FOR REFORM

With the accession to the throne of the young Edward VI in 1547, Cranmer's time had arrived. He immediately began to transform the Church of England into a decidedly Protestant Church. In 1547, Cranmer published his: *"Book of Homilies"* which required the clergy to preach sermons emphasizing Reformed doctrines. In 1549, he published the first *"Book of Common Prayer"* which was revised in 1552 by a second edition, which was more clearly Protestant. In 1553, Cranmer produced *The 42 Articles* as the doctrinal statements that moved the Church of England even more towards a Reformed, Calvinist direction. These were later revised into *The 39 Articles*, which under Queen Elizabeth became the official foundational statement of the Church of England worldwide. By Thomas Cranmer's immense learning, ecclesiastical authority and hard work, he dominated the religious revolution, which propelled England into the Reformed Camp.

King Edward VI of England.

THE BOOK OF COMMON PRAYER

None of the Reformers, neither Luther, Calvin nor Zwingli, thought it unscriptural to use set prayers. As there are set prayers in the Old Testament (such as the Psalms) and in the New Testament (such as The Lord's Prayer), their concern was to have good, Scriptural prayers.

Cranmer called it *"The Book of Common Prayer"* because it was intended for the whole nation. Both clergy and laity alike and for all classes of society. To Cranmer, carefully thought out phrases based on Scripture were more likely to express one's best intentions than the suggestions and feelings of the moment. His intention was to have these prayers fixed so that people could get to know them, think about them, memorize them and let these prayers fully enter into their understanding. The goal was to reform all teaching and prayer in the Church, by replacing the unBiblical superstitions of Catholicism with Biblical doctrines and Scriptural worship. The public liturgy was also intended to keep in check the radical individualism of preachers who may allow their prejudices or personalities to predominate. The Prayer Book was to help keep services God centred and Bible based.

DISASTER STRIKES

As the young King Edward VI approached death in July 1553, Thomas Cranmer became fatally involved in royal politics. He supported the Protestant, Lady Jane Grey (the great niece of Henry VIII), as the new sovereign. Nine days after being proclaimed Queen, Jane Grey was deposed and beheaded by her cousin Mary.

PERSECUTION UNDER BLOODY MARY

With Queen Mary's accession, the English Reformation began to unravel. Cranmer's deadly enemy, Stephen Gardiner was appointed Chancellor and Reginald Pole became the new Archbishop of Canterbury. Parliament repealed the acts of Henry VIII and Edward VI and reintroduced the Heresy Laws. Bloody Mary then began a relentless campaign against the Protestants. Along with the Reformers Nicholas Ridley, the Bishop of London and Hugh Latiner, The Bishop of Worcester, Cranmer was moved to Oxford in March 1554 to stand trial.

IMPRISONMENT AND DISGRACE

After a torturous imprisonment, Cranmer was subjected to a long and tedious trial where, as a result of the debilitating, enfeebling mental torture, isolation and physically exhausting imprisonment, Cranmer was often outmanoeuvred in the debates. In February 1556, in a ceremony designed to humiliate him, Cranmer was degraded from his episcopal and priestly offices. The symbol of his Archbishop Hood was stripped from his back, the chalice was pulled away from his hands, the Gospels and Epistles were taken away from him, his priestly tunic and

Archbishop Thomas Cranmer led through Traitor's Gate into the Tower of London.

stole were stripped from his body. A barber shaved his head and the tops of his fingers.

He was also forced to witness the excruciatingly slow and painful death, by burning, of Bishops Latimer and Ridley. After extensive mental and physical torture, the long trial and lonely imprisonment Cranmer was wearied to the point where he signed a statement of recantation, recognizing the Bishop of Rome, the pope, as the Vicar of Christ and placing himself under the authority of Queen Mary.

CONDEMNED

However, the vindictiveness of Queen Mary and Cardinal Pole was still not appeased. They still wanted to humiliate and punish Cranmer further for all the havoc he had wrecked upon Catholicism in England. They determined that he must be burned at the stake – after making one more public rejection of the Protestant Faith. On the morning of 21 March 1556, Cranmer was escorted from his cell amidst fierce rain and dark skies. The weather forced the formalities preceding the burning to be moved indoors, to St. Mary's Church. There Cranmer was forced to stand, in ragged threadbare clothes, before the pulpit, while Henry Cole spoke of Cranmer's *"crimes"* and the need for his death.

Cranmer stands firm in Oxford: *"As for the pope, I refuse him as Christ's enemy."*

CRANMER'S COURAGEOUS CONFESSION

Cranmer was then invited to *"openly express the true and undoubted profession of your faith."* Cranmer took off his cap, thanked the people for their prayers and exhorted them in four points: To care less for this world and more for the next, to obey their sovereigns out of the fear of God, to do good to all people and to be concerned for the poor.

Then he declared: *"As I am come to the last end of my life, whereupon hangeth all my life past and all my life to come...I shall therefore declare unto you my very Faith, how I believe, without any colour or dissimulation."* He then recited The Nicene Creed. Then he declared: *"I have come to the great thing that troubles my conscience more than any other thing that I ever said or did in my life and that is setting abroad of writings contrary to the truth, which here now I renounce and refuse, as things written with my hand contrary to the truth which I thought in my heart and written for fear of death and to save my life if it might be – and that is all such bills which I have written or signed with my own hand since my degradation, wherein I have written many things untrue. And for inasmuch as my hand offended in writing contrary to my heart, therefore my hand shall first be punished; for if I may come to the fire it shall be first burned."*

As loud rumblings spread through the shocked congregation, Cranmer continued: **"as for the pope, I refuse him as Christ's enemy and Anti-Christ, with all his false doctrines.** *And as for the sacrament..."* At this, Cranmer was being heckled and interjected, ordered to stop. However, he continued: *"Teacheth so true a doctrine of the sacrament that it shall stand at the Last Day before the Judgment!"* Cranmer was silenced at this point and dragged from the stage.

But the Friars did not have to pull him to the stake, because Cranmer rushed to the stake, giving his captors a hard time keeping up with him. In front of the stake Cranmer knelt on the bare ground and prayed. Then he clasped the hands of friends who stood nearby and bade them farewell.

STEADFAST AT THE END

He was bound to the stake with a steel band around his waist. As the fire was kindled and the flames leapt up, Cranmer stretched out his right arm and held his hand in the flame stating: *"This hand hath offended."* He continued to hold his hand out until it had been

21 March 1556 - Thomas Cranmer burned at the stake.

burned to a stump. His last words were: *"Lord Jesus, receive my spirit!"* He then collapsed and was consumed in the flames. For his courage and steadfastness at the end, Protestants in England forgave his vacillations and political manoeuvring. As one historian put it: *"His fame has been brightened by the fire that consumed him."*

Cranmer's *Homilies*, *The 39 Articles* and *The Book of Common Prayer* stand as enduring monuments to his Faith, which, however weak, was, without doubt, sincere and real.

"This is a faithful saying: for if we die with Him we shall also live with Him. If we endure, we shall also reign with Him. If we deny Him, He will also deny us. If we are faithless, He remains faithful; He cannot deny Himself." 2 Timothy 2:11-13

"As for the pope, I refuse him as Christ's enemy and anti-Christ, with all his false doctrines!"

CHAPTER 9
THE POLITICANS BEHIND THE ENGLISH REFORMATION

KING HENRY VIII

In 1513, 22 year old King Henry VIII waged a crusade in Europe on behalf of pope Julius II, who had promised Henry recognition as a *"most Christian King"* if he would *"utterly exterminate the King of France."* In 1521, Henry authored a book, *"The Seven Sacraments"* attacking Martin Luther and defending

Luther's writings being burned by order of the young King Henry VIII.

Catholicism's view of the Sacraments. For this, the pope gave Henry the title *"Defender of The Faith."*

Henry was a Renaissance man, he was fluent in Latin, French and Spanish, an accomplished musician, theologian and Humanist scholar. Yet, despite Henry's strong loyalties to the pope, expressed in both blood and ink, Henry did much to open England to the Reformation.

It was not so much that Henry embraced the Protestant Faith, as much as he came to reject the authority of the pope over English affairs. Henry was determined to have a male heir to the throne, to protect England from going through the kind of devastating civil war that his father had come to power through (The War of the Roses). Henry ended up going through six wives, two of whom lost their heads as a result of losing his favour.

CHANCELLOR THOMAS CROMWELL

Yet, England ended up officially Protestant, which was to a large extent thanks to Thomas Cromwell, Henry's Chancellor. After exposing the corruptions and degeneracy of the monks and friars, Cromwell dissolved hundreds of monasteries between 1536 and 1539. Through this he also swelled the Crown's treasury.

Thomas Cromwell

Cromwell also succeeded in gaining Henry's authorization for circulating copies of the Bible in English. Cromwell succeeded in transforming the nation's Catholic clergy into leaders of a Reformed Church of England. This was done carefully and with much court intrigue. Cromwell survived 11 years in the king's service, but ultimately fell out favour with the king and was executed on Tower Hill, 28 July 1540.

KING EDWARD VI

Upon the death of Henry VIII in January 1547, his 9 year old son, Edward VI ascended to the throne. Edward's uncle, Edward Seymour, The Duke of Somerset became Lord Protector of the realm. The Duke of Somerset was, like Edward, a Protestant with strong Calvinist sympathies. He directed reforms, which dismantled all the restrictions that had been placed on the printing of Scriptures and rapidly filled ecclesiastical positions with devout Protestants, such as John Hooper, Nicholas Ridley and Hugh Latimer. The *"Book of Common Prayer"* was authorised to reform worship and *"The 42 Articles"* to reform doctrine within the Church of England.

King Edward VI

Bishop Latimer preaching before King Edward VI.

England was not a Protestant nation at the close of the reign of Henry VIII. It was estimated that the majority of those living in London and the South Eastern part of England were Lutherans. But the West and North of England was still solidly Catholic. It was estimated that approximately three quarters of the total population were Catholic. However, during the brief reign of Edward VI tremendous progress was made in advancing the Reformation in England.

Within months of Edward becoming King, Parliament passed a law providing that communicants should be allowed to partake of the wine as well as the bread. In 1548, it was decreed that images should be removed from churches. In 1549, the celibacy of the clergy was done away with and marriage for priests and bishops was declared lawful. Also, in 1549, Parliament passed The Act of Uniformity making the use of *The Book of Common Prayer* compulsory in church services. The use of Latin in church services was abolished and substituted with English.

By 1552, *The Prayer Book* had been revised and a new creed had been formulated by Archbishop Cranmer, with the help of six other Theologians, of which John Knox was one. *The 42 Articles* (which was later revised to *The 39 Articles*) laid a thoroughly Protestant and Evangelical doctrinal foundation for the Church of England.

Most of the Catholic practices in worship had already been discarded. Prayers for the dead had ceased. The Communion table had taken the place of the altar. And in the Lord's Supper common bread was used instead of the wafer. The Church of England followed the Zwinglian practice of the bread and the wine being symbols of Christ's Body and Blood.

But just as the Reformation in England seemed to be succeeding, its triumphant progress was halted and Catholicism regained most of the ground that it had lost during the reign of Edward VI.

In 1553, when he was only 16 years old, Edward VI died of poisoning.

Just before he died, Edward changed the Order of Succession, which his father, Henry VIII had laid out. To prevent his ferociously Catholic half-sister, Mary, undoing the Reformation work that he had set in motion, Edward named his cousin, Lady Jane Grey to succeed him as Queen of England. Unfortunately, Queen Jane's reign lasted only 9 days before she was overthrown and imprisoned in the Tower of London.

COUNTER REFORMATION

Mary Tudor ascended the throne of England determined to undo all the work of the Reformation in England and to return the country to Catholicism.

For a time, the Protestant Reformation had swept everything before it. Now, it seemed that the Reformation movement had been brought to a standstill. The Peasants' Revolt in Germany and the extremism and fanaticism of the Anabaptist revolutionaries, had, to many, discredited the movement. Divisions between the Lutherans in Germany and the Reformed Churches in Switzerland also undermined the ongoing progress of the Reformation.

Lady Jane Grey

These divisions were exploited by Charles V, who in 1546, the year that Luther died, launched a concerted attack against the Protestant princes of Germany.

The Roman church had also been busy developing its own Counter Reformation. The Council of Trent had drawn up a list of forbidden books. This list, called *The Index*, was to protect Catholic readers from books that the Catholic church regarded as *"false"*, or *"harmful."* Protestant writings were put on *The Index* and the spread of Protestant ideas was seriously curtailed, particularly in Southern and Eastern Europe.

The Inquisition, or *"Holy Office,"* was granted more sweeping powers to detect and punish those who espoused Protestant doctrines. The Grand Inquisitor was accountable directly to the pope. The Inquisition effectively crushed the sparks of the Reformation in Spain and Italy. All those who were identified as having Protestant sympathies, or involvement, were jailed, killed or pursued into exile.

In addition, the Catholic church now had The Society of Jesus, or the *Jesuits* as they are better known. Founded by a Spanish soldier, Ignatius Loyola and Francis Xavier, the Jesuits became the most dedicated soldiers of the pope to undermine the work of the Reformation and to win Protestant areas back to Roman Catholicism. The Jesuits succeeded in recovering most of Poland, Austria and Southern Germany for Rome. The Jesuits are credited with keeping Belgium and Ireland faithful to the pope. The Jesuits also performed extensive missionary work to extend Catholic control in the Americas and Asia.

Protestants were burned at the stake as *"heretics"* in Spain, Italy, France, England and Scotland. Yet, the Dutch Protestant suffered even worse persecutions at the hands of the Catholic Inquisition.

TRIBULATION IN HOLLAND
Under king Philip II of Spain, more than 18,000 Protestants were executed in the Netherlands. In an attempt to force them to confess to *"heresy,"* both men and women were mercilessly tortured.

At that time, Spain was the most powerful country in the world. Holland was occupied by Spain. In 1566, Philip II issued a proclamation demanding that all his subjects accept the decrees made by the Council of Trent. Early in 1567, to crush the flourishing Protestant Faith in Holland, Philip sent in the Duke of Alva, who unleashed a reign a terror upon the Dutch Protestants. In 1568, the Inquisition condemned all three million inhabitants of the Netherlands to death as *"heretics."*

PROTESTANT RESISTANCE

Under the leadership of William, Prince of Orange, the Dutch Protestants rose up in resistance against Spain. William of Orange and his courageous Dutch resistance fighters, became the inspiration of Protestants worldwide. The courage and tenacity of these Dutch Davids resisting the Spanish Goliaths attracted admiration and support, particularly from Protestant England.

When the city of Leyden was besieged by Spanish troops, starvation and plague took a heavy toll. But the Protestants of Leyden refused to surrender. In July 1574 William ordered the dykes broken to chase out the Spanish occupiers, by flooding the land. Although heavily outnumbered, the Dutch succeeded in outmanoeuvring the Spanish, especially at sea. By 1581, the united 7 Northern provinces of the Netherlands declared independence from Spain. The Dutch Protestant fight for freedom continued until 1648 when their independence from Spain was finally recognised.

23 May 1568 - The Battle of Heiligerlee was a decisive Dutch victory over the Spanish invaders.

FIGHT FOR SURVIVAL

Until 1562, Protestants endured severe persecution and many martyrs were burned at the stake throughout Europe. From 1562 to 1648, Protestants throughout Europe had to fight for survival. Until the Peace of Westphalia in 1648, German, Danish and Swedish Lutherans and Dutch Calvinists had to fight for their lives against a relentless series of campaigns to crush them. In 1584, William, Prince of Orange, was murdered by an assassin's bullet. Queen Elizabeth of England survived numerous attempts to assassinate her. Religious freedom was only achieved in England, Scotland, Holland and Germany by much sacrifice, vigilance and by force of arms.

"... Proclaim liberty throughout all the land to all its inhabitants ..."
Leviticus 25:10

The Father of Dutch liberties, William the Silent, Prince of Orange - monument at the Hague.

CHAPTER 10
ANNE ASKEW
A DAUGHTER OF THE REFORMATION

Anne (1520 – 1546) was born during the reign of King Henry VIII to an honoured knight, Sir William Askew.

ATTRACTIVE
Anne was described as attractive in form and faith, a beautiful and high-spirited young woman, well educated, with unusual gifts and *"very pious."* Her father arranged that she should be married to the son of a friend, Thomas Kyme, to whom her deceased sister had originally been promised.

FAITHFUL
Anne endeavoured to be a faithful wife and bore her husband two children. However, despite an initially happy marriage, her husband, Kyme, threw her out of the home because of her Protestant Faith.

Anne Askew: *"Attractive in form and faith."*

DEDICATED
Anne had acquired a copy of the English Bible and had studied it enthusiastically. She abandoned her formal Catholic religion for the life-changing Protestant Faith in a personal Lord and Saviour, Jesus Christ. Her enthusiastic witness drew the attention of the priests who warned her husband about her *"sedition."* When challenged she confessed that she was no longer a Romanist, but *"a daughter of the Reformation."* At this, her husband threw her out of the home. However, he acknowledged that he had never known a more devout woman than Anne.

ARRESTED
In 1545, Anne was examined by church leaders concerning her beliefs. Her answers were full of wisdom and quotes from the Holy Scriptures and she often out-manoeuvered the inquisitors pointing out the contradictions in their own position. This only served to enrage them more. Lord Bonner was determined to see her burned for *heresy*.

Calm and steadfast under interrogation and torture, Anne Askew answered every challenge of her inquisitors with bold and Biblical Faith.

BLAMELESS

After failing to prove any heresy, he resorted to insinuating that she was immoral. Looking him full in the face, Anne answered calmly: *"I would, my lord, that all men knew my conversation and living in all points; for I am so sure of myself this hour, that there is none able to prove any dishonesty in me. If you know any who can do it, I pray you bring them forth."* He could not find anyone who could question her morals and so he had to have her released.

INTERROGATED

Thomas Wriothesley, the Lord Chancellor of England, was determined to crush the Reformation. He summoned her before the council and subjected her to an examination that lasted five hours. One of the council, Mr. Paget, challenged Anne: *"How can you avoid the very Words of Christ, take, eat, this is My Body which is broken for you?"*

STEADFAST

Anne answered: *"Christ's meaning in that passage is similar to the meaning of those other places of Scripture, 'I am the Door', 'I am the Vine'. 'Behold the Lamb of God.' 'That Rock was Christ.' And other such references to Himself. We are not in these texts to take Christ for the material thing which He is signified by, for then we will make Him a door, a vine, a lamb, a stone, quite contrary to the Holy Ghost's meaning. All these indeed signify Christ, even as the bread signifies His body in that place."*

IMPRISONED

Anne was charged and imprisoned in Newgate Prison. Her enemies were determined to see her burn. On 28 June, she was taken to Guild Hall to be examined again by the council. She was taunted with being a heretic. She responded that she had done nothing for which the Law of God required her death.

Anne Askew in Newgate Prison.

FAITHFUL

When asked directly if she denied the doctrine of Transubstantiation, that the sacrament of the Eucharist was the actual body and blood of Christ, Anne responded: *"God is a Spirit, not a wafer cake. He is to be worshipped in spirit and in truth – John 4:24 – and not by the impious superstitious homage paid to a wafer converted, by popish jugglery, into a god."*

CONDEMNED

That very day, 28 June, the council condemned Anne Askew to be burned to death at the stake.

TORTURED

However, before that sentence was to be carried out, Lord Wriothesley ordered her to be stretched on the rack. As the levers were turned and the torture began, Anne remained silent. Wriothesley was so angered by his lack of success that he ordered the torture to be increased. Then the officer of the rack was so moved by the sight of this pious woman enduring such torture in silence, he refused to intensify the torture. Wriothesley himself grabbed the levers and mercilessly stretched her body until her joints were pulled asunder and her bones were broken. Yet, despite the intense sufferings, all the cruelties of her enemies failed to change the patient sweetness of Anne's Christian demeanour.

MARTYRED

When the day of her execution arrived, Anne was so crippled as a result of her tortures on the rack that she had to be carried in a chair to the stake. One who witnessed her death wrote: *"She had an angel's countenance and a smiling face."* She was offered one last chance at a pardon if she would renounce the doctrines of the Reformation and embrace Catholicism. This she boldly refused. *"I believe all those Scriptures to be true which He hath confirmed with His most precious Blood. Yea and, as St. Paul sayeth, those Scriptures are sufficient for our learning and salvation that Christ hath left here with us; so that I believe we need no unwritten verities with which to rule His Church."*

COURAGEOUS

All who witnessed her noble martyrdom were impressed and inspired by the courage of this beautiful woman who gladly gave her life for Christ of one as the truest and purest witnesses of the Gospel of the Christian Church.

"Only let your conduct be worthy of the Gospel of Christ...Stand fast in one spirit, with one mind striving together for the Faith of the Gospel and not in any way terrified by your adversaries, which is to them a proof of their perdition, but to you of salvation and that from God. For to you it has been granted on behalf of Christ not only to believe in Him, but also to suffer for His sake."
Philippians 1:27 – 29

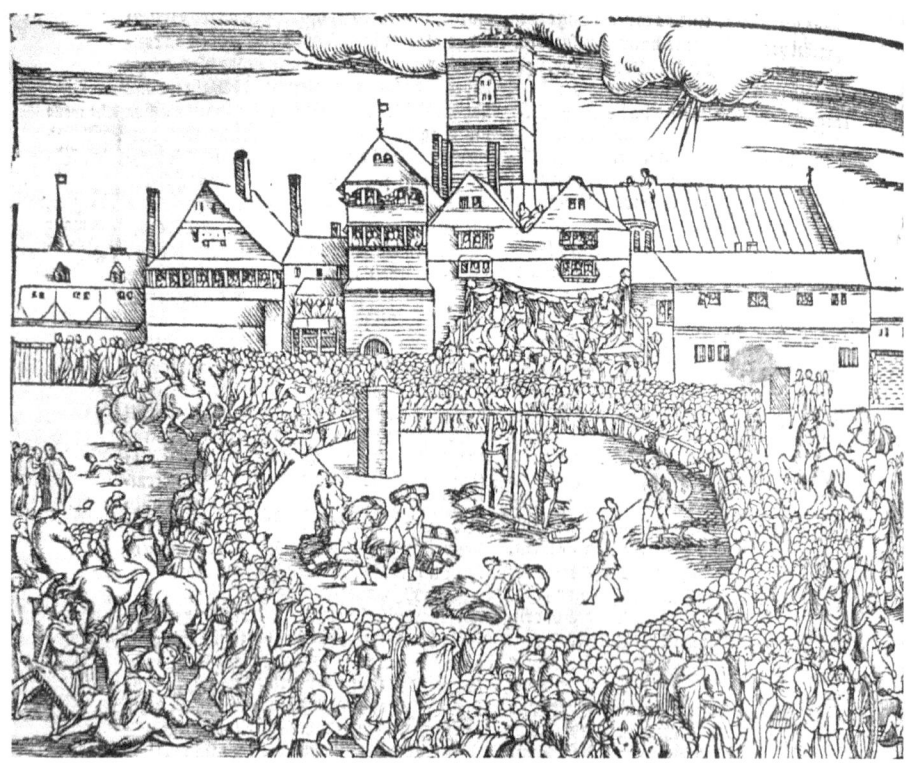

The woodcut in Foxe's Book of Martyrs depicting the martyrdom of Anne Askew and others, at Smithfield.

Chapter 11

Bloody Mary and The Martyrs of the English Reformation

Queen Mary is remembered as the ruler who failed to return England to the Catholic Church. As *Foxe's Book of Martyrs* (*Acts and Monuments*) recorded, not the hundreds of prominent executions carried out under Blood Mary, nor the cruelties, torment, torture and oppression of the Inquisition were sufficient to crush the Protestant Reformation in England.

In fact, the end result of Mary's attempts to return England to Catholicism were rather to convince the vast majority of Englishmen in their resolution and determination never again to succumb to such tyranny, superstition, intolerance or error ever again. By trying to exterminate the Reformation, Bloody Mary only succeeded in entrenching it.

Bloody Mary, persecutor of the Church.

JOHN ROGERS

As Bible translator, prominent Protestant preacher and Reformer, John Rogers was lead to the stake in January 1555, he was asked once more to recant. Rogers replied that what he had preached from the pulpits he would seal now with his blood.

"Then thou art a heretic!" exclaimed the Sheriff.

"That shall be known on the Day of Judgement," replied Rogers.

"Well, I will never pray for you," said the Sheriff.

John Rogers

"I will pray for you," responded Rogers.

As he walked to the stake, Rogers sang Psalms. He was met by his wife and 11 children, one an infant in her arms. As John Foxe observed: *"This sad sight did not move him, but he cheerfully and patiently went on his way to Smithfield, where he was burned to ashes in the presence of a great number of people."* Rogers was the first of hundreds of prominent Protestant leaders executed during the reign of Bloody Mary.

But instead of the crowds being intimidated into submission to the crown and Catholic Church, these burnings seemed to fuel their discontent and swell the ranks of the Protestants. Instead of the condemned Reformers being humbled and discredited by recanting and submitting to the demands of the Inquisition, the Protestants all died with tremendous courage and resolution, using the stake as their final pulpit. As Rogers declared: *"Sealing my testimony with my blood."* The unintended consequences of Mary's persecutions were to inspire more sympathy for the Protestants and aversion to their Catholic persecutors.

THOMAS CRANMER

Even Thomas Cranmer, the most loyal of subjects, was driven to defy the queen. Distraught that his faith had been considered treasonable, the fallen Archbishop recanted and then fearing the fires of hell more than the wrath of the queen, he withdrew his recantation and died a martyr – steadfast and resolute. As it has been pointed out, by making a hero even out of this unheroic man, the queen and cardinal demonstrated how counter-productive persecution could become.

SPANISH INQUISITION

By way of contrast, in Spain, the Inquisition, the shame of public humiliation and the fear of a torturous death by burning, drove many accused to confess and submit. In February 1486, for example, 750 recants were welcomed back to the Catholic faith in the Toledo Cathedral, amidst cheering crowds. But such demonstrations never took place in England.

BISHOPS RIDLEY AND LATIMER

In England, spectators generally sympathized with the victims, admired their courage and often embraced their Faith. As Bishop Ridley was threatened with the stake, unless he recanted, Ridley responded: *"Well, so long as the breath is in my body, I will never deny my Lord Christ and His known truth. God's Will be done in me."* As the piles of wood and sticks around them was lighted, Bishop Latimer said: *"Be of good comfort, Master Ridley and play the man! We shall this day light such a candle, by God's grace, in England, as I trust shall never put out."* Indeed, Bloody Mary and her persecutors succeeded only in alienating the people of England from Roman Catholicism and entrenching the Reformation. **"On this rock I will build My Church and the gates of hell shall not prevail against it."** Matthew 16:18

When Mary was crowned Queen of England, the Emperor of the Holy Roman Empire, Charles V proposed that she marry his heir, Prince Philip of Spain and accept, together with the Prince, £60,000 a year. For Mary to marry the heir to the Emperor opened the way to her becoming an Empress and sharing the greatest position in Europe. However, it would also end the independence of England, bringing it under foreign rule.

LADY JANE GREY

Mary had her cousin, the Protestant Lady Jane Grey (16 years old) and her 17 year old husband, along with about 100 of their followers, beheaded. This removed the immediate challenge to the throne.

Beheading of the courageous Protestant Lady Jane Grey.

THE CLEAR AND PRESENT DANGER OF SPAIN

In July 1554, Prince Philip of Spain arrived abroad an elaborate galley accompanied by a fleet of 125 ships. His entourage included 20 of Spain's top nobility, along with their wives and servants and a bodyguard numbering several hundred soldiers. Twenty carts carrying 96 chests loaded with £3 million in gold ducats accompanied him. Mary was herself half Spanish and now marrying a Spanish king with his lavish Spanish court surrounding him, it became apparent to many Englishmen that the throne of England had been hijacked by Spain.

Mary then called for Cardinal Reginald Pole to come to England and assist her in turning the nation back to Catholicism. (In one election, Pole had failed to become pope by only two votes). Mary instructed Parliament to formally return England to Catholicism. In response, Pole granted the nation *"absolution"* in St. Paul's Cathedral.

Prince Philip of Spain

Medieval statutes providing for *"heretics"* to be tried in church courts and handed over to civil authorities for execution, were restored. All Protestant laws were abolished by a Second Statute of Repeal.

BISHOPS HOOPER, RIDLEY, LATIMER AND CRANMER

John Hooper, former Bishop of Worcester was jailed for having married and for refusing to put his wife aside. Four of the most prominent Protestant Bishops – Hooper, Ridley, Latimer and Cranmer were burned at the stake, followed by hundreds of other *"heretics."*

RESISTANCE TO ROME DEEPENS

Horror, anger and resentment grew throughout England. Sincerely held religious convictions cannot be changed by decree. The books of Luther, Calvin and other Reformers had already circulated throughout England. Protestant refugees fled to Germany and Switzerland. A stream of pamphlets against Catholicism were smuggled back into England. Small house fellowships, Bible study groups and prayer meetings met in cellars, cemeteries and private homes. Thousands of English Protestants found refuge in Geneva, Frankfurt and Straßburg. Resistance to *"Bloody Mary"* and her campaign to convert England to Catholicism deepened and grew.

Work on the Geneva Bible began. As more and more burnings of Protestant leaders were ordered, riots erupted. The unpopular Spanish Prince Philip, disenchanted with the obviously infertile Queen Mary and the open resentment of the English to his Spanish court, departed for Spain.

FRUSTRATION AND FAILURE

Mary, humiliated by the failure of her marriage, inability to bear a child and the obvious failure of her campaign to return England to Catholicism unleashed her bitterness upon a rebellious England.

DEATH WISH

Mary's father-in-law, Charles V, gave Queen Mary the advice that it had required him to send 30,000 Protestants to terrible deaths to suppress *"the heresy of Lutheranism"* from spreading on the continent and she would have to do the same in England!

THE COUNTER PRODUCTIVE COUNTER REFORMATION

65 year old, Bishop of London, Ridley and 80-year-old Bishop Latimer of Worcester were sent to the stake. The sight of these grey-haired patriarchs singing Psalms in the flames *"until his lips were burned away"* shocked all of England. A 60-year-old widow was similarly burnt to death. Then a young blind woman, a rope maker's daughter, was sentenced to death by bishops she could not see. With every burning, resistance to Catholicism deepened and commitment to the Reformation doctrines spread. Mary's Counter Reformation was counter productive.

In early 1556, Charles V abdicated and handed the crowns of Castile, Aragon, Sicily and the West Indies over to Philip II. His brother, Ferdinand became the Emperor of the Holy Roman Empire..

At this time, King Philip II was at war with France and facing widespread revolt in the Netherlands, so he sought to restore his relationship with his wife, queen Mary of England. If she would send English troops and Calvary to the Netherlands, he would return to her. So, English foot and horse soldiers were dispatched to the Netherlands for Philip's use in suppressing the Dutch Protestants. Next, Philip wanted England to declare war on France. Mary insisted on Philip's return first.

Philip returned 18 March 1557 and found that Mary had become a gaunt, aged woman whose hold on the throne was tenuous. From her side, Mary also found Philip greatly changed, aged before his time. Her hopes of restoring Catholicism to England rested on having a Catholic heir, which her barrenness made impossible. Philip openly brought his current mistress (his cousin, the Duchess of Lorraine) with him to England. Mary's humiliation was complete.

Her personal popularity had vanished in the flames of her vicious persecutions. Now her increasing of taxes had brought her English subjects to the point of rebellion. Mary threatened and cajoled her Council to declare war on France. Once this was secured, Philip left, 6 July 1557. He never returned to England. Mary ended her days in great agony, in fever and mentally deranged. As *"Bloody Mary"* lay dying in England, Charles V was also suffering, in excruciating pain, feverish and in fear, full of regrets. Charles V, the Emperor who Luther had defied, died 21 September 1558. Bloody Mary followed him into eternity on 17 November 1558. Twelve hours later, her Archbishop of Canterbury, Cardinal Pole, died of a similar fever in Lambeth Palace.

DEFEAT AND RETREAT

1559 began with the Catholic cause in defeat and retreat. Emperor Charles V had died in Spain. His sister, Mary, the former regent of the Netherlands also died. Mary of Lorraine, the regent of Scotland, was out of power and on the run, with the Protestants in hot pursuit. *"Bloody Mary"* and her determined attempt to return England to the papacy was shattered.

Queen Elizabeth

REVERSAL OF FORTUNES
Protestant Elizabeth Tudor was crowned in her stead, Queen of England on 15 January 1559. John Knox returned from exile to Edinburgh, Scotland, on 2 May 1559. The Reformation had triumphed in Britain.

"... Be faithful until death, and I will give you the crown of life."
Revelation 10:2

CHAPTER 12
PHILIPP MELANCHTHON
THE TEACHER OF GERMANY

When Philipp Melanchthon delivered his first lecture at the University of Wittenberg, in 1518, Dr. Martin Luther was impressed. Melanchthon was the new Professor of Greek and although he stuttered during his presentation, his call for Theologians to go *"back to the sources, back to the Holy Scriptures"* echoed the convictions of Luther's heart.

Philipp Melanchthon

LEIPZIG
Melanchthon became an invaluable support to Professor Martin Luther's Reformation work. He accompanied Luther to the Leipzig debate in 1519. In 1521, Melanchthon published *Loci Communes*. This was the first structured presentation of Reformation doctrine and it became a standard textbook for Lutheran Theology for over a century.

AUGSBURG
Melanchthon was the leading Theological figure at the Diet of Augsburg, 1530. Melanchthon wrote and read out the *Augsburg Confession* before the Emperor Charles V.

WITTENBERG
Luther stated that without Melanchthon's methodological skills, much of his own work would have been lost.

Melanchthon's extensive efforts to reform, establish and develop schools and colleges earned him the title: *"The Teacher of Germany."*

The Greatest Century of Reformation

Bible Translation with Martin Luther.

The Monument to Philipp Melanchthon in Wittenberg.

CHAPTER 13
GUILLAUME FAREL
FIERY DEBATER AND EVANGELIST

A MAN OF ACTION
Guillaume Farel (1489-1565) was a dynamic man of action who gave his whole life to spreading the Gospel of Christ. Farel was one of the most important leaders of the French Reformation from its beginnings.

BY GRACE ALONE
While studying under Professor Jacques Lefevre at Sorbonne University in Paris, Farel came to faith in Christ. Professor Lefevre had published a Latin translation of and commentary on *The Epistles of St. Paul*. As he taught that it is God who saves by grace alone, Farel said his eyes were opened and his heart believed.

LEADER OF THE FRENCH REFORMATION
When Luther's Reformation writings came to France, Farel was one of the most prominent leaders in the French Reformed movement. When persecution forced him to flee from France in 1523, he became the leader of a group of Evangelists who preached in French speaking Switzerland.

Guillaume Farel was one of the most effective Evangelists of the Reformation.

WINNING SWITZERLAND TO CHRIST

Farel's energetic efforts were central in opposing Catholicism and promoting the Protestant Reformation in Basel, Bern, Lausanne and Geneva. Everywhere he proclaimed the supremacy of the Scriptures and the need to return to a purified Faith, which was based on the Bible alone. With great skill in debating and Evangelistic zeal, Farel succeeded in winning most of French speaking Switzerland to the Protestant Faith.

THE SCOURGE OF THE PRIESTS

Farel's powerful preaching was described as full of fire and fury. The pope is antichrist. The Mass idolatry. His sermons were cannon blasts. His oratory gripped whole cities. Farel was called *"The scourge of the priests."*

FEARLESS UNDER FIRE

Several priests attempted to assassinate Farel. After one attempt on his life failed, Farel whirled around and declared to the priest who had fired the bullet: *"I am not afraid of your shots!"*

A CHURCH PLANTER AND AUTHOR

Many new churches were established and organised under his energetic leadership. Although more of an orator than a writer and a man of action rather than a Theologian, Farel did provide the newly created churches with discipleship books in French. In his *"Summary"* Farel showed how Christian doctrine should be practically applied to everyday life and he drew up the first liturgy for French-speaking Reformed churches.

21 May 1536 - The Citizens of Geneva voted in favour of the Reformation.

THE WALDENSIANS

Farel crossed the Alps to participate in a Synod of the Waldensians. He recruited these believers to the Reformation movement and convinced them to have the Scriptures translated and printed. This was the first French translation of the Holy Scriptures and was published in 1535.

NEUCHATEL

After winning Neuchatel to the Reformation, he introduced the book publisher, Pierre de Vingle, to Neuchatel who, just between 1533 and 1535, published 20 Protestant books, which spread the Faith far and wide.

PRACTICAL FAITH

Farel was a man of deep devotion, personal piety and a very practical faith. He taught that true Christianity functions through charity.

WINNING TOWNS THROUGH DEBATES

Farel's practice was to go into the market places of Catholic towns and preach the Gospel. When attempts were made to arrest him, he challenged the local priests, or bishop, to a public debate. Inevitably, Farel won these debates. He then would appeal directly to the masses to vote on whether they were in favour of converting to the Protestant Faith, or whether they wanted to remain with Roman superstitions.

CONFRONTATIONAL

On such missions, Farel's confrontational style and tactics provoked violent reactions. In one town, the bishop tried to have him drowned in the fountain! On occasion, Farel resorted to his fists to eject the papists and seize their pulpits. It is significant that in the Reformation Wall monument, in Geneva, Farel is the only one of the Reformers depicted with a Bible in his left hand (not his right) and his right hand in a fist. Farel was ridiculed, beaten, shot at and abused, but he never gave up. Farel was a fighter.

READY TO DISPUTE

In the summer of 1535, Farel seized the church of La Madeleine and the Cathedral of St. Peter (in Geneva). Farel declared: *"I have been baptized in the Name of the Father, the Son and the Holy Ghost...I go about preaching Christ - why He died for our sins and rose again for our justification. Whoever believes in Him will be saved; unbelievers will be lost. I am bound to preach to all who will hear. I am ready to dispute with you..."*

Destroying Idols

In response to his vehement sermon against idolatry, there was a wave of destroying superstitious religious images, statues and idols throughout Geneva. Altars were demolished, the mass was abolished and images were removed from churches.

Geneva Chooses for Reformation

On 21 May 1536, a General Assembly of the citizens of Geneva voted in favour of the Reformation and made the Protestant Faith the official religion of the city.

Revolt against Savoy

With Geneva in revolt against the Duke of Savoy and its bishop, waves of political and religious turmoil swept the city and emotions were high. Surrounded by mountains in the control of Catholic France and the Duke of Savoy, the Reformation in Geneva was very vulnerable. Farel knew his limitations and he prayed for a man who would be capable of discipling this distracted and debauched city.

A Decisive Detour

It was at this decisive point that 27-year-old, French Reformer, John Calvin was forced by a local war to detour through Geneva. He expected to be in the city for only one night. But Farel heard of this famous scholar and author of *"The Institutes"* and he rushed over to recruit him.

A Contest of Wills

But Calvin was not interested. The more Farel explained his plans and described the situation in Geneva, the less Calvin felt inclined to stay. He realized that to accept Farel's challenge would involve him in controversies and conflict and his timid nature shrank from such un-scholarly activities. Calvin's mind was set on studying in Straßburg, but Farel insisted that he stay in Geneva. Others observing this escalating argument could not have appreciated what a dramatic impact the result of this contest of wills would have on world history.

Confronting Calvin

When, at last, Calvin pleaded his inexperience, general unsuitability for the pastorate and his need for further study, Farel rose from his chair and stretched himself out to his full height. As his long red beard swept his chest, Farel directed his piercing eyes at the young man seated before him. He thundered: *"May God curse your studies if now, in her time of need, you refuse to lend your aid to His Church!"*

Called to Geneva

Calvin was visibly shaken and, as he said later, he was struck with terror. In Farel's voice of thunder, Calvin had heard the call of God. There and then he yielded and consented to stay in Geneva. Just as Barnabas was used to mobilise Saul for ministry, so Farel recruited Calvin.

Calvin's Closest Friend

Farel probably was Calvin's closest friend through the years. They endured much together, including being expelled from Geneva in 1538. Again it was the persuasions of Farel that convinced Calvin to accept Geneva's requests for him to return in 1541.

Sola Scriptura! Farel holding high the Bible.

Pioneer Pastor

For the last 27 years of his life, Farel pastored the church in Neuchatel, one of the first towns that he had won to Christ. Farel's dynamic faith, missionary vision and evangelistic campaigns had in large measure been used of God to win much of French speaking Switzerland to Christ. And it was he who ensured that Calvin became the pastor, educator and Reformer of Geneva.

"Whoever confesses Me before men, him the Son of Man also will confess before the Angels of God." Luke 12:8

Chapter 14
John Calvin
A Heart Aflame and a Mind Renewed

The exiled French Reformer, John Calvin, became the most influential man of his age and his teachings have proven to be some of the most influential in the shaping of Great Britain and the United States of America.

Prominent Calvinists
Some of the greatest philosophers, writers, Reformers and Christian leaders in history have described themselves as Calvinists. Some of Calvin's influential disciples include: John Knox, William the Silent, Oliver Cromwell, John Owen, John Milton, Richard Baxter, Jonathan Edwards, David Brainerd, George Whitefield, William Carey, William Wilberforce, Sir Isaac Newton, Lord Shaftesbury, Charles Spurgeon, David Livingstone, Andrew Murray, the Covenanters in Scotland, the Huguenots of France, the Pilgrim Fathers who emigrated to New England and the Boer Voortrekkers of South Africa.

John Calvin

A Heritage of Freedom
The Reformation teachings of John Calvin were foundational in the development of modern Europe and North America. Calvin's concept of the separation of church and civil government – where each stand independent of each other yet recognise each other's Divine authority, supporting each other within their own spheres – transformed Western Civilisation. Calvin's ideals of religious toleration, representative government, constitutionalising the monarchy, establishing the rights and liberties of citizens and the Christian Work ethic – in which secular society is seen as sacred (whereby the arts, crafts, sciences and industries are all developed for the glory of God) led to the industrial and scientific revolutions developing the most productive and prosperous societies in history.

141

A Strong Doctrine for Tough Times

Calvin's Reformation teachings dominated European and American history for the rest of the 16th and 17th centuries – setting the agendas and inspiring most of the greatest social reformers. The record of history is that in every fight for freedom, whether the Puritans in England, or the Dutch fighting for freedom from Catholic Spain in the Netherlands, the Calvinists were in the forefront of political and military resistance to tyranny.

Resilience

It is an interesting historical observation that one of the most enduring characteristics of Calvinism was that it thrived in those countries where opposition was the greatest.

Following Luther

John Calvin was a second-generation Reformer. He carefully and consciously built upon the solid foundations laid by Martin Luther and Ulrich Zwingli. Calvin looked to Luther as his father in the Faith, with great respect. Luther was very aware of the up and coming distinguished scholar and author, John Calvin and praised his *Institutes*.

However, while their foundations were the same, Luther's central focus was justification by faith, whereas Calvin's focus was primarily the sovereignty of God. These Reformers shared an overwhelming sense of the majesty of God. Luther focused on the miracle of forgiveness, while Calvin went on to give the assurance of the impregnability of God's purpose. If Luther's central Biblical text was: **"the just shall live by faith,"** Calvin's was: **"Thy will be done on earth as it is in Heaven."**

Skilled in Logic and Law

John Calvin was born at Noyon, Picardy, on 10 July 1509. (He was 25 years younger than Martin Luther). Calvin entered the University of Paris at age 14,

Calvin was a scholar, author, pastor and Reformer.

studied Law and graduated at age 19 with a Master of Arts degree. He was described as having a brilliant writing style and a remarkable skill in logical argument. In later years, it was said that while people may not have liked what Calvin said, they could not have misunderstood what he meant!

From Law to Outlaw

While Calvin was engaged in further studies at Orleans University he experienced what he described as a *"sudden conversion"* from papal prejudice to Protestant conviction. With this spiritual quickening, Calvin launched into preaching, teaching and counselling amongst his peers. This in turn drew the attention of the state and soon Calvin was on the run as an outlaw, living under aliases and having to move frequently to avoid arrest.

The Institutes

In Basel, Calvin produced the first edition of his Institutes. *The Institutes of the Christian Religion* has been described as *"the clearest, most logical and most readable exposition of Protestant doctrines that the Reformation age produced."*

The full title of this 1536 edition of *The Institutes* reads: *"Basic Instruction in the Christian Religion comprising almost the whole sum of Godliness and all that it is needful to know of the doctrine of salvation. A newly published work very well worth reading by all who aspire to Godliness. The preface is to the most Christian King of France, offering to him this book as a Confession of Faith by the author, Jean Calvin of Noyon."*

This first edition was 516 pages long – divided into 6 chapters on The Ten Commandments, The Apostle's Creed, The Lord's Prayer, The Sacraments (true and false) and Christian Liberty.

The Institutes was an immediate success and catapulted Calvin into international prominence. To the French Protestants no one had spoken so effectively on their behalf and so with the publication of *The Institutes*, Calvin assumed a position of leadership in the Protestant cause in the French-speaking world.

An Accidental Detour

And so it was as a respected young author that Calvin arrived in Geneva a mere 5 months later. Calvin never intended to spend more than one night in Geneva. He was heading for Straßburg and was compelled to take a deviation to avoid a local war. The Protestants in Geneva recognised him and Guillaume Farel (the red headed Evangelist and Reformer who had won Geneva over to the Protestant Cause after a marathon debate with the papists just 2 months previously) rushed over to persuade Calvin to stay. But Calvin had other plans. As he later observed: *"Being by nature a bit antisocial and shy, I always loved retirement and peace..."* Calvin planned a life of seclusion, study and *"literary ease."*

CHALLENGED, CONVICTED AND CALLED

Farel would have none of this. He threatened Calvin with a curse: *"You are following only your own wishes and I tell you, in the Name of God Almighty, that if you do not help us in this work of the Lord, the Lord will punish you for seeking your own interests rather than His."* Convicted by Farel's serious threat of imprecations, gripped by the fear of God and ashamed by his selfish plans to avoid controversy and conflict, Calvin agreed to stay.

Guillaume Farel's bold threats and insistence convicted Calvin to accept the call to Geneva.

THE REFORMER OF GENEVA

For the next 28 years, apart from 3 years of banishment, Calvin devoted himself to evangelising, discipling, teaching and nurturing the churches in Geneva. Calvin's dedication to duty and intense drive set the highest standards of Christian work ethic. During those two and a half decades in Geneva, Calvin lectured to Theological students and preached an average of 5 sermons a week, in addition to writing commentaries on almost every book in the Bible, as well as various other Theological books. His correspondence alone fills 11 volumes.

PRODUCTIVITY DESPITE ILL HEALTH

Calvin was never physically strong and by the age of 30 he had broken his health. He would not sleep more than 4 hours a night; Even when ill, he kept four secretaries busy with his French and Latin dictation. He ate little, only one meal a day, suffered from intense migraine headaches, was frequently ill with fever, gallstones, chronic asthma and tuberculosis – yet he maintained a steady discipline of study, preaching, producing a river of Theological treatises, a massive amount of correspondence and sustained constant counselling, labour in the courts and received a stream of visitors. How Calvin managed to remain so productive while suffering from such chronic bad health is one of the mysteries of history.

DISCIPLING A CITY

Calvin's goal in Geneva was a well-taught, faithful church, dedicated to honouring God by orthodox praise and obedient holiness. He prepared a Confession of Faith to be accepted by everyone who wished to be a citizen, planned an educational programme for all and insisted on effective church discipline, including excommunication for those whose lives did not conform to Biblical standards. His was the most strenuous programme of moral discipline in the Protestant world. And quite a lot more than the City Fathers of Geneva had bargained for. In April 1538, the City Council expelled Calvin and Farel.

EXILE AND RETURN

For the next 3 years Calvin pastored a church of French refugees in the German city of Straßburg. These were the happiest years in Calvin's life. He married a widow, Idelette, was honoured by the City of Straßburg as a respected teacher of Theology and was made the City's representative to important religious conferences in Germany. However, the city of Geneva urged His return. In September 1541, with great reluctance, he once again took up the burden of discipling Geneva. Calvin succeeded in turning Geneva into a model example of a disciplined Christian community, a refuge for persecuted Protestants from all over Europe and a centre for ministerial training.

20 April 1538 - swords were drawn and pikes brandished threatening Calvin in St. Peter's as he refused to serve communion to the Libertines.

PREDESTINATION AND PERSEVERANCE OF THE SAINTS

Calvin considered Divine election to eternal life the deepest source of confidence, humility and moral power. While Calvin taught that one could not know with a certainty who were God's elect, he believed that three tests could be adequate for effective church discipline. A true Christian, John Calvin taught, could be recognised by his or her public profession of faith, active participation in church life, including participation in the two sacraments of Baptism and the Lord's Supper and by an upright moral life.

Knox described Calvin's Geneva as "the most perfect school of Christ since the Apostles."

LAW AND GRACE

Calvin taught that though Christians were no longer condemned by the Law of God, the true Christian finds in the Law God's pattern for moral behaviour. Man is not justified by works, but no man who is justified is without works. No one can be a true Christian without aspiring to holiness in his or her life. Calvin set justification by faith in a God-centred, sanctification orientated covenantal frame.

LIFE CHANGING AND LIBERATING

This rigorous pursuit of moral righteousness, both personally and in society, was one of the primary features of Calvinism. It made character a fundamental test of genuine Christianity and explains Calvinism's dynamic, social activism. God calls His elect for His own purposes. To Calvin, the consequence of Faith is strenuous effort to build God's Kingdom on earth.

FAITH AND FREEDOM

Calvin taught that no man, whether pope or king, has any claim to absolute power. Calvin encouraged the development of representative governments and stressed the right to resist the tyranny of unbelievers. Calvinist resistance to totalitarianism and absolutism (the arbitrary abuse of power by leaders) was a key factor in the development of modern limited and constitutional governments. The Church has the obligation, under Almighty God, to guide the secular authorities on spiritual and ethical matters. As a result, Calvinism rapidly assumed international dimensions.

HOLLAND

In Holland, Calvinism provided the rallying point for opposition to the oppression of Catholic Spain, which was occupying their country at that time.

SCOTLAND

In Scotland, Calvin's disciple, John Knox, taught that Protestants had the right and duty to resist, by force if necessary, any leader who tried to prevent their worship and mission.

ENGLAND

The Puritans in England established the supremacy of Parliament and constitutionally limited the power of the throne.

AMERICA

In North America, England's 13 colonies established the United States of America on Calvin's principles of representative government, separation of powers and the rule of Law, *Lex Rex*.

EVALUATING CALVIN

John Calvin stands out as one of the finest Bible scholars, one of the greatest systematic Theologians and one of the most profound religious thinkers in history. John Calvin was Bible-centred in his teaching, God-centred in his living and Christ-centred in his Faith. He integrated the confessional principles of the Reformation – Scripture alone is our authority, salvation is by the grace of God alone, received by faith alone. Christ alone is the head of the Church, everything should be done for the Glory of God alone – with supreme clarity and conviction.

Calvin's last sermon at St. Peter's Church in Geneva.

BIBLE BASED

The *Institutes* shows that Calvin was a Biblical Theologian. Nothing was in the *Institutes* which Scripture was not shown to support. As Calvin made clear in his Preface to the second edition, the *Institutes* is meant to be a general preparation for Bible study. Calvin was a systematic Theologian who interpreted Scripture with Scripture. As a second-generation Reformer he laboured consciously to confirm and conserve what those who preceded him, Luther, Zwingli, Melancthon, Bucer and others, had established. He spoke as a mainstream spokesman for the true universal Church.

A MONUMENTAL MASTERPIECE

The final edition of the *Institutes*, published in 1559, contained 80 chapters and more than 1000 pages. The *Institutes* stands as the finest textbook of Theology, apology for the Protestant Faith, manifesto for the Reformation, handbook for Catechism, weapon against heresy and guide to Christian discipleship. It is a systematic masterpiece, which has earned itself a permanent place amongst the greatest Christian books in all of history.

THE FIRST BIBLE COMMENTARIES

In addition to writing the *Institutes*, John Calvin produced some of the finest Bible commentaries. He wrote commentaries on every book in the Bible, except for Revelation. A theme that binds all of Calvin's works together is to know God and to make Him known.

TO KNOW GOD

He deals with what can be known about God (Theology) and how to know God personally (Devotion). Calvin's motto was *Prompte et sincere in opere Dei* (promptly and sincerely in the service of God). His emblem was of a heart aflame in the hand of God. This is what Calvin wished to be and this, in fact, was what he was: a heart aflame for God who sought to be

Farel, Viret, Beza and Calvin.

faithful in the service of God, renewing his mind according to the Word of God. To him it was not enough to know about God, but essential that one knew Him personally, whole-heartedly, with a heart aflame for God. Not for Calvin the dry-as-dust, cold-hearted, external and empty religion, which epitomises so many of those who claim to follow him. Calvin's faith was intense, passionate and wholehearted.

To the question: **What does it mean to know God?** Calvin answered: To know God is to acknowledge Him as He has revealed Himself in Scripture and through Christ – worshipping Him and giving Him thanks, humbling ourselves before Him as foolish and depraved sinners, learning from His Word, loving God for His love in adopting and redeeming us, trusting in God's promises of pardon, glorifying what God has accomplished through Christ, living in obedience to God's Law and seeking to honour God in all our human relationships and in all connections with God's creatures.

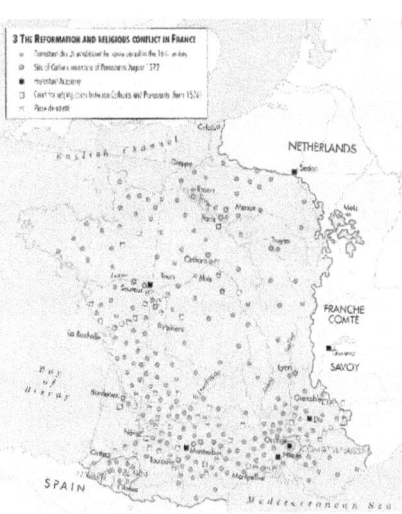

Over 2,000 Reformed congregations were established in France by pastors and evangelists trained by Calvin.

To the question: **From where comes our knowledge?** Calvin answers: From the Holy Spirit, speaking in and through the written Word of God by uniting us to the Risen Christ for abundant life.

A Reason to Sing and a Message to Give

Calvin viewed music as a gift of God and encouraged congregational Psalm singing, even putting to music a number of the Psalms himself. Calvin was an Evangelist who worked diligently to bring the lost to repentance and faith in Christ.

A World to Win

Calvin's vision is attested to by the fact that during his ministry over 2,000 Reformed churches were established in France alone – with half a million church members in congregations led by pastors and evangelists he had trained and sent out. Calvin sent missionaries throughout Europe and even as far afield as Brazil.

In his *Institutes*, Calvin wrote of *"the magnificence"* of Christ's reign

St. Peter's Church, Geneva.

prophesied in Daniel 2:32-35; Isaiah 11:4; Psalm 2:9 and Psalm 72 where Christ will rule the earth. *"Our doctrine must tower unvanquished above the glory and above all the might of the world, for it is not of us, but of the Living God and His Christ"* Who will *"rule from sea to sea and from the river even to the ends of the earth."*

HAVE YOU READ CALVIN?

If you have never read Calvin's *Institutes*, or benefited from his commentaries, perhaps this would be a good opportunity to invest the time in studying these treasures.

A CALL TO SUFFER AND SERVE – CHANGING CULTURES FOR CHRIST

Calvin's concept of the Christian life as a militant pilgrimage leading safely home by a predestined path of service and suffering – as we fulfil our cultural calling – has produced some of the most humble, hard-working heroes of the Faith. Has your mind been renewed by the Word of God? Is your heart aflame with devotion to Christ? And are you applying the Lordship of Christ to all areas of life, *promptly and sincerely in the service of God?*

"It is better to trust in the Lord than to put confidence in princes."
Psalm 118:9

Calvin and Beza with students at the Academy in Geneva.

CHAPTER 15

JOHN KNOX
AND THE REFORMATION IN SCOTLAND

REFORMATION IN SCOTLAND
As the books of Martin Luther and Tyndale's translation of the New Testament entered Scotland, they were received with great interest. Students at St. Andrews University began to take their Faith seriously. Patrick Hamilton, a student at St. Andrews, wrote a book that was condemned as *heretical*. He fled to Germany, met with Luther and soon returned to Scotland. Hamilton began preaching the Protestant Faith with great boldness.

THE BETRAYAL OF PATRICK HAMILTON
By an act of Parliament, 17 July 1525, the importation of Luther's books into Scotland was prohibited. In 1528, the Archbishop of St. Andrews summoned Hamilton for *"a debate."* However, he had no intention of debating Hamilton; it was a trap. Before any of his friends could come to Hamilton's defence, a church court hurriedly found him guilty of *"heresy."*

MARTYRDOM
While most heresy trials took weeks, Hamilton's was rushed through in less than 12 hours. It took 6 long, excruciatingly painful hours for Hamilton to die by burning at the stake. Patrick Hamilton was Scotland's first Protestant martyr. He was just 24 years old. His death inspired widespread interest in the Reformation and an intensified opposition to Catholicism. Hamilton's last words were: *"How long, O Lord shall darkness cover this realm? How long will you suffer this tyranny of men? Lord Jesus, receive my spirit!"*

Scotland's first Protestant Martyr, Patrick Hamilton.

151

Holding a double handed broadsword, John Knox stands behind Reformer George Wishart.

CONVERSION

In 1543, the Regent for the infant Mary Queen of Scots initiated a pro-English and pro-Protestant, policy. The Regent encouraged Bible reading and promoted preaching by Reformers. It was through the preaching of Thomas Guilliame, a converted friar, that John Knox was converted in 1543. The exhilarating effect of this newfound Faith and freedom, the joy of experiencing God's grace in Christ, transformed Knox forever. Soon, however, the Scottish authorities reversed their initially pro-Reformation policies and began to threaten Protestants.

THE COURAGE OF WISHART

Tall, handsome and well-mannered George Wishart became the spokesman for Scotland's growing Protestant movement. Wishart travelled throughout the country proclaiming Reformation doctrines with skill and conviction.

Scottish Reformer George Wishart.

PERSECUTION

Cardinal David Beaton, Archbishop of St. Andrews, had 5 Protestants executed in 1544 and twice tried to have the popular Wishart murdered. After one failed attempt on his life, out of concern for his safety, the Protestants organised for Wishart to move his location daily to avoid capture. John Knox, armed with a large double handed, broadsword was part of the bodyguard appointed to travel with Wishart. Those who came to a service by George Wishart found, instead of the normal mass in Latin, congregational singing and a fiery, hour-long sermon in their own tongue.

SACRIFICE

In 1546, believing his arrest imminent and unavoidable, Wishart dismissed his bodyguard saying, *"One is sufficient for a sacrifice."* Wishart was condemned as a heretic, strangled and burned by order of Cardinal Beaton. As the fire was lit, Wishart declared: *"This flame hath scorched my body, yet hath it not daunted my spirit. But he who from yonder high place beholdest us with such pride, shall, within a few days, lie in the same as ignominiously as now he is seen proudly to rest himself."*

Cardinal David Beaton

REVENGE

Within 2 months of the execution of Wishart, 16 Scottish nobles assassinated Beaton in a most brutal way. Before being struck down Beaton was admonished: *"Repent thee of thy former wicked life, but especially of the shedding of the blood of that notable instrument of God, Master George Wishart, which... cries for vengeance... We from God are sent to avenge it... Thou hast been and remain an obstinate enemy against Jesus Christ and His holy Evangel."*

ST. ANDREWS

Then a group of ardent Protestants, the Castilians, took over the city of St. Andrews and garrisoned themselves in the castle there. Although Knox was not part of either the assassination, or this conspiracy, he decided to join the men to minister to them. Impressed by Knox's teaching abilities, they asked him to become the castle's chaplain. (Although, Knox had studied Law and Theology at the University of St. Andrews and had been ordained, because of the excess of priests in Scotland, he had ended up becoming a tutor and had not previously served as a parish priest.) Knox was overwhelmed, reduced to tears and declined the offer, not feeling worthy.

CALLED

Over the next few days, the congregation persisted in extending to him the call. Then, while attending a local church service in St. Andrews, Knox heard Dean John Annand affirming Catholicism, claiming that it was *"the Bride of Christ."* Knox stood up in his pew and interrupted him, declaring that the Roman church was no Bride of Christ, but a prostitute. The Roman papacy had degenerated further from the Faith of the Apostles than the Jews had from Moses when they had crucified Christ.

STRIKING AT THE ROTTEN ROOTS OF ROME

At this, the congregation loudly demanded that Knox justify his remarks in a sermon the following Sunday - which he did. Knox declared that the Roman church had become the synagogue of Satan. He pulled no punches and one observer noted that while others snipped at the outer branches of the papacy, Knox *"struck at the root to destroy the whole!"* This was the beginning of the public career of one of the most powerful preachers of the Reformation era.

CAPTURED AND CONDEMNED

The French fleet laid siege to St. Andrews Castle, which surrendered in July 1547. The rebels were taken to Rouen, in France. Knox and most of the Protestants were condemned for life to serve as galley slaves. A life sentence in the galleys was considered the next most severe punishment after execution. Knox said little about his time in the galleys, but two words that he used to describe it were: *"torment"* and *"affliction."* During his time in the galleys he contracted kidney infection and stomach ulcers, which afflicted him for the rest of his life.

Many Protestants were condemned to be galley slaves for the French.

GALLEY SLAVE

About 150 galley slaves, or *forsairs*, rode 6 to the oar. The 25 oars were each about 45 feet long. The rowers were kept chained to the oar, when not doing other duties. The *comites* on the ships carried whips to ensure that the convicts and prisoners of war pulled their weight. Galley slaves were considered a cheap and expendable form of fuel for ships. Knox was 33 years of age when he was condemned to the galleys. His strong character, which was evidenced throughout the rest his life and ministry served him well throughout this ordeal.

Rejecting Idolatry

On one occasion, while mass was being celebrated on the galley and the *Salve Regina* (O, Holy Queen) was sung, a statue of the Virgin Mary (*Nostre Dame*) was handed around for all on board to kiss. He refused: *"Trouble me not; such an idol is accursed!"* When this statue was again thrust before Knox's face to kiss, he grasped it and threw the idol overboard declaring: *"Now, let our lady save herself. She is light enough, let her learn to swim!"*

Steadfast

Knox admitted that the prisoners on these galleys were *"miserably treated."* They were also placed under pressure to renounce Protestantism and embrace Catholicism. Knox was steadfast in rejecting all forms of Catholicism.

Release and Freedom

The English Protestant government of King Edward VI took a direct interest in the plight of these prisoners and, in February 1549, after 18 months as a galley slave, Knox was released. This was probably at the direct intervention of King Edward VI, as part of a prisoner exchange.

Knox the Puritan

Knox spent the next 5 years in England as an honoured guest. He was granted preaching opportunities in Berwick and Newcastle. In 1551, Knox was appointed a royal Chaplain of King Edward VI. As Chaplain, he had the opportunity to preach before the king and contributed to the preparation of the second *"Book of Common Prayer"* (BCP). Knox, for example, insisted that the statement be included that *"kneeling at the Lord's Supper does not imply any adoration of the bread and wine, nor is such adoration intended or permitted. On the contrary, it is stated explicitly, firstly that the natural body and Blood of Christ are in Heaven, not on earth and, secondly, that at the Lord's Supper both the bread and the wine stay the same as they are. To adore them is idolatry."* When Knox was invited to become Bishop of Rochester, he declined.

John Knox, the King's Chaplain.

BLOODY MARY AND EXILE

When King Edward VI died, 6 July 1553, the future of Protestants in England looked bleak. Mary Tudor made clear her intention to reinstate Catholicism as the national religion. Knox described Mary as the *"wicked English Jezebel."* Knox, along with thousands of other English Protestants, sought refuge in Protestant Germany and Switzerland.

SWITZERLAND

Early in 1554 Knox travelled to Geneva, where he met John Calvin. Knox described Calvin's Geneva as *"the most perfect school of Christ that ever was on earth since the days of the Apostles."* Knox also met Heinrich Bullinger in Zürich.

FRANKFURT

Knox settled in Frankfurt where a group of English and Scottish exiles asked Knox to be their pastor. This plunged Knox into distressing quarrels and controversies over what liturgy should be used. Knox had become critical of the *"Book of Common Prayer"* (BCP) and even about Calvin's *"Genevan Order of Service"* (GOS), so he drew up a new Order of Service, which became known as the *"Book of Common Order"* (BCO). However, this was rejected by a large majority of the congregation. By March 1555, the congregation was split and the majority proposed Knox's dismissal. Some members of the congregation convinced the city authorities to prohibit Knox from preaching and to expel him from the city. It is interesting to note that although his *"Book of Common Order"* was rejected by the exiles in Frankfurt, in 1560 it became the official worship book of the Church of Scotland.

THE LORDS OF THE CONGREGATION

While Knox was in exile in Europe, Protestant congregations were forming back in Edinburgh, Dundee, St. Andrews, Perth and Brechin. Most of these were clandestine meetings and many used the English *"Book of Common Prayer."* In December 1557, a group of Scottish nobles drew up a covenant to *"set forward and establish the most blessed Word of God and His Congregation,"* to renounce Catholicism and to establish the Protestant Faith as the official religion of Scotland. This group became known as the *"Lords of the Congregation."*

GENEVA AND SCOTLAND

After being expelled from Frankfurt, Knox helped co-pastor an English congregation in Geneva. In August 1555 he returned to Scotland and spent 9 months preaching extensively throughout the land. The Catholic bishops summoned him to Edinburgh in May 1556 to face legal charges. Knox returned to Geneva where he assisted members of his congregation in a new translation of the Bible into English. This became known as the *"Geneva Bible."*

WHEN IS IT RIGHT TO FIGHT?

Knox asked Calvin whether it was permissible to resist by force a monarch who was *"idolatrous."* Calvin maintained that individuals might refuse to obey commands contrary to God's Law, yet he could not accept revolt. However, Knox was coming to believe that Christians had the obligation to revolt against a tyrannical monarch. A ruler's highest obligation was to preserve pure Faith and worship. In Knox's *"A Godly Letter"* (1554) he taught that the nation could incur corporate guilt for tolerating evil. If the people permitted Catholicism to remain, the nation would be subjected to Divine judgment and plagues. God punished the entire tribe of Benjamin, for example, not because all were adulterers, but because some were tolerated.

IDOLS FOR DESTRUCTION

In his 1549 leaflet: *"A Vindication That The Mass is Idolatry,"* Knox taught that idolatry entails not only worshipping what is not God, but also in trusting anything besides God. To honour anything in religion contrary to God's Word is to lean on something other than God. That is idolatry. *"The mass... is an abomination."* The mass promoted a false atonement based on works.

Iconoclasts protest against statues in church as idols - objects of worship - by smashing them.

REBELLION AGAINST GOD

Since the Law of God never changes, He would respond to sin in Scotland as He did in ancient Israel, e.g. raising up a Jehu to slay an idolatrous ruler. Knox demanded that God's Law be upheld in Scotland. If the people obeyed the unjust commandments of evil rulers, they would receive a far more terrible punishment from God than any ruler could inflict upon them for treason. Not to revolt against an idolatrous ruler was *"plain rebellion against God."*

FROM SEPARATION TO VICTORY

Knox maintained that, when in a minority, the faithful are only required to separate themselves from idolatry. However, when the believers are in a dominant position and reasonably unified, they must not simply separate from idolatry, they must also abolish it. If exterminating idolatry meant overthrowing a tyrannical ruler, then that was necessary. Knox's sermons and writings on the subject were full of Scriptural examples: Abraham, Moses, Deborah, Samuel, Elisha, Hezekiah, Jehu, Elijah, Amos, Isaiah, Josiah, Jeremiah and many other passages dealing with the Covenant, purifying national religion, resisting authorities who promoted idolatry and the Sovereignty of God. *"If princes exceed their bounds...there is no doubt that they may be resisted with power."*

THE MINISTER OF JUSTICE

Luther was protected by Prince Fredrick of Saxony, Zwingli by the mayor and council of Zürich, Calvin had the support of the Geneva City Council, the English Reformation at that time had King Edward VI. However, since no civil authority in Scotland was able to provide protection for Protestants, Knox believed that the abusive powers should be overthrown. In this Knox stands alone amongst the leading Reformers of the 16th Century. He openly challenged the standard interpretation of Romans 13, held by such Reformers as Luther, Zwingli, Tyndale and Calvin.

A CALL FOR RESISTANCE

In his 1555 *"Admonition to England,"* Knox condemned those leaders who had connived to restore the nation to Catholicism under Queen Mary Tudor. *"Had She... been sent to hell before these days, then should not their iniquity and cruelty so manifestly have appeared to the world."*

In 1558, Knox published his most notorious *"The First Blast of the Trumpet Against the Monstrous Regiment of Women"* aimed directly at *"Bloody Mary,"* - The Queen of England at that time.

Knox stated that no woman could be a legitimate ruler - certainly not one who persecuted true Christians. *"Bloody Mary"* was a rebel against God, *"a traitoress and rebel against God."* Knox declared that it was against the Law of God and nature for such a woman to rule any kingdom, because it subverted both the Divine and natural order. He called for the faithful to *"remove from honour and authority that monster in nature."*

In his, *"Appellations To the Nobility and Commonality of Scotland"* he extended to the common people the right and duty to rebel against tyranny.

CONTROVERSY

John Calvin severely disapproved of Knox's *First Blast* and banned its circulation in Geneva. Within weeks of its publication, *"Bloody Mary"* died and the Protestant Queen Elizabeth ascended to the English throne. Many saw Knox's bold stand against the tyranny of *"Bloody Mary"* vindicated by her sudden removal and the accession of a Protestant Queen to the throne.

However, most saw it as a monumental political mistake and distanced themselves from Knox. Knox admitted: *"My First Blast has blown from me all my friends in England!"*

Queen Elizabeth I was appalled at Knox's tract. Knox's explanation that *"the monstrous regiment of women"* that he was referring to were *"Bloody Mary"* Tudor of England, Mary of Guise and Mary Queen of Scots, did not seem to repair the breach. Nor did Knox's public statement of support for the new Queen Elizabeth I as the Protestant Queen of England repair the damage of his once strong links to the Church of England.

REFORMATION SWEEPS SCOTLAND

In May 1559, Knox arrived in Perth. His fiery sermon against Catholic idolatry was so effective that when the service was over, the congregation immediately began to demolish altars, smash images, statues and crucifixes. They removed all the superstitious trappings of Romanism. Then the Lords of the Congregation militarily occupied Perth, Sterling, St. Andrews and by the end of June, Edinburgh. There, Knox was elected minister at St. Giles Kirk in High Street. His Reformation preaching reverberated throughout Scotland.

Knox preaching to an armed congregation eager to bring about Reformation by force.

THE FRENCH OUTMANOEUVRED

To counter Mary of Guise and her French troops, the Scottish Lords of the Congregation drew up the Treaty of Berwick, February 1560, with the English. The Treaty was so effective that on 6 July 1560 the French and English both agreed to leave Scottish soil. Without French interference, the future of the Reformation in Scotland was assured!

THANKSGIVING AND CONFESSION

Later that month the Scottish Parliament met at St. Giles, in Edinburgh, for a great Thanksgiving service where Knox preached to them. The Parliament then ordered Knox and 5 of his colleagues to write a confession of faith. Hurriedly put to paper in 4 days, *The Scots Confession* is vibrant and spontaneous, filled with prophetic and militant language. It was adopted by Parliament and remained, for 90 years, the Scottish churches' official Theology. (In 1647, it was superseded by The Westminster Confession.)

FAITH IN ACTION

The Scots Confession stands out in how it specifies practical Christian ethics. It urges good citizenship, honourable living and a commitment to social justice in these words: *"To have one God, to worship and honour Him, to call on Him in our troubles, to reverence His Holy Name, to hear His Word and believe it, to share in His Holy sacraments.*

"The second kind is: to honour father, mother, monarchs, rulers and superior powers; to love them, support them, obey their orders providing they are not contrary to God's Commandments, save the lives of the innocent, overthrow tyranny, defend the oppressed, keep our bodies clean and holy, live in soberness and temperance, deal justly with all men in word and deed and finally, to subdue any desire to harm our neighbour... Contrary acts are sins." (Article 14)

A HIGHER DUTY

The Scots Confession not only permits the overthrowing of tyrants, but makes such action mandatory. Tyrants are defined as the real rebels to the King of kings. Article 13 defines workers of iniquity as: *"filthy persons, idolaters, drunkards and thieves... murderers, oppressors and cruel persecutors."* *The Scots Confession* makes clear that no civil power is absolute. Civil leaders are permanently on probation and no Christian should give unqualified and absolute allegiance to any government. Christians must reserve the right of just rebellion against tyrants.

John Knox and the Reformation in Scotland

TOUGH TIMES DEMAND TENACIOUS FAITH

No other Reformation Confession ventured so far into such dangerous waters, providing theological justification for rebellion against tyrants. As Knox declared: *"Dangerous times demand vigorous faith."*

NATIONAL REFORMATION

On August 17, Parliament abolished the mass, repudiated papal jurisdiction over Scotland and rescinded all laws at variance with the Reformed Faith.

COMPREHENSIVE REFORM

Also in 1560, Knox's Treatise on *Predestination* was published in Geneva. The Geneva Bible was also published. This was the work of the English congregation that Knox had pastored. In December 1560 the *"First Book of Discipline"* drawn up by Knox and his colleagues was submitted to the General Assembly. Knox laid out plans for the comprehensive application of the Gospel to every area of Scottish life. He wanted a school in every parish, a college in every town, a university in every city and regular, organised provision for the poor.

Also in 1560, Knox's wife, Marjory, died.

MARY QUEEN OF SCOTS

Although the Reformation Parliament of 1560 had worked with John Knox to mandate a Calvinist Scotland, the return of the Catholic Mary queen of Scots in 1561 put that in jeopardy. As queen, she refused to assent to the new order and Scotland remained officially Catholic. Mary Stuart was heir to England's throne if Elizabeth died. With her strong ties to Philip II of Spain and the Guises in France, the Catholic threat to Scotland's emerging Reformation was serious.

Mary, murder and immorality.

THE PAPIST THREAT

The Scots were well aware that in the Netherlands Protestants were being tortured, beheaded, hanged, drowned, burned and buried alive by the Vatican's heavy hand. They had recently witnessed the wave of horrible executions under *"Bloody Mary"* in neighbouring England. As rumours circulated that Mary Stuart would marry Don Carlos, the son of Philip II of Spain (the arch persecutor of Protestants), Knox preached a withering sermon declaring that: *"all papists are infidels!"*

A CLEAR AND PRESENT DANGER

Philip II was well aware that Mary Stuart was the Vatican's best hope of restoring Catholicism to England: *"She is the one gate through which religion can be restored in England. All the rest are closed."*

IMMORALITY AND INTRIGUE

Mary Stuart married Lord Darnley of England, hoping to unite the Catholics of England and Scotland. When the queen became pregnant, her young husband accused the queen of adultery with her private secretary, David Rizzio. Lord Darnley (now King Henry) participated in the murder of Rizzio, 9 March 1556. On 15 June 1556, Mary Stuart delivered a son: James Charles Stuart (who grew up to become James I of England).

Mary queen of Scots was heard to complain: "I am more afraid of the prayers of John Knox than of an army of ten thousand!"

MURDERING HER HUSBAND

In revenge for voicing his suspicions, Mary Stuart arranged through her boyfriend, the Earl of Bothwell, the assassination of her husband, King Henry (Lord Darnley). Mary coaxed Henry back to Edinburgh, lulled his suspicions and arranged for him to be blown up by explosives. Both Protestants and Catholics in Scotland were outraged. Mary had Bothwell stand a mock trial, at which he was acquitted, then gave him Dunbar Castle and various lands to his associates.

CONFRONTING THE QUEEN

Knox was called before the Queen's Council - where he voiced his suspicions. Then he confronted Bothwell with charges of adultery, complicity in murder and rape. When Bothwell married queen Mary, May 1567, the nation became convinced that she had helped murder her husband. There were widespread calls for her to be deposed and the people turned against her. Knox demanded that the queen stand trial for murder and adultery - both capital crimes. Mary Stuart was forced to abdicate and the nobles organised a swift coronation of the infant, James VI of Scotland (later he would become James I of England and of the United Kingdom).

THE REFORMATION TRIUMPHS IN SCOTLAND

At this coronation, Knox preached from the pulpit about the baby Joash who was anointed and crowned while queen Athaliah cried *"treason"* from her palace! The sermon included details from the Bible as to how the nobles had gone from the coronation of Joash to kill Athaliah, to tear down the temples of Baal and to restore the rule of the prophets in the land. While Knox was calling for the trial of Mary Stuart, she escaped and raised an army of 6,000 Catholics. However, when her army was confronted by the disciplined Protestants, Mary's army melted. She fled to England and sought the protection of her cousin, Elizabeth. Bothwell fled to Denmark.

The end of Mary's reign in Scotland.

JAMES STUART

James Stuart, Mary's half-brother, became Regent of Scotland. James Stuart (1531-1570) had been an influential figure in Scottish politics. By age 19, he was already a member of the Privy Council. He became Mary queen of Scots' Chief Advisor when she returned to Scotland. However, as he was won over to the Protestant Faith and became a member of the Lords of the Congregation, he used his power to maintain and extend the influence of Protestantism. When Mary was forced to abdicate in 1567 and her infant son, James VI was crowned, Stuart was appointed Regent. He was described as: *"a Puritan with natural charm and diplomacy."*

The Duke of Alva

OPPRESSION AND INSURRECTION

At the same time, Europe was boiling. The Spanish Duke of Alva had fallen upon the Calvinist rebels of Holland with fire and sword. 8,000 Dutch Protestants were executed. Another 30,000 had their property confiscated. Then in 1568, the Inquisition condemned all 3 million Dutch Protestants to death as *"heretics!"* The Dutch valiantly resisted and declared independence. Philip II was facing a great revolt. Along with the war in the Netherlands and civil war in France, a papal bull excommunicating Elizabeth inspired a Catholic uprising under the Earls of Northumberland and Westmoreland. The Catholic armies of Northumberland destroyed Bibles and prayer books, re-instituted the mass in Durham Cathedral and moved to rescue Mary Stuart to make her queen of England.

REMOVING THE THREAT

Elizabeth's army crushed the Catholic rebellion and after numerous other intrigues and conspiracies to assassinate her and place Mary on the English throne were exposed, Elizabeth reluctantly agreed to Mary's trial and execution.

ASSASSINATION

The assassination in February 1570 of the Protestant Regent of Scotland, James Stuart, plunged Scotland into civil war. Later that year, Knox suffered a stroke. But he continued to

James Stuart

preach throughout the last months of his life. Even as his health was deteriorating, he insisted on being carried to the pulpit.

SUCCESS

Before he died, in 1572, Knox had the joy of seeing the Reforms of 1560 ratified by the Scottish Parliament. Papal authority in Scotland was outlawed. All future rulers of Scotland were to swear to uphold the Reformed doctrine. The day before he died Knox said: *"I have been fighting against satan, who is ever ready for the assault; I have fought against spiritual wickedness and have prevailed."* The dedicated labours of John Knox resulted in Scotland becoming the most Calvinist nation in the world.

THE VERDICT OF HISTORY

Otto Scott in *"The Great Christian Revolution"* summarizes his achievements: *"Knox had humbled a reigning monarch, toppled a government, ousted a hierarchy, converted the people and could regard, towards the close of his life, the landscape transformed by his efforts and the teaching of his mentor, Calvin. Knox's triumph in Scotland...severed a tentacle of France and lessened the threat to the Reformation of England."*

John Knox - a man who neither feared nor flattered any flesh.

FEARLESS

At his grave, one man declared: *"Here lies a man who neither flattered, nor feared, any flesh."*

DYNAMIC

One of Knox's followers had declared that his preaching was *"able in one hour to put more life in us than 500 trumpets continually blustering in our ears."*

STALWART

The 19th Century historian, Thomas Carlyle, describe Knox as: *"a most surprising individual to have kindled all of Scotland, within a few years, almost within a few months, into perhaps the noblest flame of sacred human zeal and brave determination, to believe only what it found completely believable and to defy the whole world and the devil at its back, in an unsubduable defense of the same."* To Carlyle, Knox was the very epitome of stalwart leadership, *"the most Scottish of Scots... nothing hypocritical, foolish and untrue can find harbour in this man... fearing God and without any other fear."*

UNCOMPROMISING

Douglas Wilson in his biography of Knox *"For Kirk and Covenant"* describes Knox as: *"like Daniel in the Old Testament, he was forthright in his condemnation of sin, unguarded in his pronouncement of truth and single-minded in his adherence to the Word of God. Like King Josiah, in ancient Israel, he did what was right in the sight of the Lord, never turning aside to the right hand or to the left. Like the great general Joshua, he dutifully obeyed the clear commands of Scripture, always steadfast and unwavering. But such character traits and such stands, however compelling, are inevitably costly. It nearly cost Knox everything during his lifetime and it has earned him the odium and ire of virtually every secular historian in the years since... a simple compromise here or there might well have saved him from imprisonment, exile and anathema. But he refused to compromise. He could have tried to work within the system. He could have tried conciliation, accommodation, or negotiation. But he refused to compromise, risking everything for the sake of principle."*

GOD'S FIREBRAND

John Calvin described Knox as: *"God's firebrand"* and as a *"brother... labouring energetically for the Faith."*

"Give me Scotland, or I die!"

Mary Stuart, queen of Scots, had been heard to declare, trembling and in tears: *"I am more afraid of the prayers of John Knox than of an army of 10,000."*

John Knox's famous prayer: *"Give me Scotland or I die!"* was thoroughly answered in his lifetime.

"I have fought the good fight, I have finished the race, I have kept the Faith."
2 Timothy 4:7

CHAPTER 16
PIERRE VIRET
FRENCH EVANGELIST AND REFORMER

Pierre Viret entered the University of Paris at the same time as Ignatius Loyola and about the time that Calvin was graduating. It was during his university studies that Viret was challenged by the new Protestant ideas and personally committed his life to Christ.

UNDER FIRE
Farel then challenged young Viret to become a minister of the Gospel and to preach and work for the Reformation in his home village of Orbe. Viret succeeded in winning Orbe over to the Gospel. However, when he was invited to preach in Payerne, a band of Catholics attempted to kill

Pierre Viret

him and he escaped with severe wounds. Viret survived numerous attempts on his life, including by poisoning and shooting.

WINNING GENEVA FOR CHRIST
In 1534, Viret joined Farel in a mission to Geneva. For the next 2 years, Farel and Viret preached Salvation and Reform until the city of Geneva was in an uproar. Viret performed the first evangelical baptism in Geneva and took part with Farel in the marathon debate that convinced the Council of Geneva to formally renounce Catholicism and embrace the Reformation. Viret was with Farel when he confronted Calvin with the call to remain in Geneva and become its pastor.

LAUSANNE FOR CHRIST
After Calvin accepted the call to disciple Geneva, Viret left to help consolidate the Reformation in Lausanne. Viret's ministry in Lausanne flourished as he founded an academy to train Protestant leaders. Viret taught and supervised at this academy. He also established ministries to care for the poor, particularly widows and orphans.

EXILE
In 1559, when the Bernese exiled Viret, he returned to Geneva, bringing with him many of the ministers, all but one of the faculty of the academy and nearly 1,000 of his parishioners. The Genevans loved Viret and elected him their minister.

167

MISSION TO FRANCE

In 1561, in response to news of the harsh persecution of Christians in France, Viret requested leave from the Geneva Council to minister in France. Viret travelled to Lyon and then to Nimes, where he regularly preached to crowds of many thousands. Riots followed his sermons, but within a few months Nimes was solidly Protestant. Invitations to minister in churches throughout France poured in. Viret travelled continuously preaching to huge crowds. In Montpellier Viret saw most of the faculty of the medical college convert to Christ.

DISCIPLESHIP DESPITE CIVIL WAR

In Lyon, despite civil war, the plague and ill health, Viret was able to disciple the city and bring moral order. He preached daily to large crowds, counselled soldiers, wrote at least 12 books, including his monumental *"Instruction Chrestienne."* Along with his itinerant preaching, Viret wrote many Gospel pamphlets and maintained regular correspondence with other leaders of the Reformation.

UNDER THE PROTECTION OF THE QUEEN

In 1565, the King of France ordered Viret's expulsion from the country. Viret fled to Navarre where the Protestant Queen, Jeanne d' Albret (the mother of the future Henry IV of France) provided him protection. Queen Jeanne made Viret one of her Chief advisers and Superintendent of the Academy at Ortez.

UNDER THE THREAT OF DEATH

Catholic forces later captured Viret and 11 other Reformed ministers in a surprise attack. They had already executed 7 of the 12, when a counter attack by Protestant forces rescued Viret and returned him to his intense and productive ministry.

PRODUCTIVE AND POPULAR

Pierre Viret was undoubtedly the most popular Protestant preacher in 16th Century France. He had a great reputation for personal piety, Bible based ministry, a gentle spirit and a compassionate pastoral heart. Viret was the author of more than 50 popular books.

TRIUMPH AMIDST TRAGEDY

Viret suffered much. He lost his first wife, two daughters and a son in the plague in Lausanne. He later lost two other daughters and his second wife to the plague during his ministry in France. Viret was a sensitive and eloquent preacher, whose Bible based messages won many thousands to Christ.

"In mighty signs and wonders, by the power of the Spirit of God... I have fully preached the Gospel of Christ." Romans 15:19

CHAPTER 17
ALBRECHT DÜRER
EVANGELIST AND REFORMER IN ART

Albrecht Dürer

Albrecht Dürer (1471 - 1528) was the oldest son and third of 18 children born to a goldsmith in Nuremberg, Germany. His father, Albrecht Dürer, the elder, worked hard in his precious metals business, but faced severe trials and suffered the loss of many of his children. Only three of his 18 children survived to adulthood. Yet Mr. Dürer was an honest man who trusted in God and handled his trials with courage and faith.

BROUGHT UP TO LOVE AND HONOUR GOD

His son, Albrecht wrote: *"My father lived an honourable Christian life. He was a man patient of spirit, mild and peaceable to all and very thankful toward God... He was a man of few words and a God fearing man... This man, my dear father, was very careful of his children to bring them up to love and honour God."*

APPRENTICED IN ART

Albrecht was trained as an apprentice in his father's goldsmith shop, but his longing was to be an artist. So in 1486 his father sent Albrecht to study for three years at the studio of the famous Michael Wolgemuth. Then Dürer spent the following few years travelling from town to town with other artists to develop his craft. In Mainz, where just 35 years earlier, Johannes Gutenberg had invented the Printing Press, Dürer worked with the famous Erhard Reuwich, whose book *Travels in The Holy Land* was full of sketches depicting the architecture, clothing and landscape of Israel.

169

MARRIAGE AND MASTERS

In 1494, Albrecht returned to Nuremberg and married the beautiful Agnes Frey. Together they spent the next 11 years in Nuremberg where Albrecht developed woodcut illustrations and copper plate engravings. In 1505 he travelled to Venice to study alongside some of the great Renaissance masters.

A DISCIPLE OF MARTIN LUTHER

As Martin Luther launched his Reform, Dürer paid close attention. When Prince Frederick of Saxony sent Dürer one of Luther's books in 1520, Dürer wrote to him and thanked him: *"I pray and humbly beg that you will protect the praiseworthy Dr. Martin Luther for the sake of Christian truth. It matters more than all the riches and power of this world, for with time everything passes away; only the truth is eternal. And if God helps me to*

come to Dr. Martin Luther, then I will carefully draw his portrait and engrave it in copper for a lasting remembrance of this Christian man who has helped me out of great distress. And I beg your worthiness to send me as my payment anything new that Dr. Martin Luther may write in German."

In his journal, Dürer describing Luther as: *"enlightened by the Holy Ghost to be the continuer of the true Faith... he has suffered... for the Christian truth against the unchristian papacy, which works against the freedom of Christ, exacting from us our blood and sweat, therewith to nourish itself in idleness, while the people famish."*

CHRIST CENTRED

Dürer returned to the Netherlands in 1521 and spent the remaining years of his life in pursuit of his ministry in art, engraving, painting, devoting all of his work to various aspects of the life of Christ, the Resurrection and the last Day of Judgement.

ARTIST OF THE REFORMATION

It is in part due to Dürer's influence and to the spiritual and intellectual character of Nuremberg, that it was the first free city to become officially Protestant. Dürer was also one of the first artists publicly to identify with the Reformation. Dürer developed a special relationship with Philipp Melanchthon. Dürer wrote: *"No man can ever execute a beautiful picture relying on his own imagination, unless he has stirred his mind from a study of Divine work in nature...the mysterious treasure welled up in the* heart is made known by the man's work – for the mind and the heart must be in union with the life and power of God and then the artist's hand will form that thing of beauty which is indeed a joy forever."

THE GOSPEL IN ART

Dürer has provided the church with some of the most striking works representing the life and ministry of Christ in pictures. Clearly, Albrecht Dürer was a humble and dedicated Christian who loved the Saviour with all his heart. His art proclaims the greatest story ever told.

"Declare His glory among the nations, His wonders among all peoples. The Lord is great and greatly to be praised..."
1 Chronicles 16:24 – 25

The Four Horsemen of The Apocalypse.

CHAPTER 18

HOW THE REFORMATION CHANGED THE CHURCH

In the book of Judges we read about another generation, which arose, which knew neither the Lord nor what He had done (Judges 2:10). Today, it appears that a generation has arisen, which like Israel under the Judges, knows little of either the Lord nor of what He did during the time of the Protestant exodus and the struggles in the wilderness, which followed in the 16th and 17th century. Sometimes this is from a cowardly dislike of controversy and confrontation. But few people seem to understand either the evils from which the Reformation delivered us, or the blessings which the Reformation won for us.

THE REFORMATION DELIVERED THE CHURCH FROM GROSS IGNORANCE AND SPIRITUAL DARKNESS
The church, before the Reformation, was a church without the Bible. And a church without a Bible is as useless as a lighthouse without light, a candlestick without a candle, or a motor vehicle without an engine. The priests and people knew scarcely anything about God's Word or the way of salvation in Christ.

Bishop J.C. Ryle described the situation: *"The immense majority of the clergy did little more than say masses and offer up pretended sacrifices, repeat Latin prayers and chant Latin hymns (which of course most of the people could not understand), hear confessions, grant absolutions, give extreme unction and take money to get dead people out of purgatory."*

Bishop Latimer observed: "When the devil gets influence in a church, up go candles and down goes preaching."

Martin Luther burning the papal bull excommunicating him, along with books of canon law.

Quarterly sermons (that is, once every three months) were prescribed to the clergy, but not insisted upon. Latimer noted that while the mass was never left unsaid for a single

Sunday, sermons might be omitted for 20 Sundays in succession. Indeed, to preach much was to incur the suspicion of being a *heretic*.

Bishop Hooper, who along with Bishop Latimer was burned alive at the stake under Queen Mary, did a survey in 1551 and found that out of 311 clergy in his Diocese, 168 were unable to repeat the Ten Commandments, 31 of those 168 could not even say in which part of the Scripture the Ten Commandments were to be found, 40 could not tell where the Lord's Prayer was written and 31 of the 40 did not even know who the author of the Lord's Prayer was!

THE REFORMATION DELIVERED THE CHURCH FROM CHILDISH SUPERSTITIONS

The Roman Catholic church, before the Reformation, taught its members to seek spiritual benefit from so-called relics of dead saints and to treat them with divine honour. Calvin's *"Inventory of Relics"* and Hobart Seymour's *"Pilgrimage to Rome"* catalogue some of the ludicrous swindles, which were perpetrated by the church of Rome. This included pieces of wood *"of the true cross"* enough to load a large ship, thorns professing to be part of the Saviour's crown of thorns, enough to make a huge faggot, at least 14 nails said to have been used at the Crucifixion, four spearheads – each purporting to be the one which pierced our Lord's side, at least three seamless coats of Christ, for which the soldiers cast lots, Saint James's hand, bones of Mary Magdalene, toenails from Saint Edmund, some bread, purported to have been used by Christ at the Last Supper, a girdle of the Virgin Mary and milk from the Virgin Mary! The Royal Commissioners of Henry VIII examined a vial at the Abbey in Gloucestershire, which was said to contain the blood of Christ! The Commissioners found that it contained the blood of a duck.

There were literally thousands of profane and vile inventions, fabrications and deceptions, which Roman priests imposed on the people before the Reformation. They must have known that they were deceiving the people, yet they persisted in presenting these lies and requiring that the ignorant laity believe them. Sometimes the priests induced dying sinners to give vast tracts of lands to abbeys and monasteries, in order to atone for their bad lives. In one way or another, they were continually separating sinners from their money and accumulating property and wealth in the hands of the Roman church.

The power of the priests was practically despotic and was used for every purpose except the advancement of the Christian Faith. It seemed that their primary object was power. To them confession had to be made.

Without their absolution and extreme unction no professing Christian could be saved. Without their masses no soul could be redeemed from purgatory. In short, they were, to all intents and purposes, the *mediators between Christ and man*. To please and honour the Roman church was a devout Christian's first duty. To injure them was the greatest of sins. One of the indulgences issued in 1498, with the authority of the pope, claimed: *"To absolve people from usury, theft, manslaughter, fornication and all crime whatsoever, except smiting the clergy and conspiring against the pope!"*

A starving man in a famine may be reduced to eating rats and rubbish, rather than die of hunger. Similarly, a conscience-stricken soul, deprived of God's Word, should not be judged too harshly by us, if they struggled to find comfort in the most debasing superstition. However, we must never forget that it was from such superstitions which the Reformation delivered us.

Tetzel selling indulgences.

THE REFORMATION DELIVERED THE CHURCH FROM BLATANT IMMORALITY

Before the Reformation, the lives of the clergy were simply scandalous. There were brothels in the Vatican. The popes, cardinals and bishops openly consorted with prostitutes and engaged in the most debauched orgies. The local priests became notorious for gluttony, drunkenness and gambling. As Bishop Ryle pointed out: *"To expect the huge roots of ignorance and superstition, which filled our land, to bear any but corrupt fruit, would be unreasonable and absurd."*

175

Contemporary art depicted friars as foxes preaching with the neck of a stolen goose peeping out of the hood behind; as wolves giving absolution, with the sheep partly concealed under their cloaks; or as apes sitting on a sick man's bed with a crucifix in one hand and with the other hand in the suffering person's pocket! Such public contempt in art reflects the scorn with which the clergy were held at the time.

Bishop Ryle pointed out: *"But the blackest spot on the character of our pre-Reformation clergy in England is one of which it is painful to speak ... their horrible contempt of the 7th Commandment ... the consequences of shutting up herds of men and women in the prime of life, in monasteries and nunneries, were such that I will not defile my paper by dwelling upon them ... if ever there was a plausible theory weighed in the balance and found utterly wanting, it is the favourite theory that celibacy and monasticism promote holiness ... monasteries and nunneries were frequently sinks of iniquity."*

The report of the Royal Commissioners, under Henry VIII, declared: *"That manifest sin, vicious, carnal and abominable living, is daily used and committed in abbeys, priories and other religious houses of monks, canons and nuns and that albeit many continual visitations have been had, by the space of 200 years or more, for an honest and charitable reformation of such unthrifty, carnal and abominable living, yet that nevertheless, little or none amendment was hitherto had, but that their vicious living shamefully increased and augmented."*

It was observed that: **"There is no surer recipe for promoting immorality than fullness of bread and abundance of idleness."** Ezekiel 16:49. It is from such superstition, corruption, immorality, ignorance and idolatry that the Reformation freed the church.

The interior of the Schlosskirche, Wittenberg.

THE REFORMATION GAVE THE CHURCH BACK THE BIBLE

In 1519, six men and a woman were burned at Coventry for teaching their children the Ten Commandments, The Lord's Prayer and The Apostle's Creed in English. Nothing seems to have alarmed and enraged the Roman priesthood as much as the spread of Bibles in the local language. It was for the crime of translating the Bible into English that the Reformer, William Tyndale, was burned at the stake. Of all the aspects which combined to make up the Reformation, no other aspect received such bitter opposition as the translation and circulation of the Scriptures. The translation of the Bible struck a blow at the root of the whole Roman Catholic system. The Bible, as the only rule of faith and conduct, freely available in the local languages, was a threat to all the superstitions and abuses of the medieval Roman popery. With the Bible in every parish church, every thoughtful man soon saw that the religion of the priests had no basis in Holy Scripture.

THE REFORMATION OPENED THE ROAD TO THE THRONE OF GRACE

The way of salvation had become blocked up and made impassable by heaps of superstitious rubble. *"He who desired to obtain forgiveness had to seek it through a jungle of priests, saints, Mary worship, masses, penances, confession, absolution and the like, so that there might as well have been no throne of Grace at all."* J.C. Ryle

The Reformers hacked their way through this huge jungle of papal obstruction and cleared the way for every heavy-laden sinner to go straight to the Lord Jesus Christ for remission of sins.

THE REFORMATION RESTORED BIBLICAL SIMPLICITY TO WORSHIP

Before the Reformation, the laity were only present at church services as passive, ignorant spectators. The elaborate, theatrical presentations of the sacraments were a solemn farce because the ceremonies and prayers were in Latin. The laity could bring their bodies to the services, but their minds, understanding, reason and spirit could take no part at all. For this reason, the 24th Article of the Church of England declared: *"It is a thing totally repugnant to the Word of God and the custom of the primitive church to have public prayer in the church or to minister the sacraments in a tongue not understood of the people."*

Mary queen of Scots confronted by Reformer John Knox.

THE REFORMATION GAVE A BIBLICAL UNDERSTANDING OF THE OFFICE OF A MINISTER

Before the Reformation, the concept of the Christian ministry was sacerdotal. That is it was imagined that every clergyman was a sacrificing priest. The clergy were understood to hold the keys of Heaven and to be practically the mediators between God and man.

The Reformers brought the office of the clergy down to its Scriptural level. They stripped it entirely of any sacerdotal character. They cast out the words *"sacrifice"* and *"altar."* They taught that the clergy were pastors, ambassadors, messengers, witnesses, evangelists, teachers and ministers of the Word and sacraments. The Reformers taught that the chief business of every Christian minister is to preach the Word and to be diligent in prayer and the reading of the Scriptures. The Reformers taught the immense superiority of the pulpit to the confessional. For this reason, where the altar used to be, the Lord's Table was placed, with an open Bible, or a pulpit, showing the centrality of God's Word in the worship of Protestant churches.

THE REFORMATION RESTORED A BIBLICAL UNDERSTANDING OF HOLINESS

Before the Reformation, it was believed that a monastic life and vows of celibacy were the only ways to escape sin and to attain sanctification. Multitudes of men and women poured into the monasteries and convents under the vain idea that this would please God and ensure their eternal salvation.

The Reformers struck at the root of this fallacy by establishing the great Scriptural principle that true religion was not to be found in retiring into convents and monasteries and fleeing from the difficulties of daily life, but in manfully facing up to our difficulties and doing our duty diligently - in every position to which God calls us. It is not by running away from the world that we fulfil God's call, but by courageously resisting the devil, the flesh and the world and overcoming them in daily life. That is how true holiness is to be exhibited. For this reason, the Reformers dissolved the monasteries and convents in their areas and freed the inmates to be reintegrated into normal life.

St. Peter's Church, Geneva

The Reformers also ordered that the Ten Commandments be set up in every parish church and taught to every child and that our duty towards God and our neighbour be set forth in the Catechism. They insisted that you cannot become saints by shirking your duties in society.

A HERITAGE OF FAITH AND FREEDOM

We must continually thank God for the Reformation. It lit the flames of knowledge and freedom, which we must ensure are never allowed to be extinguished, or to grow dim. We need to continually remember that the Reformation was won for us by the blood of many tens of thousands of martyrs. It was not only by their preaching and praying and writing and legislation, but by their sacrifices that our religious liberty, freedom of conscience and Christian heritage was won.

The Reformation Monument, Geneva.

SET FREE TO SERVE CHRIST

The Reformation found church members steeped in ignorance and left them in possession of knowledge. It found them without Bibles and left them with the Bible in every parish. It found them in darkness and left them in light. It found them bound in fear and left them enjoying the liberty and peace, which only Christ can give. It found them strangers to the Blood of Christ's Atonement, to faith, grace and holiness and left them with the key of all those blessings in their hands. It found them blind and left them with spiritual eyes to see. It found them slaves to superstition and set them free to serve Christ.

NEVER RETURN TO IGNORANCE, IDOLATRY AND IMMORALITY

As Bishop Ryle declared: *"Are we to return to a church which boasts that she is infallible and never changes – to a church which has never repented her pre-Reformation superstitions and abominations – to a church which has never confessed and abjured her countless corruptions? Are we to go back to gross ignorance of true religion? Shame on us, I say, if we entertain the idea for a moment! Let the Israelite return to Egypt, if he will. Let the prodigal go back to his husks among the swine. Let the dog return to his vomit. But let no Englishman with brains in his head, ever listen to the idea of exchanging Protestantism for popery, or returning to the bondage of the church of Rome. No, indeed! ... God forbid! The man who counsels such base apostasy and suicidal folly, must be judicially blind. The iron collar has been broken; let us not put it on again. The prison has been thrown open; let us not resume the* yoke and return to our chains ... Let us not go back to ignorance, superstition, priest craft and immorality."

COUNT YOUR MANY BLESSINGS

If you have a Bible in your own language and enjoy to read and study God's Word, never forget that you owe that Bible to the Reformation. Brave men and women died that you could have the freedom to delight in God's Word.

If you know the joy of sins forgiven and new life in Christ, if you are walking by faith and enjoying peace with God, never forget that you owe this priceless privilege to the Reformation.

If you enjoy Church services, Scripture choruses, Hymns, prayers and sermons in your own language, remember that for this you are also indebted to the Reformation.

If you appreciate the Biblical and practical sermons of your pastor and his counsel, never forget that for this you are indebted to the Reformation.

The Reformation is the source of many blessings. We need to ask if we are on the side of the Reformers, or of those who burned them and the Bible?

"...*Contend earnestly for the Faith which was once for all delivered to the saints.*" Jude 3

Martin Luther and Johann Eck at the Leipzig Debate, 1519.

The Schlosskirche in Wittenberg.

CHAPTER 19

HOW THE REFORMATION CHANGED THE WORLD

HOW LUTHER REFORMED MARRIAGE AND THE FAMILY

Martin Luther, the German Reformer, is generally remembered as the Theological professor, the Bible translator, the writer, even as the composer of hymns. However, Martin Luther was also a husband and a father of six children. He provided the church its first and most prominent example of a pastoral family.

While still a celibate priest, Luther wrote extensively on marriage. He saw marriage as an institution in as much crisis as the church - and no less in need of reform.

Martin Luther was a leading defender of the dignity of women and the foundational importance of marriage. Luther placed the home *"at the centre of the universe."* His teaching on marriage and the family (and his personal example) were so radical and so long-lasting that it profoundly and permanently altered the home. If his innovations do not seem so radical to us, it is because of his success in establishing these principles as Christian ideals.

Martin Luther's marriage to Katherine Von Bora in 1524 provided the Church with its first model of a pastoral family.

For a thousand years, the single, celibate life had been upheld as the Christian ideal. Sex, though grudgingly permitted inside marriage, was not to be enjoyed. As the Church father, Jerome, declared in the 4th century: *"Anyone who is too passionate a lover with his own wife is himself an adulterer."* Augustine advocated sexual relations within marriage to be without emotion and primarily for procreation. A catechism of the Catholic Church written in 1494, applies the third deadly sin (impurity) to married people enjoying sex within marriage!

Martin Luther, however, declared war on Greek philosopher Aristotle's depiction on women as *"botched males."* Luther also criticised Jerome, Cyprian, Augustine, Gregory and other Church fathers for *"never having written anything good about marriage."*

Luther and the first generation of Protestant Reformers rejected this tradition of over a thousand years, of ascetic sexuality - in both their Theology and their lives. The Reformers rejection of the celibate ideal of the Middle Ages was as great a revolution in the home as their teachings were in the Church. Luther literally transferred the praises and esteem that Christians had traditionally heaped upon the celibate monks and nuns, to marriage and the home.

Marriage as Ministry

Luther described marriage as the only institution where a chaste life could be maintained. He insisted that *"one cannot be unmarried without sin."*

Luther led his family in the singing of hymns.

"Marriage pervades the whole of nature." Luther taught that nothing was more natural and necessary than marriage, *"For all creatures are divided into male and female."*

Luther actively encouraged fathers to remove their daughters from convents. Protestant towns and territories dissolved the cloisters and nunneries and freed women from the sexual repression, cultural depravity, dominance by male clergy and Catholic practices. Wherever the Reformation succeeded, monks and nuns who wished to marry received automatic permission to do so.

Luther had a high regard for the ability of women to shape society by moulding its youth and civilising its men through the institution of marriage. *"A companionable woman brings joy to life"* Luther wrote. *"Women tend to and rear their young, administer the household and are inclined to compassion. God has made them compassionate by nature, so that by their example men may be moved to compassion also."*

Celebrating Christmas at Luther's home.

Parenthood is the School of Character

Luther also wrote: *"People who do not like children are swine, dunces and blockheads, not worthy to be called men and women, because they despise the blessings of God, the Creator and Author of marriage."*

"Love begins when we wish to serve others." There is no better school for humility and for loving sacrificial service than marriage and parenthood.

Luther wrote that his entrance into the monastery was *"a cowardly act"*. He saw marriage and fatherhood as an essential requirement for effective pastors. Luther had six children (Hans, Elizabeth, Magdalene, Martin, Paul and Margaretha).

Luther urged parents to always discipline their children with forethought and caution, taking into account the unique personality of each. He taught that: *"no power on earth is so noble and so great as that of parents."*

Marriage and Divorce

Luther also wrote: *"There is no bond on earth so sweet nor any separation so bitter as that which occurs in a good marriage."*

"A wife is easily taken, but to have abiding love, that is the challenge. One who finds it in his marriage, should thank the Lord God for it. Therefore, approach marriage earnestly and ask God to give you a good, pious girl, with whom you spend your life in mutual love. For sex alone establishes nothing in this regard; there must also be agreement in values and character."

Because of the importance attached to companionship in marriage the Reformers endorsed, for the first time in the Western Christendom, genuine divorce and remarriage. Although they viewed marriage as a spiritual bond transcending all other human relationships, a marriage could definitely end this side of eternity and a new one begin for separated spouses. *"Christ permits divorce for adultery and compels none to remain unmarried thereafter; and St. Paul would rather have us remarry than burn now with lust and later in hell."*

The Protestants, in contrast to the Catholics, generally permitted divorce and remarriage on five grounds: adultery, wilful abandonment, chronic impotence, life-threatening hostility and wilful deceit. The Straßburg Reformer, Martin Bucer, declared that no proper marriage exists where affection is not regularly shared and where all conversation has ceased.

Protestant marriage courts did not permit divorce and remarriage to occur without first making every effort to re-unite the estranged couple and to revive the dead marriage. However, the Reformers held that the community formed by husband and wife was so fundamental to society, that when all conversation, affection and respect between a husband and wife had irretrievably broken down, it could not be allowed to continue. The marriage bond was so important that one had to fight to save it and failing success in genuine restoration, the marriage should be recognised to have come to an end.

Never before had women been empowered to divorce abusive husbands. Women from all over Europe fled to Protestant areas, particularly Geneva, to find protection and freedom from abuse.

Katherine - The Prototype Pastor's Wife

Luther wrote: *"Women have narrow shoulders and wide hips. Therefore they ought to be domestic. Their very physique is a sign from the Creator that He intended them for the home."* Luther also wrote: *"In domestic affairs, I defer* to Katie, otherwise I am led by the Holy Spirit!"

Luther's wife, Katherine, was smuggled out of a cloister, hidden in an empty herring barrel. She became a model housewife and an accomplished businesswoman. Luther dubbed her: *"the morning star of Wittenberg"* as her day began at 4:00am. Even in his last will and testament, Luther revolutionised the home by ignoring the prevalent practice of appointing a male trustee to administer the estate. Luther directly designated his wife Katherine *"heir to everything."*

Luther wrote: *"It is impossible to keep peace between man and woman in family life if they do not condone and overlook each other's faults, but watch everything to the smallest point. For who does not at times offend?"*

HOSPITALITY

Luther's home was described as *"half home, half hotel."* The Luther's housed up to 30 people in their home at a time - students, orphans, the sick and former monks and nuns. Even on his wedding night, Luther could not refuse a person in need. At 11:00pm, after all the guests had left, the radical Reformer and critic of Luther, Andreas Karlstadt, knocked at the door. Karlstadt was fleeing the Peasants' War and needed shelter. Luther took him in.

This picture commemorated the time Luther locked himself in his study for 4 days. Here Katherine had the door removed from its hinges.

FOCUS ON THE FAMILY

Luther not only made the Bible part of the daily routine in the home, but he also made the singing of hymns central. He played the flute and the lute and led his children in singing hymns of praise. He also introduced the Catechism to explain the faith to children, incorporating Scripture memorisation in the daily routine. Perhaps it is time for us to recognise Martin Luther as the true and original founder of Focus on the Family.

REFORMING WORSHIP

Congregational singing remains one of Martin Luther's most enduring legacies. *"Next to the Word of God, music deserves the highest praise,"* wrote Luther. *"I am not of the opinion that all arts are to be cast down and destroyed on account of the Gospel, as some fanatics suggest. On the other hand, I would gladly see all arts, especially music, in the service of Him Who has given and created them."*

Luther himself was a well-trained musician with a fine voice. He played the lute, composed intricate hymns and was well acquainted with the work of the leading composers of his day. *"I always love music; who so has skill in this art, is of a good temperament, fitted for all things. We must teach music in schools; a schoolmaster ought to have skill in music, or I would not regard him. Neither should we ordain young men as preachers, unless they have been well exercised in music."*

Luther insisted that we are to *"praise God with both word and music." "God has preached the Gospel through music."* The common people need to hear and sing the Word of God in their own language, so that they might be edified. (Before the Reformation such singing as had been done in Churches was in Latin and sung by choirs).

Luther produced a Catechism to explain the Faith to children and incorporate Scripture memorisation in the home.

"Let everything be done so that the Word of God may have free course." Luther loved to cite examples like Moses who praised God in song following the crossing of the Red Sea and David who composed many of the Psalms. *"Music is a vehicle for proclaiming the Word of God,"* declared Luther.

Urging pastors to write German hymns based on the Psalms, Luther advised *"use the simplest and most common words, preserve the pure teaching of God's Word and keep the meaning as close to the Psalm as possible."*

Luther wrote a variety of hymns, intended for Church services and for devotions at home. To teach the Catechism, he wrote two hymns on the Ten Commandments, a hymn for the Apostles' Creed, one for The Lord's Prayer and others for baptism and the Lord's Supper. Through these hymns, Luther demonstrated his on-going desire to teach the Faith, especially to children, through music.

A Mighty Fortress is our God

In 1527, during one of the most trying times of Luther's life, (he suffered severe illness for 8 months of that year) with his entire body in pain, the plague had erupted in Wittenberg and he watched many friends die. Then his own son became ill. Even though his wife was pregnant, Luther's house was transformed into a hospital. During that horrific year, surrounded by sickness and death, Luther took time to remember the 10th anniversary of his publication against indulgences. *A Mighty Fortress is our God*, based on Psalm 46, was composed during this time of severe trial. It has endured as one of the most popular and most translated hymns in history: **"And though this world with devils filled, should threatened to undo us, we will not fear for God has willed, His truth to triumph through us. The prince of darkness grim? We tremble not for him. His rage we can endure, for lo his doom is sure, one little Word shall fell him."**

Luther made singing a central part of Protestant worship. He dispensed with the choir and assigned all singing to the congregation. Luther would often call the whole congregation into the church during the week for congregational rehearsals so that the people could learn new hymns.

"Let everything that has breath praise the Lord." Psalm 150:6

The Reformation and Science

Modern Science as a discipline is a fruit of the Reformation. As **Francis Bacon**, the father of the scientific method, once put it: *"There are two books laid before us to study; to prevent us falling into error; first, the volume of the Scriptures which reveal the will of God; then the volume of the Creatures, which express His power."*

Historian Robert G. Frank points out: *"The predominant forms of scientific activity can be shown to be a direct outgrowth of a Puritan ideology."*

The great astronomer **Johannes Kepler** (1571-1630), the founder of Celestial Mechanics declared: *"My wish is that I may perceive the God whom I find everywhere in the external world in like manner within me."* Kepler was a *"brilliant mathematician and astronomer,"* he contributed to the scientific revolution with his work on the planetary orbits, laws of motion and the scientific method. Kepler's accomplishments formed the foundation of modern theoretical astronomy.

Kepler saw astronomy as a glimpse of God's glory. Kepler argued: *"Truth in religion is based on the Word of God in Scripture, while truth in natural science is based on evidence and reason."* Kepler viewed all of science as man attempting to ***"think God's thoughts after Him."*** Kepler was the father of the modern satellite and of modern space travel.

Sir Isaac Newton (1642-1727), the father of calculus and dynamics, was a scientific genius and a dedicated Christian. Newton formulated the theory of gravitation and the laws of motion. He discovered that white light is composed of the colours of the spectrum. He made vital contributions to mathematics, astronomy and physics. Newton maintained that there were two key sources of knowledge - one revealed in the Bible and the other revealed in nature. Newton believed that in order to *"truly know the Creator, one must study the natural order of things."* Newton dedicated his life to know **the Word of God** (the Bible) and to know **the works of God** (creation).

Blaise Pascal (1623-1662) made vital contributions to mathematics and technology that helped with the development of the computer. Pascal invented the first adding machine. In his honour, a computer language is named after Pascal.

Charles Babbage (1792-1871), the father of modern day computer science, described the world as a great computer and God as the programmer. Babbage was essentially a mathematician and regarded mathematics as the best preliminary preparation for all other branches of human knowledge. He believed that the study of the works of nature, with scientific precision, was a necessary and indispensable preparation for the understanding and interpreting their testimony of the wisdom and goodness of the Divine Author.

Samuel F.B. Morse (1791-1872) was the man responsible for the development of the modern telegraph and the Morse code. This was one of the greatest innovations in the world of communication. Samuel deeply absorbed his family's Calvinism, which he eventually translated and applied to all his scientific work. In 1844, he astonished the US Congress, gathered in the Supreme Court chamber, by sending words from Numbers 23:23: *"What hath God wrought?"* The first inter-city telegraph line in the world communicated these Words of Scripture to inaugurate this great invention. Morse, as an inventor, saw his work as a service to the Lord. He laid the foundations for the development of modern communications.

In the realm of physics, **Sir Michael Faraday** is acknowledged as one of the greatest scientists of all times. He discovered electro-magnetic induction, without which we could have no motors or engines. He invented the generator. Faraday was a devout Christian who declared: *"The Bible and it alone, with nothing added to it nor taken away from it by man, is the sole and sufficient guide for each individual, at all times and in all circumstances. Faith in the Divinity and work of Christ is the gift of God and the evidence of this faith is obedience to the commandments of Christ."*

William Thompson, 1st Baron of Kelvin, one of the greatest scientists, mathematical physicists and engineers of all times, formulated the metric temperature scale. He formulated the first and second laws of thermodynamics. Lord Kelvin was the first scientist who used the concept of energy and the first scientist elevated to the House of Lords. He declared: *"With regard to the origin of life, science positively affirms Creative power."*

Joseph Lister, the English surgeon who developed antiseptic surgery and the use of chemical disinfectants, stated: *"I am a believer in the fundamental doctrines of Christianity."*

Karl von Linnaeus (1707-1778) was the pioneer of modern botany. He laid the foundation of natural history by devising a system of classification whereby any plant or animal could be identified and related to an overall plan. He introduced the method of naming each type of living being with universal terms that could be recognised in any language. He used the Bible to provide the framework for scientific classification of plants and animals.

James Simpson (1811-1870), the founder of gynaecology and anaesthetics, was inspired by the Scriptural passage that God had made Adam fall into a deep sleep before taking the rib from him, to develop chloroform and pioneer the beginnings of modern surgical anaesthetics. Before this, operations were conducted on conscious patients.

Matthew Fontaine Maury (1806-1873), the father of modern oceanography and hydrology, derived many of his ideas from the Bible. He was the first person to chart shipping routes throughout the world, pioneered the establishment of sea-lanes and made possible the laying of electric cables across the ocean floor. Maury was inspired by a verse from the Bible (Psalm 8:8, which speaks of the fish that passed through *"the paths of the seas"*). Maury declared that: *"The Bible is true and science is true ... the Bible is authority for everything it touches ... God is the Great Architect Who planned it all."*

A BIBLICAL WORLDVIEW GAVE BIRTH TO SCIENCE

It has been pointed out that science could not have developed amongst those who worship Allah, because of Islam's fatalism. Nor could science have been birthed from Hinduism or Buddhism, because of their belief that the world is an illusion. Neither could modern science have risen in our modern humanistic culture, because of the humanist's belief that life is irrational and illogical. By rejecting the notion of absolutes, humanists reject the very foundation of science. If there are no absolutes in nature, then results in experimentation can only be relative. If everything is relative, then engineering and other branches of science, become impossible.

A proper, philosophical base for investigating the universe was needed and only the Christian doctrine of Creation has provided that base. The Creator established Laws for people and Laws for the natural world. A created universe was expected to have design, order and purpose. Man using his created, rational mind, could study this ordered universe in a rational way and seek to discover its laws. Modern science is based upon this assumption of scientific law. In addition, the moral laws given by the Creator established the ethical basis for science. Scientists must be honest and truthful. If this universe were not created, if it is merely the product of chance, then no intelligence would be involved. There could be no reason to expect such a universe to operate in a rational or consistent way. Man's mind would also be the product of chance and would not be capable of reason or logic. Hence, a materialistic philosophy could not provide any foundation for science. Many ardent atheists dominate science today, but they are working off the foundations and pre-suppositions of Christianity.

The irrefutable fact is that **Christianity gave birth to modern science.** The scientific revolution began in the Protestant Reformation and the Bible played a vital part in the development of scientific discovery. Every major branch of science was developed by a Bible-believing Christian. The Bible essentially created science.

When we get into a car, start the engine, turn on the lights, drive to hospital, receive an anaesthetic before an operation and have an effective operation done in a germ-free environment, we need to remember that we owe it to the Reformation.

As Isaac Watts declared in his great Christmas carol: *"Joy to the World,"* Jesus makes His blessings flow *"far as the curse is found." "No more let sins and sorrows grow, nor thorns infest the ground; He comes to make His blessings flow, far as the curse is found, far as the curse is found, far as, far as, the curse is found."*

The Publication of The 95 Theses in Wittenberg, 1517.

The Reformation and Education

The phenomenon of education for the masses has its roots in Christianity. Christianity is a teaching religion. The greatest universities worldwide were started by Christians in fulfilment of the Great Commission of our Lord Jesus Christ.

The roots of education for the common person goes back to the Reformation and, especially, to John Calvin. *"The modern idea of popular education - that is, education for everyone - first arose in Europe during the Protestant Reformation."* (Dr. Samuel Blumenfeld - Is Public Education Necessary?)

American educator, Dr. Samuel Blumenfeld, came to Christ through reading Calvin's *Institutes of the Christian Religion*. As Blumenfeld did his research on education, he found that, when it came to the concept of education for the common man, all roads led to Calvin. It was as he read the primary documents that he came to place his faith in Christ.

"Wherever Calvinism has gone, it has carried the school with it and has given a powerful impulse to popular education. It is a system, which demands intellectual manhood. In fact, we say that its very existence is tied up with education of the people." (Dr. Loraine Boettner - *The Reformed Doctrine of Predestination*).

Calvin's Academy at Geneva was the model for many of the early colleges and universities established by the Puritans and their successors in America.

Calvin advocated that the purpose of education is for people to know God and to glorify Him as God - that in our vocation and in our life we might know *"the knowledge of God, the Creator and Redeemer."* The content of education must begin with the Scriptures and continue into God's Creation.

In Geneva, Calvin promoted education for everyone, which has become the pattern for our day. When John Knox fled from Scotland and sought freedom from persecution in Geneva, he declared that Geneva had become the greatest school of Christ since the time of the Apostles.

Calvin emphasised the importance of education having moral relevance. Calvin also was insistent that it was the parents' responsibility to educate their children. Therefore the control of education should remain with the parents.

Of America's first 126 universities, 123 were Christian. This included Harvard, Yale, Princeton, etc.

The Reformation also produced some of the greatest works of literature. **William Shakespeare** (1564-1616) was one of the world's greatest writers. Scriptural quotes and Biblical images from the Geneva Bible permeate Shakespeare's writings.

Similarly, **John Bunyan** (1628-1688) gave the world one of the greatest novels ever written - *Pilgrim's Progress*. This parable of the Christian life is one of the all-time most published and widely read books in the history of the world.

John Milton (1608-1674) author of *Paradise Lost* and *Paradise Regained* was the secretary to Oliver Cromwell and also a Puritan.

Many music critics declare that **Johann Sebastian Bach** was the greatest musician that ever lived. J.S. Bach was an unsurpassed genius and is acknowledged as the father of modern music. He left no musical form as he found it, says one critic. On the other hand, with every form he touched, he seemed to have said the last word. Bach's teaching notebooks and violin books have been the basis for music theory and practice ever since. Johan Sebastian Bach was a Protestant Christian, a Lutheran. Most of his library consisted of Protestant writings, including all of Luther's writings. Bach taught his pupils that music is an act of worship and all musicians need to commit their talents to the Lord Jesus Christ.

As one critic said: *"Bach is to music what Shakespeare is to literature. They are both the greatest."* And they were both Protestant Christians.

The Wittenberg marketplace in Luther's day.

FREE ENTERPRISE AND THE WORK ETHIC

Along with some of the greatest art and literature, the Reformation brought about the greatest industrial advances and prosperity ever experienced in history.

The Protestant work ethic, which helped to bring about great prosperity in Western Europe and North America, arose mostly through the Protestant Reformers - particularly John Calvin. *"The most dynamic businessmen were to be found in Protestant Holland and the most vigorous industrial growth in Protestant England, both states heavily tinctured with Calvinism."* (Historian Richard Dunn).

Max Weber, in his famous book: *"The Protestant Ethic and the Spirit of Capitalism"* (1905), attributed the Capitalist Revolution to Calvinism, its worldly asceticism and Protestant work ethic.

Calvin upheld the right of private ownership of property, taught the Biblical concept of stewardship and promoted free enterprise. By promoting the Protestant work ethic, Calvin unleashed all the powers that capitalism has produced. As a result, the free enterprise system has generated the highest standards of living, the longest life expectancy and the greatest advances in industry and medicine ever experienced in history.

For these and so many other reasons, the Reformation in Europe during the 16th century has to be seen as one of the most important epochs in the history of the world. The Reformation gave us the Bible - now freely available in our own languages. The Reformation also pioneered the now-almost universally acknowledged principles of religious freedom, liberty of conscience, the rule of law, separation of powers and constitutionally limited Republics. All of these foundational principles were unthinkable before the Reformation. The Reformers emphasis on God's sovereignty, that Scripture alone is the final authority, that Christ alone is the head of the Church, that justification is by God's grace, on the basis of the finished work of Christ, received by faith alone. Their teachings on the depravity of man, the Covenant and Church government has influenced law and liberty throughout the Western world and beyond. All of us are beneficiaries of this tremendous movement for Faith and Freedom. It is time that we re-examined the history and the principles of the Reformation.

"If I profess with the loudest voice and clearest exposition every portion of the truth of God, except precisely that point which the world and the devil are at that moment attacking, then I am not confessing Christ, however boldly I may be professing Him. Where the battle rages, there the loyalty of the soldier is proved; and to be steady on all the battle front besides is mere flight and disgrace if he flinches at that point." Martin Luther

Reformation Monument in Geneva.

The Schlosskirche, Wittenberg, Germany.

CHAPTER 20
LUTHER'S PRACTICAL PROGRAMME TO REVIVE YOUR PRAYER LIFE

The German Reformer, Professor Martin Luther, taught that prayer should be living, powerful, strong, mighty, earnest, serious, troubled, passionate, vehement, fervent and ardent.

THE HARDEST WORK OF ALL
Luther described prayer as: *"The hardest work of all – a labour above all labours, since he who prays must wage almighty warfare against the doubt and murmuring excited by the faint-heartedness and unworthiness we feel within us... that unutterable and powerful groaning with which the godly rouse themselves against despair, the struggle in which they call mightily upon their faith."*

THE DAILY BUSINESS OF A CHRISTIAN
"Audacious prayer, which perseveres unflinchingly and ceases not through fear, is well pleasing unto God," wrote Luther. *"As a shoe maker makes a shoe, or a tailor makes a coat, so ought a Christian to pray. Prayer is the daily business of a Christian."*

REFORMING PRAYER
In 1535, Luther wrote and published: **"A Simple Way To Pray,"** dedicated to his barber, Peter Beskendorf. His barber had asked him for some guidelines on how he might improve his prayer life. In response, Luther wrote this 35-page book which became so popular that 4 editions were printed that first year alone.

Martin Luther has been described as one of the most dedicated men of prayer in all of history. The historical records show that Luther prayed for 3 to 4 hours each day. In the 16th Century, the Church of Rome had buried Biblical prayer under layers of institutional, mystical and theological error. Prayer for most in the 16th Century was a mechanical, religious rite, a legalistic work, requiring little thought. Luther worked hard to reform prayer. He spent long, solitary nights in fervent prayer and fasting.

GUIDELINES FOR PRAYER
In *"A Simple Way To Pray"* Luther wrote: *"First, when I feel that I have become cool and joyless in prayer, because of other tasks or thoughts (for the flesh and the devil always impede and obstruct prayer), I take my Psalter, hurry to my room...and as time permits, I say quietly to myself and word for*

word *The Lord's Prayer, The Ten Commandments, The Apostles Creed and ... some Psalms...*

*"It is a good thing to let prayer be your first business in the morning and the last at night. Guard yourself carefully against those false, deluding ideas that tell you, 'wait a little while. I will pray in an hour, first I must attend to this or that'...**Those who work faithfully, pray twice...Christ commands continual prayer: ask and it will be given to you, seek and you shall find; knock and it will be opened to you...pray without ceasing**... we must unceasingly guard against sin and wrong doing, something one cannot do unless one fears God and keeps His Commandments...we become relaxed and lazy, cool and listless towards prayer. The devil who besets us is not lazy or careless and our flesh is too ready and eager to sin and is disinclined to the spirit of prayer.*

"When your heart has be warmed by such recitation to yourself (of The Ten Commandments, the Words of Christ, etc.)...Kneel or stand with your hands folded and your eyes towards Heaven and speak or think as briefly as you can.

"O Heavenly Father, dear God, I am a poor, unworthy sinner. I do not deserve to raise my eyes or hands toward You or to pray. But, because You have commanded us all to pray and have promised to hear us and through Your dear Son, Jesus Christ has taught us both how and what to pray, I come to You in obedience to Your Word, trusting in Your gracious promises."

Luther recommended that our prayers be numerous, but short in duration. Luther taught that we should pray: *"Brief prayers...pregnant with the Spirit, strongly fortified by faith...the fewer the words, the better the prayer. The more the words, the worse the prayer. Few words and much meaning is Christian. Many words and little meaning is pagan."*

The Lord's Prayer and the Psalms were tools which Luther considered most important for any Christian's prayer life. *"A Christian has prayed abundantly who has rightly prayed The Lord's Prayer."* The Lord's Prayer is the model prayer of Christianity and it is not essentially a prayer of one individual, but a common prayer that binds all Christians together, uniting us with all believers, past, present and future, whether in Heaven, or on earth, in a Biblical Kingdom focused prayer.

PRAYING THE PSALMS
Luther taught that praying the Psalms brings us: *"into joyful harmony"* with God's Word and God's Will. *"Whoever begins to pray the Psalms earnestly and regularly will soon take leave of those other light and personal*

little devotional prayers and say, 'Ah, there is not the juice, the strength, the passion, the fire which you find in the Psalms. Anything else tastes too cold and too hard.'"

STRUCTURE PRAYER

Luther also recommended that we structure our prayers according to The Apostle's Creed and the Catechism, to connect doctrine and devotion. He also recommended praying according to The Ten Commandments, meditating on each item as instruction, thanksgiving, confession and petition. By meditating on the instruction, giving thanks for the blessings that flow from these principles, confessing where we have personally failed in obeying and applying these commands and as petition to being able to honour and obey God's Word in our daily lives, would revive our prayer lives.

SPIRITUAL WARFARE

Luther lived daily exposed to what he called the *"Anfechtung,"* the unbridled, vicious assault of satan. At times, it seemed as if the whole world was against him, as well as the flesh and the devil. In the midst of this spiritual warfare, Luther's enriching approach to prayer strengthened him. The Apostle's Creed, The Lord's Prayer, The Ten Commandments, The Catechism and the Psalms deepened and focused his prayer life.

In his preface to the *"Larger Catechism,"* Luther wrote: *"We know that our defence lies in prayer. We are too weak to resist the devil and his vassals. Let us hold fast to the weapons of the Christian; they enable us to combat the devil... our enemies may mock at us. But we shall oppose both men and the devil if we maintain ourselves in prayer and if we persist in it."*

OUR FIRST PRIORITY

Luther recommended a set time for personal devotions, early morning or at night and warned against postponing them for any *"more urgent business."*

FLINT FOR THE FLAMES

He thought that one should see The Ten Commandments as a school textbook, a songbook, a penitential book and as a prayer book. He advised that one take The Ten Commandments as one's structure for prayer on one day, a Psalm or a chapter of the Holy Scripture for another day and use them *"as flint and steel to kindle a flame in the heart."*

Praying the Lord's Prayer

"*A Simple Way To Pray*" gives some examples of the intercessions Luther was inspired to pray on the basis of The Lord's Prayer: "***Hallowed be Thy Name.*** *Yes, Lord God, dear Father, Hallowed be Your Name, both in us and throughout the whole world. Destroy and root out the abominations, idolatry and heresy of all false teachers and fanatics who wrongly use Your Name and in scandalous ways take it in vain and horribly blaspheme it…Dear Lord God, convert and restrain them… restrain those who are unwilling to be converted so that they may be forced to cease from misusing, defiling and dishonouring Your Holy Name and for misleading the poor people. Amen.*

"***Thy Kingdom Come.*** *O dear Lord, God and Father, convert them and defend us… so that they with us and we with them may serve You and Your Kingdom in true faith and unfeigned love and that from Your Kingdom which has begun, we may enter into Your eternal Kingdom. Defend us against those who will not turn away their might and power for the destruction of Your Kingdom so that when they are cast down from their thrones and humbled, they will have to cease from their efforts. Amen.*

"***Thy will be done on earth as it is in Heaven.*** *O dear Lord, God and Father, You know that the world, if it cannot destroy Your Name or root our Your Kingdom, is busy day and night with wicked tricks and schemes, strange conspiracies and intrigues, huddled together in secret counsel, giving mutual encouragement and support, raging and threatening and going about with every evil intention to destroy Your Name, Word, Kingdom and children… for Your sake gladly, patiently and joyously enable us to bear every evil, cross and adversity and thereby acknowledge, test and experience Your benign, gracious and perfect Will…*

"***Give us this day our daily bread.*** *Protect us against war and disorder. Grant to all rulers' good counsel and a will to preserve their subjects in tranquillity and justice. O God, grant that all people be diligent and display charity and loyalty towards each other. Give us favourable weather and good harvests…*

"***Forgive us our trespasses as we forgive those who trespass against us.*** *O dear Lord, God and Father, enter not into judgement against us because no person living is justified before You. Do not count it against us as a sin that we are so unthankful for Your ineffable goodness, spiritual and physical, with that we stray so many times each day. Do not look upon how good or how wicked we have been but only upon the infinite compassion, which You have bestowed upon us in Christ, Your dear Son. Amen. Also, grant forgiveness to those who have harmed or wronged us, as we forgive them from our hearts… we would much rather that they be saved with us. Amen*

"**Lead us not into temptation.** Keep us fit and alert, eager and diligent in Your Word and service, so that we do not become complacent, lazy and slothful as though we had already achieved everything. In that way the fearful devil cannot fall upon us, surprise us and deprive us from of Your precious Word or store up strife and factions among us and lead us into other sin and disgrace…"

"**And deliver us from evil.** This wretched life is so full of misery and calamity, of danger and uncertainty, so full of malice and faithlessness… but You, dear Father, know our frailty. Therefore help us to pass safely through so much wickedness and villainy…"

WARM WHOLEHEARTED WORSHIP

Luther warned: *"I do not want you to recite all these words in your prayer. That would make it nothing but idle chatter and prattle. Rather do I want your heart to be stirred and guided concerning the thoughts, which ought to be comprehended, in The Lord's Prayer. These thoughts may be expressed, if your heart is rightly warmed and inclined toward prayer, in many different ways than with more words or fewer… listen in silence and under no circumstances obstruct them. The Holy Spirit Himself preaches here and one Word of His sermon is far better than a thousand of our prayers. Many times I have learnt more from one prayer than I might have learned from much reading and speculation."*

He warned against: *"A cold and inattentive heart,"* teaching that prayer requires *"the full attention of all one's senses and members… concentration and singleness of heart…"*

SPIRITUAL DISCIPLINE

Luther taught that in praying through The Ten Commandments *"I think of each Command as first, **instruction**, which is really what it is intended to be and consider what the Lord demands of me so earnestly. Second, I turn it into a **thanksgiving**; third a **confession**; and fourth a **prayer**."*

He taught the importance of Spiritual disciplines, including solitude, silence, listening, meditation, journalling, praying and obeying.

DEEPER DEVOTION

May God be gracious to use the example and teachings of Martin Luther to revive our prayer lives, to discipline, sharpen and focus our prayers in a Biblical and Kingdom focused way. As we work through The Lord's Prayer, The Ten Commandments, The Apostle's Creed, The Psalms and The Catechisms, may the Lord be merciful to revive our prayer lives, deepen our devotional lives and use us more effectively for the extension of His Kingdom and for His eternal glory.

*"**Lord, teach us to pray…**"* Luke 11:1

APPENDIX 1
THE PEOPLE OF THE REFORMATION

PRE-REFORMERS:

John Wycliffe	(1324-1384) Professor of Oxford University, Pastor and Bible Translator.
Jan Hus	(1369-1415) Rector of Prague University, Pastor of Bethlehem Chapel. Martyred.
Girolamo Savonarola	(1452-1498) Dominican Monk and Reformer of Florence. Martyred.

REFORMERS:

Martin Luther	(1483-1546) Augustinian Monk, Professor of Wittenberg University, Reformer and Bible Translator.
Ulrich Zwingli	(1484-1531) Parish Priest, Bible Translator and Reformer of Zürich. Killed in battle.
William Tyndale	(1494-1536) Oxford and Cambridge graduate, Tutor and Bible Translator. Martyred.
Guillaume Farel	(1489-1565) Evangelist and Debater who won whole cities to Christ.
John Calvin	(1509-1564) Brilliant Scholar, Author, Pastor, Professor and Reformer of Geneva.
John Knox	(1514-1572) Pastor and Reformer of Scotland.
Pierre Viret	(1511-1571) French Pastor and Evangelist.
Philipp Melanchthon	(1497-1560) Professor of Greek and Hebrew at the University of Wittenberg. Author of *The Augsburg Confession*. Luther's successor.
Thomas Cranmer	(1489-1556) Archbishop of Canterbury, Author of *The Book of Common Prayer*. Martyred.
Heinrich Bullinger	(1504-1575) Pastor, Prolific Author, and Reformer of Zürich. Zwingli's successor.
Theodore Beza	(1519-1605) Professor of Greek and Rector of the Geneva Academy. Calvin's successor.
Martin Bucer	(1491-1551) Pastor and Reformer of Straßburg. Calvin's mentor.
Gaspard de Coligny	(1519-1572) Military hero and leader of the French Huguenots. Murdered.

ALLIES OF THE REFORMERS:

Prince Frederick III of Saxony	(1463-1525) The Elector of Saxony who protected Luther.
George Spalatin	(1484-1545) Chaplain and secretary to Prince Frederick.
Prince John of Saxony	(1468-1532) Dedicated Lutheran, co-founder of Schalkaldic League against Charles V.

ENEMIES OF THE REFORMATION:

Johann Tetzel	(1465-1519) Dominican friar and papal indulgence salesman who provoked Luther's protest.
Johann Maier Eck	(1484-1543) Professor of Theology at Ingolstadt University who debated Luther.
Charles V	(1519-1558) Holy Roman Emperor
Leo X	(1513-1521) pope
Adrian VI	(1522-1523) pope
Clement VII	(1523-1534) pope
Paul III	(1534-1549) pope
Julius III	(1550-1555) pope
Marcellus	(1555) pope
Paul IV	(1555-1559) pope
Pius IV	(1559-1565) pope
Pius V	(1566-1572) pope
Gregory XIII	(1572-1585) pope
Sixtus V	(1585-1590) pope
Fancis I	(1515-1547) king of France
Henry II	(1547-1559) king of France
Charles IX	(1560-1574) king of France
Henry III	(1574-1589) king of France
Mary I	(Mary Tudor) (1553-1558) queen of England
Mary, Queen of Scots	(1542-1567) Mary Stuart – queen of Scotland

Appendix 2
Chronology of the Reformation

1177 The dynamic Waldensian Gospel movement launched by Peter Waldo. The Waldensians translated the Gospels into French and boldly proclaimed the Word of God throughout Southern France, Northern Italy and Switzerland.

1229 The Council of Valencia places the Bible on the Index of Forbidden Books. The Waldensians come under increasingly vicious persecution.

1309 The *"Babylonian Captivity of the church"* begins with a French pope, Clement, moving the papal court to Avignon.

1328 English Reformer, John Wycliffe is born.

1337 The beginning of *The Hundred Years War* between England and France.

1346 Outnumbered English longbow men defeat huge French army at the Battle of Crecy.

1347 The beginning of *The Black Death*. The bubonic plague kills over one third of the total population of Europe.

1351 Under King Edward III, England removes the pope's power to give English benefits to foreigners.

1353 Parliament's statue of *Praemunire* forbids appeals to the pope.

1361 Wycliffe receives Master of Arts degree at Balliol College, Oxford and is ordained.

1362 English replaces French as the authorised language of the law courts in England.

1366 The English Parliament refuses to continue paying tribute to the pope.

1372 Bohemian Reformer, Jan Hus is born in Husinec.

1372 Wycliffe receives Doctorate of Theology and enters the service of the Crown.

1374 John of Gaunt, the Duke of Lancaster, returns from the French wars to become leader of the state.

1377 pope Gregory XI issues five bulls against Wycliffe.

1378 The Queen Mother ends the trial of Wycliffe at Lambeth.

1378 *The Great Schism* divides the Catholic church for 39 years when two opposing popes are elected – pope Urban VI in Rome and pope Clement VII in Avignon.
1381 Professor John Wycliffe begins intensive work on translation of the Bible into English.
1381 The Peasants Revolt and 30,000 rioters converge on London.
1382 Wycliffe suffers first stroke.
1384 Wycliffe suffers second stroke and dies.
1391 Bethlehem Chapel founded in Prague.
1401 Jan Hus appointed Dean of Faculty at University.
1402 Jan Hus becomes preacher at Bethlehem Chapel.
1409 Professor Hus elected Rector at Charles University.
1409 *The Great Schism* widens as a third pope is elected.
1410 Papal Bull prohibits preaching in private chapels. Wycliffe's books publically burned in Prague. Hus excommunicated (twice) and forbidden to preach.
1411 Hus excommunicated a third time.
1412 Hus excommunicated a fourth time. Prague threatened with an interdict. Hus goes into exile.
1413 Hus writes *"De Ecclesia"* (The Church).
1414 Sir John Oldcastle (Lord Cobham), a disciple of Wycliffe, is burned at the stake in Smithfield.
1414 Hus is summoned to the Council of Constance (The largest church council ever convened – with 5,000 delegates) and guaranteed safe conduct by the Emperor.
1415 Hus is condemned without any opportunity to respond to the charges against him and burned as a *"heretic."*
1415 English archers at the Battle of Agincourt decisively defeat an overwhelmingly superior force of French cavalry.
1417 The Council of Constance deposes all three papal rivals and elects a new pope, Martin V.
1419 Hussites organise mass worship services on Bohemian hilltops and organise for military defense.
1420 First crusade against Hussites defeated.
1421 Second crusade against Hussites defeated.
1422 Third crusade against Hussites defeated.

Chronology of the Reformation

1427 Fourth crusade against Hussites defeated.
1428 At a papal command, the remains of John Wycliffe are dug up, burned and scattered on the River Swift.
1433 Negotiations between Hussites and Catholics open at Council of Basel.
1436 Hussite - Catholic peace treaty (*Campactata*) agreed on.
1453 Constantinople, the largest city in the world, captured by the Ottoman Turks. Christian population massacred.
1455 The first book ever printed, a Bible (in Latin), is completed by Johannes Gutenberg.
1483 German Reformer, Martin Luther born in Eisleben, Germany.
1484 Swiss Reformer, Ulrich Zwingli, born in Wildhaus, in the Swiss Alps.
1492 Spanish forces liberate the city of Grenada, expelling Islamic Moors from the Iberian Peninsula.
1492 Christopher Columbus discovers America.
1494 English Reformer, William Tyndale, born at Cotswolds.
1497 German Reformer, Philipp Melanchthon, born.
1498 Italian Reformer, Girolamo Savonarola, burned at the stake, in Florence.
1501 Martin Luther enters the University of Erfurt.
1505 Luther earns MA at Erfurt; and enters the Order of Augustinian monks.
1506 Ulrich Zwingli completes Master of Arts at University of Basel; and becomes parish priest at Glarus.
1509 John Calvin born in Noyon, Picardy, France.
1510 Luther visits Rome.
1512 Luther becomes Doctor of Theology and begins lecturing at the University of Wittenberg.
1515 Zwingli witnesses the Battle of Marignano and writes an attack on mercenary service, *"The Labyrinth."*
1515 Luther begins lectures on Romans.
1516 Erasmus publishes the Greek New Testament.
1517 Luther posts his *95 Theses*.
1518 Ulrich Zwingli comes to Zürich.
1519 Luther debates with Johann Eck in Leipzig.

1520 Papal Bull *Exsurge Domine* gives Luther sixty days to recant or be excommunicated. Luther publicly burns the papal bull.

1521 Luther excommunicated by papal bull. Luther is summoned to the Diet of Worms and stands firm before the Emperor, refusing to recant. Luther declared an outlaw by the Emperor.

1522 Luther completes the translation of The New Testament into German, while hidden at Wartburg Castle.

1523 Zwingli presents his *67 Theses* at the First Zürich Disputation. The Zürich City Council authorises Zwingli to continue his Reformation work.

1524 William Tyndale travels to Germany and begins work on translating the Bible into English.

1524 The Peasants Revolt, under Thomas Munzer, erupts.

1525 The Princes decisively defeat the rebels.

1525 Martin Luther marries Katherine Von Bora and writes *"The Bondage of the Will."*

1525 Zwingli establishes The School of the Prophets (*Prophezei*).

1526 Tyndale completes the printing of the English New Testament in Worms and begins smuggling copies of these New Testaments into England.

1526 A huge Turkish army invades Hungary, sacks the capital, Budapest and carry off 200,000 Christians into Islamic slavery.

1527 First Protestant University (at Marburg) founded.

1527 Luther writes: *"A Mighty Fortress is our God"* Hymn.

1527 Imperial troops sack Rome.

1528 Bern votes to become Protestant.

1528 Tyndale writes *"The Obedience of a Christian Man."*

1529 Turks lay siege to Vienna.

1530 The Diet of Augsburg. Melanchthon presents *The Augsburg Confession*.

1531 Ulrich Zwingli is killed in the Battle of Kappel.

1531 The Schmalkaldic League of German Protestant states are formed in defense against Charles V.

1532 The Peace of Nuremberg guarantees religious toleration in the face the Turkish threat.

1533 Radical Anabaptists seize control of Munster and institute polygamy and communal ownership, amidst much bloodshed.

Chronology of the Reformation

1533 Thomas Cranmer becomes Archbishop of Canterbury.

1534 Henry VIII of England declares The Act of Supremacy, making himself the Head of the Church in England.

1535 Tyndale betrayed by Henry Phillips, arrested in Antwerp and imprisoned at Vilvoorde.

1536 Calvin publishes the first edition of *The Institutes of the Christian Religion*.

1536 *The Ten Articles* outlines early Protestant Theology in England.

1536 Bible translator and English Reformer, William Tyndale, burned at the stake at Vilvoorde.

1536 John Knox graduates from the University of St. Andrews and is ordained a priest.

1536 Calvin is persuaded by Farel to answer the call to remain and minister in Geneva.

1537 King Henry VIII authorises the distribution of Matthew Coverdale's translation of the Bible into English.

1538 Henry VIII orders English Bibles to be placed in every Parish church.

1538 Calvin and Farel are banished from Geneva.

1539 Remaining Catholic monasteries in England dissolved.

1541 Calvin is welcomed back to Geneva.

1543 John Knox converted to the Protestant Faith.

1545 John Knox becomes a bodyguard to Reformer, George Wishart.

1546 Scottish Reformer George Wishart martyred.

1546 Luther dies and Emperor Charles V seeks to crush Lutheranism in the Schmalkaldic War.

1547 Knox joins Protestant rebels at the Castle of St. Andrews, preaches his first Protestant sermon, is captured, imprisoned and condemned to the galleys in France.

1547 King Henry VIII dies and his 9-year-old son, Edward VI becomes King of England.

1549 Cranmer's *"Book of Common Prayer"* is authorised under The Act of Uniformity.

1549 Knox freed in prisoner exchange and begins preaching in England.

1552 Cranmer revises *"The Book of Common Prayer"* and issues *The 42 Articles* providing a Calvinist doctrinal foundation for the Church of England.

1553 When King Edward VI dies, Cranmer supports Lady Jane Grey, as Queen of England.

1553 Mary Tudor (*"Bloody Mary"*) enters London and seizes control. Cranmer imprisoned and convicted of *"high treason."* Lady Jane Grey beheaded.

1554 Protestant Faith and worship outlawed in England.

1555 Bishops Latimer and Ridley executed by burning at the stake in Oxford.

1555 The Peace of Augsburg allows rulers to determine the religion of their region (*Cuius Regio, Eius Religio*).

1556 Archbishop Thomas Cranmer burned at the stake in Oxford.

1558 Charles V dies, *"Bloody Mary"* dies, her half-sister, Elizabeth I becomes Queen of England and legalizes the Protestant Faith.

1559 John Knox returns from exile to Scotland.

1559 Calvin completes the final edition of the *Institutes* and establishes The Academy in Geneva.

1560 Scottish Parliament adopts the Protestant *Scots Confession*.

1561 Mary queen of Scots attempts to re-impose Catholicism on Scotland.

1563 *The 39 Articles of Religion* are issued in England.

1563 Foxe's *"Book of Martyrs"* published.

1564 John Calvin dies in Geneva.

1571 The Turkish fleet is decisively defeated at the Battle of Lepanto.

1572 St. Bartholomew's Day Massacre in France.

1579 The Dutch Provinces sign The Union of Utrecht and declare independence from Spain, forming the new country of the Netherlands.

1588 English Royal Navy defeats Spanish Armada.

1593 Henry IV of France nominally converts to Catholicism to gain the crown.

1598 Henry IV authorises the Edict of Nantes which returns civil and religious freedoms to Protestants in France.

APPENDIX 3

REFORMATION CALENDAR OF KEY EVENTS AND DATES

1 JANUARY 1484
Swiss Reformer, Ulrich Zwingli, was born 1 January 1484.

1 JANUARY 1519
On his 36th birthday, Zwingli shocked his new congregation at *Grossmünster*, in Zürich, by breaking with tradition, abandoning the Latin liturgy and beginning the first expository preaching, verse by verse through the New Testament, beginning with Matthew 1. History was made, the Swiss Reformation was launched and lives were changed.

2 JANUARY 1492
The Liberation of Spain from 8 Centuries of Islamic occupation and oppression was concluded when Ferdinand of Aragon and Isabella of Castile conquered the last Muslim fortress in Granada.

3 JANUARY 1521
Martin Luther was excommunicated by pope Leo X.

4 JANUARY 1577
Hans Bret, a baker and lay preacher in the Netherlands was tortured and burned at the stake for his Protestant Faith. Despite having his tongue clamped and cauterized by a red hot tongue screw, he boldly proclaimed the Gospel until the flames consumed his body. He was one of many thousands of martyrs who gave their lives for the Gospel of Christ in Holland during the great persecution of 1531-1578.

12 JANUARY 1519
Emperor Maximilian I of the Holy Roman Empire died.

14 JANUARY 1529
Spanish Reformer, Juan de Valdes published *Dialogue on Christian Doctrine*, which emphasized Reformation teachings on justification by faith, in Spanish. De Valdes translated into Spanish and wrote commentaries on the books of Matthew, Romans, 1 Corinthians and the Psalms. He had to flee Spain to escape from the Inquisition.

15 JANUARY 1559
Elizabeth I was crowned Queen of England, after the death of her half-sister, *"Bloody Mary"*. The Protestant Faith, which had been so fiercely persecuted under Mary, was restored in England.

213

16 January 1547
Ivan the Terrible was crowned as the first Czar of Russia.

24 January 1527
Felix Manz was executed for sedition, for attempting to undermine the authority of the City Council in Zürich.

25 January 1579
The Dutch provinces signed the Union of Utrecht and declared independence from Spain, forming the new country of the Netherlands.

26 January 1564
Pope Pius IV accepted and confirmed the decrees of the Council of Trent, including upholding the doctrines of the Mass, the seven sacraments, Purgatory, the celibacy of the priesthood and indulgences. The Council of Trent also asserted that the Bible should not be translated into the language of the people and that the Roman Church alone could interpret Scripture.

28 January 1547
England's King Henry VIII died after a 38 year reign. He was succeeded by his son, Edward VI.

29 January 1523
Zwingli presents his *67 Theses* at The First Zürich Disputation.

4 February 1555
Bible translator, John Rogers was burned at the stake in the centre of London under the reign of *"Bloody Mary"*. Rogers was a friend of Reformer, William Tyndale and ensured that his work was published under the pseudonym, Thomas Matthews. To this day, his translation is known as the Matthews Bible. Rogers was one of the first of many victims of *"Bloody Mary's"* reign of terror in England.

12 February 1554
Lady Jane Grey, the brave 16-year-old Protestant, who was Queen of England for only 9 days, was beheaded at the Tower of London.

16 February 1497
German Reformer, Philipp Melanchthon was born in Bretten, Saxony.

16 February 1519
Gaspard de Coligny was born in France. He became a great French soldier and prominent Protestant leader. He was one of the first Huguenot victims of the St. Bartholomew's Day Massacre.

18 February 1546
Martin Luther, the great Protestant Reformer, died in Eisleben on this day.

Reformation Calendar of Key Dates and Events

25 February 1570
pope Pius V excommunicated England's Queen Elizabeth I for refusing to return to Catholicism.

29 February 1528
Scottish Reformer Patrick Hamilton was burned at the stake in St. Andrews, for *"heresy."*

1 March 1546
Scottish Reformer, George Wishart was burned at the stake. He exhorted the crowds: *"Love the Word of God and suffer patiently. I know surely that my soul shall sit with my Saviour this night."*

4 March 1554
"Bloody Mary" outlaws Protestantism in England.

15 March 1517
pope Leo X authorised a plenary indulgence, in order to finance the rebuilding of St. Peters *Basilica* in Rome. It was the brazen hawking of this indulgence that outraged Luther and inspired *The 95 Theses*, which sparked the Reformation.

21 March 1556
The Archbishop of Canterbury, Thomas Cranmer was burned at the stake in Oxford.

28 March 1592
Pioneering educator, John Comenius, was born in Prague.

13 April 1598
King Henry IV of France signed *The Edict of Nantes* providing for religious toleration and ending the persecution of the Protestants.

18 April 1521
Martin Luther stands firm before the Emperor Charles V saying: *"my conscience is captive to the Word of God. I cannot and I will not recant anything, for to go against conscience is neither right nor safe. Here I stand, I cannot do otherwise. God help me. Amen."* This speech shook the world.

19 April 1526
The citizens of Straßburg, Nuremberg, Ulm and 9 other cities, along with numerous electors and princes, protested a decree of the Diet and petitioned the Emperor to allow religious freedom in Germany. From this point on, the Reformers were given the name of *"Protestants."*

21 April 1538
On Easter Sunday both Calvin and Farel, in different churches in Geneva, refused to serve communion because of the prevalent immorality in the city. Swords were drawn, tempers flared but the Reformers remained steadfast. The next day the City Council fired both ministers and ordered them to leave Geneva within 3 days.

24 April 1558
The first 2 Protestant candidates for the ministry were ordained at Gileskirk, in Edinburgh, by John Knox: Robert Campbell Sproul and James Grant. They forwarded the Reformation message with distinction.

25 April 1599
Oliver Cromwell was born in Huntington, Oxfordshire.

2 May 1559
John Knox returned from exile to Scotland.

6 May 1527
Rome fell to an army of Charles V and was plundered by the looting troops.

12 May 1587
Mary Stuart, Queen of Scots, was executed for treason.

15 May 1556
John Knox appeared at the Church of Blackfriars in Edinburgh to face charges of heresy. Knox succeeded in turning the tables on the Catholic Bishops and went on to preach to large crowds in Edinburgh.

19 May 1588
The Spanish Armada set sail to invade England.

20 May 1536
English King Henry VIII married his third wife, Jane Seymour, the day after his second wife, Anne Boleyn, was beheaded in the Tower of London.

21 May 1471
Albrecht Dürer, the great Reformed artist of Germany, was born in Nuremberg.

21 May 1536
The General Assembly of Citizens of Geneva voted in favour of the Reformation and adopted the Protestant Faith.

23 May 1498
The Italian Reformer, Girolamo Savonarola, was executed in Florence after enduring cruel tortures. He was resolute to the end.

27 May 1564
The great French Reformer, John Calvin died in Geneva. His ministry had succeeded in turning Geneva into one of the freest and most productive cities in Europe.

28 May 1453
Turkish soldiers stormed the great city of Constantinople and massacred Christians celebrating the Lord's Supper in the largest church in the world at that time, the Hagia Sophia.

24 June 1509
Henry VIII was crowned King of England.

2 July 1553
Protestant King Edward VI of England died.

6 July 1415
The Council of Constance condemned Reformer Jan Hus as a *"heretic."* On the same day he was burned at the stake.

10 July 1509
French Reformer, John Calvin was born in Noyon, Picardy, France.

11 July 1533
pope Clement VIII excommunicated King Henry VIII of England.

13 July 1536
The brilliant Renaissance academic Desiderius Erasmus died in Basel.

18 July 1504
The Swiss Reformer, Henrich Bullinger, was born.

19 July 1553
15-year-old Protestant Queen, Lady Jane Grey, was deposed as Queen of England after a reign of merely 9 days, by forces of the Catholic daughter of King Henry VIII, *"Bloody Mary."*

24 July 1567
After her defeat by the Protestants at Carberry Hills, Mary Queen of Scots abdicated.

25 July 1593
In an effort to consolidate support for his claim to the French throne, Henry IV of Navarre, converted from Protestantism to Roman Catholicism.

28 July 1540
King Henry had his chief minister, the Reformer Thomas Cromwell, executed.

29 July 1588
The English decisively defeated the Spanish Armada in the Battle of Gravelines.

15 August 1557
Agnes Prest, was martyred under the reign of *"Bloody Mary."* Agnes had memorized much of the New Testament. When she refused to return to Catholicism, she was condemned to die. Her last words were: *"I am the Resurrection and the Life, saith Christ. He that believeth in Me, though he were dead, yet shall he live."*

24 August 1572
The St. Bartholomew's Day Massacre cripples the advance of the Reformation in France.

25 August 1531
Protestant Reformer, Thomas Bilney, was martyred by order of Cardinal Wolsey. He cheerfully went to his death urging the large crowd to turn to Christ in faith.

25 August 1560
The Protestant Faith was formally adopted in Scotland.

21 September 1558
Emperor Charles V of the Holy Roman Empire died in agony.

25 September 1555
The Peace of Augsburg was signed recognizing freedom of religion for Protestants in territories where the Prince was Protestant (*Cuius Regio, Eius Religio*).

29 September 1565
Hundreds of Huguenot settlers in Florida – having fled persecution in France – were slaughtered by Spanish soldiers.

1 October 1529
The Colloquy of Marburg – first Council of Protestant Christians – was hosted by Prince Philip of Hesse, to resolve differences between the two great Reformers, Martin Luther and Ulrich Zwingli.

6 October 1536
The English Reformer and Bible translator, William Tyndale, was martyred at Vilvord. He was strangled and burnt at the stake.

7 October 1555
At the Diet of Augsburg, Charles V of the Holy Roman Empire, was compelled to recognise religious freedom for the Lutherans.

7 October 1571
The Spanish and Austrian Navies defeated the much larger Turkish fleet at the Battle of Lepanto.

10 October 1533
Nicolas Cop was elected Rector of the University of Paris. In his inaugural address he attacked the Catholic theologians who *"teach nothing of faith, nothing of the love of God, nothing of the remission of sins, nothing of grace, nothing of justification."* Cop and Calvin who wrote his speech, had to flee Paris for their lives.

11 October 1531
The great Swiss Reformer, Ulrich Zwingli died in the Battle of Kappel.

16 October 1555
Bishops Hugh Latimer and Nicholas Ridley were burned at the stake in Oxford.

31 October 1517
Martin Luther nailed *The 95 Theses* to the door of the *Schlosskirche* in Wittenberg.

2 November 1533
John Calvin escaped arrest in Paris and under hot pursuit, assumed a disguise and fled for his life.

10 November 1483
German Reformer, Martin Luther, was born in Eisleben, Saxony.

17 November 1558
The persecutor of the church, *"Bloody Mary"*, Queen of England died of fever.

24 November 1514
Scottish Reformer, John Knox, was born in Haddington, Scotland.

10 December 1520
Martin Luther publically burned the Papal Edict demanding that he recant or face excommunication. Surrounded by a large crowd of students and faculty of the University of Wittenberg, Luther declared:

"I stand fast on the truth and no other. Fear of power shall never sway me, for God is God and man is naught."

13 DECEMBER 1545
Pope Paul III convened The Council of Trent, in Northern Italy, to determine a comprehensive response to the Reformation. This Counter Reformation attempted to clean up abuses within the Roman Catholic churches, as well as reassert traditional doctrines (such as transubstantiation, purgatory, the 7 sacraments, etc.), which had been discredited.

15 DECEMBER 1417
Sir John Oldcastle was executed for protecting and advancing the Lollard Movement. He praised God from the flames as long as his life lasted.

23 DECEMBER 1531
Heinrich Bullinger took the place of slain Swiss Reformer, Ulrich Zwingli, as pastor of *Grossmünster*, in Zürich. Bullinger continued Zwingli's practice of preaching verse by verse through the books of the Bible.

27 DECEMBER 1571
Johannes Kepler, the father of modern astronomy, was born in Germany.

30 DECEMBER 1384
English Reformer, Professor John Wycliffe, died.

Wittenberg, Germany, the view from the Stadtkirche across the marketplace, with the City Hall on the right, looking towards the Schlosskirche.

APPENDIX 4

THE POPES OF ROME

"Watch out for false prophets. They come to you in sheep's clothing, but inwardly they are ferocious wolves. By their fruit you will recognise them..." Matthew 7:15-16

CORRUPTION
STEPHEN VII (896-897AD)
"He dug up a Corsican predecessor, pope Formosus (891-896), when he had been dead for over nine months.... He dressed the stinking corpse in full pontificals, placed him on the throne in the Lateran and proceeded to interrogate him personally....After being found guilty, the corpse was condemned as an anti-pope, stripped and minus the two fingers with which he had given his fake apostolic blessing, was thrown into the Tiber...." (Vicars of Christ – the Dark Side of the papacy by Father Peter de Rosa).

SERGIUS III (904-911)
Standing in his way to the throne had been Leo V, who reigned for one month before he was imprisoned by a usurper, Cardinal Christopher. Sergius had both killed. Then he exhumed his predecessor and had him beheaded, three fingers chopped off and thrown into the Tiber River.

JOHN XII (955-963)
He invented sins, it was said, that had not been known since the beginning of the world – including sleeping with his mother. John XII ran a harem in the Lateran Palace, he gambled with the offerings of pilgrims and he even toasted the devil at the high altar during the mass.

BENEDICT V (964)
Described by a church historian as *"the most iniquitous of all the monsters of ungodliness."*

BENEDICT IX (1032-44, 1045, 1047-1048)
Elected pope at age eleven, he was twice driven from his position due to his participation in plunder, immorality, oppression and murder. Church historians described him as *"That wretch, from the beginning of his pontificate to the end of his life, feasted on immorality,"* and *"a demon from hell in the disguise of a priest has occupied the chair of Peter."*

SIXTUS IV (1471-1484)
This is the pope who built the Sistine Chapel in which all popes are now

elected. Sixtus IV had several illegitimate sons, licensed the brothels of Rome and received a large amount of revenue for the papacy from these houses of iniquity, introduced the novel idea of selling indulgences for the dead to raise more revenue and sanctioned the Inquisition in Castile (Spain) by issuing a bull in 1478 (in just one year – 1482 – in one city of Andalusia, 2000 *"heretics"* were burned as a result).

ALEXANDER VI (1492-1503)

He was a murderer by age 12, he had 10 known illegitimate children, he was infamous for his drunken and immoral parties, he was known to have cardinals who had purchased their positions to be poisoned so that he could sell their positions again and increase his turnover. He spent a fortune in bribes to secure his own election as pope and he caused the Reformer Savonarola to be burned at the stake.

CRUELTY

The Romans papacy has been characterised by extreme cruelty in its persecution of those it deemed as *heretics*. In particular the Waldensians, Lollards and Albigensians were slaughtered by the forces of Rome.

In 1208 pope Innocent III declared: *"Death to the heretics!"* Great privileges and rewards were promised to those who would annihilate the *"heretics"* and to every man who killed one of them, the assurance was given that he would attain the highest place in Heaven!

The first target of this crusade against the Albigensians was the town of Begiers. All its inhabitants were killed and all the buildings burned. The monk leading this slaughter, Arnold, reported back to Innocent III *"Today, Your Holiness, twenty thousand citizens were put to the sword, regardless of age or sex."*

In Bram the papal soldiers cut off the noses and gouged out the eyes of the Albigensian *"heretics."*

In Minerve, 140 Albigensians were burned alive.

In Lavaure 400 *"heretics"* were burned at the stake.

In response, Innocent III praised the papal soldiers who had destroyed the heretics.

The successor of Innocent III, pope Gregory IX established the Inquisition in 1232. For over 600 years, spanning the reigns of over 80 popes, the Inquisition tortured and killed tens of thousands of Protestants including the Waldensians, Hussites, Lollards and Huguenots.

CONTRADICTION

Pope Gregory VII (1073-1085) declared that *"The pope cannot make a mistake."*

The First Vatican Council (1869-1870) under pope Pius IX raised the Dogma of Papal infallibility to become the official teaching of Roman Catholicism adding the usual anathema upon all who dared to disagree:

"But if anyone ....presume to contradict this assertion, let him be accused."

Yet, between 1378 and 1408, there were first two popes and then three! Gregory XII reigned from Rome, Benedict XIII from Avignon and John XXIII from Pisa.

John XXIII was described in Vicars of Christ: *"He was noted as a former pirate, pope-poisoner, mass-murderer, mass-fornicator..., adulterer on a scale unknown outside fables, simoniac par excellence, blackmailer, pimp, master of dirty tricks."*

Yet John XXIII accused his rival pope Benedict XIII of being *"a Fake"* and Gregory XII he nicknamed *"Mistake!"*

pope Pius IX, who at the First Vatican Council (1869-1870) caused the dogma of Papal Infallibility to become the official teaching of Roman Catholicism, also issued an edict permitting *"excommunication, confiscation, banishment, imprisonment for life, as well as secret execution in heinous cases."*

At the First Vatican Council, Bishop Strossmayer (himself a papist) gave a speech arguing against papal infallibility. He pointed out: *"Gregory I calls anyone anti-Christ who takes the name of Universal Bishop; and contrawise Boniface III made Emperor Phocas confer that title upon him. Paschal II and Eugenius III authorised duelling; Julius II and Pins IV forbad it. Hadrian II declared civil magistrates to be valid; Pius VII condemned them. Sixtus V published an edition of the Bible and recommended it to be read; Pius VII condemned the reading of the Bible."*

It could also be noted that while one (supposedly infallible) pope, Eugene IV (1431-1447), condemned Joan of Arc as a heretic to be burned alive, another pope, Benedict XV, in 1920, declared her to be a saint and her burning a mistake.

Yet the Dogma of Papal Infallibility declares that when a pope speaks

223

ex cathedra his words are *"as infallible as if it had been uttered by Christ Himself!"*

In plain contradiction to this *"papal infallibility"* is the Bible. The apostle Peter (from whom all popes claim their succession) never suggested that he was infallible. Indeed in his first general epistle Peter described himself simply as *"an elder"* and he exhorted his *"fellow elders"* not to act as *"lords over those entrusted to you"* (1 Peter 5:1-3).

Paul records in Galatians 2:11 *"But when Peter had come to Antioch I withstood him to his face, because he was to be blamed..."* Plainly Paul did not see Peter as infallible. Also Peter was married (Mark 1:30; 1 Corinthians 9:5). Indeed a requirement of a church leader is that he is married and bring up his children in the faith (1 Timothy 3:4-5).

The Lord Jesus taught: *"You know that the rulers of the gentiles lord it over them and those who are great exercise authority over them. Yet it shall not be so among you; but whoever desires to be first among you, let him be your slave – just as the Son of Man did not come to be served but to serve..."* Matthew 20:25-28

Jesus taught that no one is good – except God alone (Mark 10:18) and we are to call no-one on earth Father – God alone is our spiritual Father. How then can any pope be called *"his Holiness"* or *"Holy Father!"* The term Holy Father is only used once in the Bible and it is clearly addressed to God the Father in Christ's prayer (John 17:11).

It is no wonder that when Archbishop Thomas Cranmer was about to be burned at the stake, on 21 March 1556, he declared: **"As for the pope, I refuse him as Christ's enemy and Anti-Christ, with all his false doctrines."**

In the words of Martin Luther: **"Unless I am convinced by Scripture or clear reasoning that I am in error – for popes and councils have often erred and contradicted themselves – I cannot recant for I am subject to the Scriptures I have quoted. My conscience is captive to the Word of God. It is unsafe and dangerous to do anything against one's conscience. Here I stand. I cannot do otherwise. So help me God. Amen."**

APPENDIX 5
LIBEL AGAINST LUTHER

Our articles, *How the Reformation Changed the World* and *Here I Stand* received many responses from around the world, mostly very positive. However, there were also some friends who responded in surprise that we could have so positively quoted from Martin Luther, because from what they had heard, he was anti-Semitic and responsible for terrible atrocities against the Jews.

CHARACTER ASSASSINATION
I was even directed towards websites that are dedicated to depicting Luther as an *"anti-Semite"* who *"laid the foundations for the holocaust!"*

LUTHER WAS A FRIEND AND ADVOCATE FOR JEWS
The accusation that Martin Luther was an anti-Semite, responsible for massacres, reveals an ignorance of history. Luther was pro-Christ and he was zealous in evangelism. For decades he lovingly and patiently reached out to the Jewish people in his area with the Gospel. In 1523, Luther accused Catholics of being unfair to Jews in treating them *"as if they were dogs."* Luther was outraged and declared that such mistreatment made it even more difficult for Jews to convert to Christ.

LOVE YOUR JEWISH NEIGHBOUR
Dr. Luther wrote: *"I would request and advise that one deal gently with the Jews ... if we really want to help them, we must be guided in our dealings with them, not by Papal law, but by the Law of Christian love. We must receive them cordially and permit them to trade and work with us, hear our Christian teaching and witness our Christian life. If some of them should prove stiff-necked, what of it? After all, we ourselves are not all good Christians either."*

OUTRAGED BY BLASPHEMY
Fifteen years later, however, the persistent rejection of Christ and repeated blasphemies of Jewish people in his community provoked Luther to write: *"On the Jews and their Lies."* In this booklet, Luther wrote against the *"madness and blindness that blasphemes Christ"* in the Rabbinic teachings. Luther declared that he could not *"have any fellowship or patience with obstinate blasphemers and those who defame our dear Saviour."* These blasphemies included describing our Lord Jesus Christ as *"the bastard Son"* of *"that whore, Mary"* and even worse. Blasphemy was a civil crime. Luther taught that to tolerate such blasphemy was to share in the guilt for it. Therefore, he proposed measures of *"sharp*

225

mercy" which included confiscating all Jewish literature which was blasphemous and prohibiting Rabbis to teach such blasphemy.

CONTEXT IS EVERYTHING
However, to quote these reactions of Dr. Luther without explaining their local context of opposing the repeated blasphemies of Jewish individuals in his community and then to project guilt for the continent-wide, anti-Christian holocaust of World War II upon the great 16th century Reformer is ludicrous. How can any Christian Reformer of the 16th century be blamed for the evils perpetrated by humanists (who clearly rejected Martin Luther's Protestant teachings) 400 years after his death!

OPPOSING ENEMIES OF THE GOSPEL
Luther was not an anti-Semite. His arguments against Jewish individuals were Theological, not biological or cultural. He was speaking out against blasphemy and heresy, not opposing an entire race or nation of people. Nevertheless, the harsh and extreme terminology used by Luther in his writings leave many of his supporters embarrassed and confused as to how a man, who so wondrously preached the grace of God, could have seemed to be so ungracious in his writings on the Jews.

BEYOND THE BOUNDS OF MODERATION
By his own admission, Martin Luther was often harsh in opposing those who rejected Christ. *"I cannot deny that I am more vehement than I should be..."* he wrote. *"But, they assail... God's Word so atrociously and criminally that... these monsters are carrying me beyond the bounds of moderation."*

CHRIST IS OUR EXAMPLE
Luther once asked: *"What do you think of Christ? Was He abusive when He called the Jews an adulterous and perverse generation, an offspring of vipers, hypocrites and children of the devil? ...the truth ...cannot be patient against its obstinate and intractable enemies"* (Matthew 23).

VERBAL WARFARE
The few pamphlets which Luther wrote against Jewish blasphemies, pale when compared to the many books produced by Luther against the papacy. *"We should take him, the pope, the cardinals and whatever riff-raff belongs to his idolatrous and papal holiness and as blasphemers, tear out their tongues from the back and nail them on the gallows."*

FALSE TEACHERS AND FALSE SHEPHERDS
On another occasion Luther wrote: *"Why should we hesitate to use arms against these teachers of perdition, the cardinals, popes and the whole Roman*

Sodom, which corrupts the Church of God without end and wash our hands in their blood?"

SCRIPTURE ALONE IS OUR AUTHORITY
"How often must I cry out to you, coarse, stupid papists, to quote Scripture sometime? Scripture! Scripture! Scripture! Do you not hear you deaf goat and coarse...?"

BORN FOR WARFARE
Luther admitted that he was, on occasion, bull-headed, coarse-tongued and intemperate. His speech and actions were frequently intense. Luther wrote: *"I was born to go to war and give battle to sects and devils that is why my books are stormy and war-like."*

SHARP SALT
"What good does salt do if it does not bite? What good does the edge of the sword do if it does not cut?"

TOUGH SKIN
On another occasion, when he was being publicly criticised, Luther declared: *"I am a tough Saxon. I have grown a thick skin for this kind of..."*

WHOLEHEARTED REPENTANCE
The Reformer did sometimes, however, regret his outbursts. He explained to his wife, Katie: *"Why, I sometimes rage about a piddling thing not worthy of mention. ...Isn't that a shameful thing?"* Luther could repent and apologise with wholeheartedness unlike any other. He could also laugh at himself and was often cheerful and witty when everyone around him was desperate.

WE ALL SHARE THE GUILT FOR CHRIST'S DEATH
Unlike many of his time, Luther did not, however, hold Jews alone responsible for the death of Christ. As he wrote in a hymn: *"We dare not blame ...the band of Jews; ours is the shame."* Luther frequently emphasised that the blame for the death of Christ was upon each individual sinner, not least himself. Luther continued to the end of his life to maintain an eagerness and desperate longing that Jews might be won for Christ.

BEARING FALSE WITNESS
It is most disturbing that such a humble and God-fearing man, who, against all odds, gave to the church and the world, the Bible, freely available in the common tongue; who introduced congregational singing; championed justification by God's grace, received by faith, on the basis of the finished work of Christ; who stood for Sola Scriptura, that Scripture alone is our

ultimate authority; and who was so wonderfully used of the Lord to bring about the greatest Biblical Reformation and birth of freedom that the world had ever known, could be the target of such vicious slander.

DO NOT SLANDER ONE ANOTHER
The Scriptures implore us: *"Brothers, do not slander one another. Anyone who speaks against his brother or judges him speaks against the Law and judges it."* James 4:11

RESPECT OUR ELDERS
Even more, the Scriptures continually command us to respect our elders, especially our spiritual fathers. *"Rise in the presence of the aged, show respect for the elderly..."* Leviticus 19:32. *"Do not rebuke an older man harshly, but exhort him as if he were your father..."* 1 Timothy 5:1. (Exodus 20:12; Leviticus 19: 3; Deuteronomy 27:16; Proverbs 30:17; Matthew 15:4).

MALICIOUS SLANDER IS FORBIDDEN
"Therefore, rid yourselves of all malice and all deceit, hypocrisy, envy and slander of every kind." 1 Peter 2:1. There is a disturbing tendency throughout the church, seen regularly in those homes where they have *"roast pastor for Sunday lunch,"* to continually set ourselves up as judges of those who are better than us. Many have the gift of criticism and a ministry of discouragement.

SLANDER IS INSEPARABLE FROM MALICE
As the Scripture so plainly shows us, slander of every kind is inseparable from malice, deceit, hypocrisy and envy. The middle letter of pride is *"I,"* the middle letter of lie is *"I,"* the middle letter of sin is *"I,"* so too the middle letter of Lucifer is *"I."* Self-centered pride is often at the root of our desire to slander great men and women of the past and to drag down others whom God has raised up.

IGNORANT BLINDNESS
Do those who so confidently condemn Martin Luther really believe, in the light of eternity, in the sight of God, that they have served God's people and God's cause and Kingdom with even 1% as much dedication and effectiveness as Dr. Martin Luther? If they do, it betrays an ignorance of history and a blindness to their own weaknesses.

FORGIVE THEM
It is most encouraging that while Jesus was being crucified on the Cross, he prayed: *"Father, forgive them, for they do not know what they are doing."* Luke 23:34

APPENDIX 6
DID THE REFORMERS PERSECUTE THE ANABAPTISTS?

Several people have challenged us over organising **Reformation Conferences** and claimed that the Reformers persecuted the Anabaptists just because they *"were not willing to baptise babies."* One correspondent wrote that rather than celebrate the Reformation *"would it not be preferable to study the Scriptures..."*

BACK TO THE BIBLE
Here is our response:

Of course, our highest priority is to *"study the Scriptures daily to see if these things be true."* In fact that is the heritage of the Reformation. The Reformation gave us back the Bible freely available, translated into our own languages and the Reformers championed **"Scripture alone is our final authority."** The Reformation succeeded in bringing about greater freedoms than had ever been experienced before in human history.

UNDERSTAND THE TIMES
We would encourage you to read *How the Reformation Changed the World* and *How the Reformation Changed the Church*, both available on our *www.ReformationSA.org* website.

VIOLENT REVOLUTIONARIES
Those who accuse the Reformers of persecuting Anabaptists are being unfair and selective in not reporting the whole context. Anabaptists were not so much opposed and convicted for not being willing to baptise babies, but because the Anabaptists in the 1520's and 1530's were radical, violent revolutionaries.

RADICAL EXTREMISTS
While the Anabaptists claimed to be the only true Christians, they denied many key elements of the Faith. They rejected Biblical Law, Christian ministry, worship and sacraments. Anabaptists in the 16th century proclaimed socialism, egalitarianism and revolution. They claimed *"it is impossible to be Christian and wealthy at the same time"*; *"all authorities, secular and clerical, must be deprived of their offices once and for all, or be killed by the sword..."*

DEATH THREATS

Igor Shafarevich, in his book *The Socialist Phenomenon*, documents the teachings and activities of two important Anabaptist leaders, Thomas Muntzer and John of Leyden. Muntzer, an itinerant preacher and organiser of rebellions, established his revolutionary base in Muhlhausen from where he issued proclamations damning landowners, magistrates and Reformers. *"I would like to smell your frying carcass"* he wrote to Professor Martin Luther.

PEASANTS REVOLT

In 1524, Muntzer was successful in rousing up many of the peasants of central Germany in the bloody, so called Peasants Revolt, which it should be noted attracted several nobles to his side. *"Let your swords be ever-warm with blood!"* Muntzer exhorted his faithful followers. Muntzer's army of Anabaptists struck terror throughout the countryside, robbing, burning and destroying the property of the faithful, killing many thousands.

SOCIALIST UTOPIA

Frederick Engels praised Muntzer's *"robust vandalism"* and explained *"by the Kingdom of God Muntzer meant a society without class differences, private property and the state authority.... All the existing authorities...were to be overthrown, all work and property shared in common and complete equality introduced."*

ATHEISM IN RELIGIOUS DISGUISE

Engels praised Muntzer's doctrines in this way: *"Under the cloak of Christianity he preached a kind of pantheism, which curiously resembled modern speculative contemplation and at times even approached atheism. He repudiated the Bible both as the only and as the infallible revelation. The real and living revelation, he said, was reason, a revelation which existed and always exists amongst all people at all times. To hold up the Bible against reason, he maintained, was to kill the spirit with the letter, ...faith is nothing but reason come alive in man and pagans could therefore also have faith... just as there is no heaven in the beyond, there is no hell and no damnation. Similarly, there is no devil...Christ was a man, as we are, a prophet and a teacher..."*

BRUTAL OPPRESSION OF THE LIBERATORS

In 1534, Anabaptist leader Jan Matthijs seized the town of Munster. *"Armed Anabaptists broke into houses and drove out everyone who was unwilling to accept second baptism. Winter was drawing to a close; it was a stormy day and wet snow was falling. An eyewitness account describes crowds of expelled citizens walking through the knee-deep snow. They had

Anabaptist Revolutionaries in the Peasant Revolt, 1524.

not been allowed even to take warm clothing with them. Women carrying children in their arms, old men leaning on staffs. At the city gate they were robbed once more." (*The Socialist Phenomenon* – Shafarevich)

REIGN OF TERROR

Jan Matthijs and Johan Bokelson then instituted a reign of terror in Munster, ordering the socialisation of all property, ordaining *apostles of revolution* to preach throughout Europe. The communist paradise of Munster attracted thousands of Anabaptists from throughout Germany and Holland. Matthijs was killed in one of the early battles. Johan Bokelson took command and established a dictatorship in Munster. He then issued the order for holding everything in common, including wives.

VIOLATING EVERY LAW

As Frederick Engels observed: *"It is a curious fact that in every large revolutionary movement the question of free-love comes to the foreground."* No woman was allowed to be exempt – there was a law against being unmarried, which meant that every girl was forced to be passed around amongst the men. Every woman in Munster became fair game for the lusts of these Anabaptist males. Rapes, suicides, severe punishments and mass executions took place almost every day. On one notable occasion, Bokelson himself beheaded a virtuous woman who had refused his sexual advances. As he ceremoniously chopped her head off in the public square, a choir of his *wives* sang *"Glory to God in the Highest!"* (*Productive Christians in an Age of Guilt Manipulators* by David Chilton).

You Reap What You Sow

This reign of terror continued for a year and a half until the city was freed by Protestant forces who put Bokelson and his lieutenants to death for their crimes – crimes committed in the name of *love, equality and spirituality.*

Suppressing Violent Revolution

We have left out most of the sordid and horrifying details of the 1524-1525 Peasants Revolt and the 1534 Anabaptist *"Kingdom of God"* established in Munster. But these few examples should be sufficient to explain why Anabaptists were opposed. It was not that they were being persecuted for taking the Scriptures seriously, but because they were violent revolutionaries subverting the entire social order and guilty of the deaths of many thousands of innocent people.

Do Not Bear False Witness

Those who would claim that Anabaptists have changed dramatically since that time, should recognise that it is for that very reason therefore unfair to portray the Reformers as supporting the persecution of poor innocent Anabaptist pacifists, as that is plainly not the case. Yes, the Anabaptists have changed since. So we should not continue to propagate the false accusation that Reformers were persecuting pacifist Anabaptists who were seeking to mind their own business. The Anabaptists that were opposed by the Reformers in the 1520's and 1530's were violent revolutionaries guilty of abominable atrocities and abuses.

Further Reading

For further reading, I would encourage you to read our articles: *When All Men Speak Well of You* and *Why Is There So Much Hostility To the Bible and Christianity?* on our www.frontlinemissionsa.org website and obtain these outstanding books: *What If Jesus Had Never Been Born* by Dr. James Kennedy and Jerry Newcombe, *How Christianity Transformed Civilisation* by Dr. Alvin Schmidt and *The Great Christian Revolution* by Otto Scott. We all owe a tremendous debt to the Reformation in so many different ways. The Reformation was the greatest movement for Faith and freedom that the world has ever seen.

APPENDIX 7
SOME ROMAN CATHOLIC HERESIES AND INVENTIONS

Dates or approximate dates of their adoption

		A.D.
1.	*Prayers for the dead*, began about	300
2.	Making the *sign of the cross*	300
3.	*Wax candles*, about	320
4.	*Veneration of angels and dead saints* and use of *images*	375
5.	*The Mass*, as a daily celebration	394
6.	Beginning of *the exaltation of Mary* (the term *"Mother of God"* first applied to her by the Council of Ephesus)	431
7.	Priests began to dress differently from laymen	500
8.	*Extreme Unction*	526
9.	The doctrine of *Purgatory*, established by Gregory I	593
10.	*Latin language*, used in prayer and worship, imposed by Gregory I	600
11.	*Prayers directed to Mary*, dead saints and angels, about	600
12.	*Title of pope*, or universal bishop, given to Boniface III by emperor Phocas	607
13.	*Kissing the pope's foot*, began with pope Constantine	709
14.	*Temporal power of the popes*, conferred by Peppin, King of the Franks	750
15.	*Worship of the cross*, *images* and *relics*, authorised in	786
16.	*Holy water*, mixed with a pinch of salt and blessed by a priest	850
17.	*Worship of St. Joseph*	890
18.	*College of Cardinals* established	927
19.	*Baptism of bells*, instituted by pope John XIII	965
20.	*Canonization of dead saints*, first by pope John XV	995
21.	*Fasting on Fridays* and during *Lent*	998
22.	*The Mass*, developed gradually as a sacrifice, attendance made obligatory in the 11th Century	

23. *Celibacy*, of the priesthood decreed
    by pope Gregory VII (Hildebrand)   1079
24. *The Rosary*, mechanical praying with beads, invented
    by Peter the Hermit   1090
25. *The Inquisition*, instituted by the Council of Verona   1184
26. *Sale of Indulgences*   1190
27. *Transubstantiation*, proclaimed by pope Innocent III   1215
28. *Auricular of Confession* of sins to a priest (instead of God) instituted by pope Innocent III, in Lateran Council   1215
29. *Adoration of the wafer*, (Host), decreed by pope Honorius III   1220
30. *Bible forbidden to laymen*, placed on the index of Forbidden books by the Council of Valencia   1229
31. *The Scapular*, invented by Simon Stock, an English monk   1251
32. *Cup forbidden to the people* at communion
    by Council of Constance   1415
33. *Purgatory* proclaimed as a dogma by the Council of Florence   1439
34. The doctrine of *Seven Sacraments* affirmed   1439
35. The *Ave Maria*
    (part of the latter half was completed 50 years later
    and approved by pope Sixtus V end of the 16th Century)   1508
36. *Jesuit* order founded by Loyola   1534
37. *Tradition* declared of equal authority with the Bible
    by the Council of Trent   1545
38. *Apocryphal* books added to the Bible by the Council of Trent   1546
39. *Creed of pope Pius IV* imposed as the official creed   1560
40. *Immaculate Conception* of the Virgin Mary, proclaimed
    by the pope Pius IX   1854
41. *Syllabus of Errors*, proclaimed by pope Pius IX and ratified by the Vatican Council: condemned freedom of religion, conscience, speech, press and scientific discoveries, which were all disapproved by the Roman Church and asserted the pope's temporal authority over all the civil rulers   1864
42. *Infallibility of the pope* in matters of faith and morals, proclaimed by the Vatican Council   1870
43. *Assumption of the Virgin Mary* (bodily ascension to Heaven), proclaimed by the pope Pius XI   1950

Add to these many other un-Biblical inventions: monks – nuns – monasteries – convents – forty days lent – holy week – Palm Sunday – Ash Wednesday – All Saints day – Candlemas day – fish day – meat days – incense – holy oil – holy palms – St. Christopher medals – charms – and still others.

Thus throughout the centuries the Roman Catholic system progressively departed from the simplicity of the Gospel and Book of Acts Christianity. It has been a departure so radical and far-reaching that it has produced a drastically anti-evangelical church. The Roman Catholic religion, as now practised, is the outgrowth of centuries of error. Human inventions have been substituted for Bible truth and practice.

The Jan Hus Memorial in Prague.

236 Monument to the Father of the Printing Press: Johannes Gutenberg in Straßburg.

APPENDIX 8

Is Celebrating the Reformation Anti-Catholic?

Some have suggested that celebrating the great spiritual Revival and birth of freedom achieved by the Reformation is unnecessarily divisive and antagonistic to our Catholic neighbours and brethren. This is an unfortunate and unjustified assumption.

The purpose of celebrating the Reformation is not to re-open old wounds or to blame present day Roman Catholics for what popes and their followers may have done four to five centuries ago.

The purpose of celebrating the Reformation is to focus on the tremendous courage and convictions of those Reformers who restored to us the Bible, freely available in our own languages. The battle cries of the Reformation: *Scripture alone is our authority, Christ alone is the Head of the Church, salvation is by the grace of God alone, received by faith alone*, is positive and beneficial to all.

Roman Catholics have immeasurably benefited from the Reformation themselves. The bold actions of the Reformers forced the Roman Catholic church to institute major reforms which radically improved the moral standards of the clergy, cleared up many of the abuses and ultimately even pressured the Second Vatican Council to allow Roman Catholic laity to read the Bible in their own language.

The Protestant Reformation brought about the greatest birth of freedom and Bible study ever. The Reformation teachings produced the most productive, prosperous and free nations in history. Everyone has benefited from the sacrifices, courage, faith and love of the Reformers.

Some have suggested that in celebrating the Reformation we are saying that Roman Catholics cannot be saved. Yet, many of the Reformers that we have focused on: John Wycliffe, Jan Hus, Martin Luther, Ulrich Zwingli and William Tyndale, among many others, were themselves ordained Roman Catholic priests. Of course we believe that Roman Catholics can be saved: by the grace of God, received by faith, on the basis of Christ's Atonement on the Cross of Calvary, through Scripture, which is the power of God for the salvation of everyone who believes.

The ongoing relevance of the Reformation in applying the Word of God to all areas of life should also be clear to us. Many Reformed believers through the centuries have tackled different threats and challenges. In the Middle Ages, in the time of Luther, the greatest political power was the Holy Roman Empire and the only ecclesiastical authority in Western and Central Europe was the Roman Catholic church. Naturally his focus was the abuses, corruptions and superstitions prevalent in the system under which he lived.

William Carey confronted the superstitions, corruptions and abuses of Hinduism, **David Livingstone** confronted the atrocities, superstitions and abuses of Animism and the Islamic slave trade. **Charles Spurgeon** confronted liberals within the Baptist Union. **Gresham Machan** dealt with abuses, corruption and liberalism within the Presbyterian Church, USA. **Eric Liddell** battled Secularists and Humanists within the Olympic Committee and Shintoism of the Japanese empire; **Richard Wurmbrand** confronted the atrocities and abuses of Communism. Reformed Christians are not anti-Catholic, they are pro-Christ.

In our commitment to study, believe, preach and apply the Bible to all areas of life, we cannot flinch from confronting whatever abuses and threats face us, no matter from which quarter it comes.

We are not anti-Catholic. Some of our friends and colleagues in the fight for the right to life of pre-born babies are Roman Catholic. Many of the churches that we deliver Bibles and aid to, in Muslim and Communist countries, are Roman Catholic. Roman Catholics are frequently our allies in the battle against the greatest threats confronting us today: Secular Humanism, Communism, Materialism and Islam. But the message and ministry of the Reformers is of immense importance and relevance for us today. They dealt with primary issues of authority, salvation and God's Word. Our Faith and freedoms are at stake.

In the words of Martin Luther: *"If I profess with the loudest voice and clearest exposition every portion of the truth of God's Word, except precisely that point which the world and the devil are at that moment attacking, then I am not confessing Christ, however boldly I may be professing Him. Where the battle rages, there the loyalty of the soldier is proved; and to be steady on all the battle front besides is mere a flight and disgrace – if he flinches at that point."*

APPENDIX 9

THE CHALLENGE OF ISLAM ACCORDING TO THE REFORMERS

In expounding Daniel 9, Martin Luther noted that among others, the prophet Daniel was talking about the Muslim Turks, who at that time were invading Europe: *"In the latter part of their reign, when rebels have become completely wicked, a stern-faced king, a master of intrigue will arise. He will become very strong, but not by his own power. He will cause astounding devastation ...He will cause deceit to prosper and he will consider himself superior. When they feel secure, he will destroy many and take his stand against the Prince of princes. Yet he will be destroyed, but not by human power."* Daniel 9: 23-25

Luther wrote that the *"two regimes, that of the pope and that of the Turk, are ... antichrist."*

John Calvin in a sermon on Deuteronomy 18:15 maintained that Muhammad was one of *"the two horns of antichrist."*

In his commentaries on Daniel 7:7-18, Calvin put forward the theory that the Muslim Turks were the little horn that sprang up from the beast. As the Turks had conquered much of the old Roman Empire, much of the prophecies concerning Rome could apply to the Muslim world. Islam was one of the two legs of the later Roman Empire described in Daniel 2.

Commenting on Daniel 11:37, Calvin wrote that Muhammad *"allowed to men the brutal liberty of chastising their wives and thus he corrupted that conjugal love and fidelity which binds the husband to the wife ...Mohamet allowed full scope to various lusts – by permitting a man to have a number of wives ...Mohamet invented a new form of religion."* (Commentaries on the Book of the Prophet Daniel – John Calvin).

Luther noted that Christ warned about false prophets coming from the desert (Matthew 24:24-26) and this certainly included Muhammad.

Commenting on 2 Thessalonians 2:3-12, Calvin wrote that ... *"the sect of Muhammad was like a raging overflow, which in its violence tore away about half of the church."*

In his commentary on 1 John 2:18-23, Calvin states that the Turks *"have a mere idol in place of God."*

239

Luther observed from 1 John 2:18-22 and 4:1-3, *"Who is the liar? It is the man who denies that Jesus is the Christ. Such a man is antichrist – he denies the Father and the Son."* (1 John 2:22). The Muhammadans deny both the Fatherhood of God and the Deity of Christ – hence they are liars. They testify against the truth of God's Word.

In 1 John 4:3-6: *"but every spirit that does not acknowledge Jesus, is not from God. This is the spirit of antichrist ... this is how we recognise the spirit of truth and the spirit of falsehood"*, Calvin noted that *"Muhammad too asserts that he has drawn his dreams only from Heaven ... False spirits claim the Name of God."*

Luther observed that the Muslim Turks want *"to eradicate the Christians."*

The 1637 Calvinist Dordt Bible in Dutch, comments on Revelation 16:12 that the Muslim nations of the East would still unite with one another in a Pan-Islamic *Jihad* against the West.

The 1643 Westminster Assembly's *"Larger Catechism"* calls on Christians to ... *"pray, that the kingdom of sin and satan may be destroyed, that the Gospel propagated throughout the world ..."* It's *"Directory for the Public Worship of God"* instructs congregations to *"pray for the propagation of the Gospel and Kingdom of Christ to all nations, for the conversion of the Jews, the fullness of the gentiles, the fall of antichrist and the deliverance of the distressed Churches abroad from the tyranny of the anti-Christian faction and from the cruel oppression and blasphemies of the Turk."*

Commenting on Revelation 9:1-11, the Dutch Dordt Bible of 1637 suggests that Muhammad is *"Apollyon"* (which is Greek for the Hebrew word *"Abaddon"* which means destroyer) and the army of locusts and scorpions are the Arab and Saracen armies which wage *Jihad* in Muhammad's name.

In his Institutes (Book 2, chapter 6:4), Calvin writes: *"So today the Turks, although they proclaim at the top of their lungs that the Creator of Heaven and earth is their God, still, while repudiating Christ, substitute an idol in the place of the true God."*

Jonathan Edwards, the first President of Princeton University, wrote in his *A History of the Work of Redemption*: *"The two great works of the devil which he ...wrought against the Kingdom of Christ are ...his Anti-Christian (Romish or Papal) and Mahometan (Muslim or Islamic) kingdoms ...which have been and still are, two kingdoms of great extent and strength. Both together swallow ...up the Ancient Roman Empire; the (Papal) kingdom of Antichrist swallowing up the Western Empire and satan's Mahometan kingdom the Eastern Empire... In the Book of Revelation (chapters 16-20) ...it is in the destruction of these that the glorious victory of Christ at the introduction of the glorious times of the Church, will mainly consist..."*

In a sermon on 2 Timothy 1:3, Calvin explained: *"The Turks at this day, can allege and say for themselves: 'We serve God from our ancestors!' ...It is a good while ago since Mahomet gave them the cup of his devilish dreams to drink and they got drunk with them. It is about a thousand years since those cursed hellhounds were made drunk with their follies... Let us be wise and discreet! ...For otherwise, we shall be like the Turks and Heathen!"* (*Sermons on Timothy and Titus* – John Calvin).

Calvin pointed out that the reign of antichrist will be destroyed by the Word of God (2 Thessalonians 2:8). *"Paul does not think that Christ will accomplish this in a single moment ... Christ will scatter the darkness in which antichrist will reign, by the rays which He will emit before His coming – just as the sun, before becoming visible to us, chases away the darkness of the night with its bright light.*

"This victory of the Word will therefore be seen in the World. For 'the Breath (or Spirit) of His Mouth' means simply His Word ...as in Isaiah 11:4, the passage to which Paul appears to be alluding... It is a notable commendation of true and sound doctrine that it is represented as being sufficient to put an end to all ungodliness and as destined at all times to be victorious over all devices of satan. It is also a commendation when ...a little further on ...the preaching of this doctrine, is referred to as Christ's 'coming' to us." (*Commentary on Second Thessalonians* - John Calvin).

"The Kingdoms of the world have become the Kingdom of our Lord and of His Christ and He shall reign for ever and ever."
Revelation 11:15

"All nations will come and worship before You..." Revelation 15:4

"The desert tribes will bow before Him and His enemies will lick the dust ...All kings will bow down to Him and all nations will serve Him." Psalm 72: 9-11

Appendix 10
The Five Points of Calvinism in the Teachings of Christ

Calvinistic soteriology is commonly summarised by the acronym TULIP:

Total depravity,
Unconditional election
Limited atonement
Irresistible grace
Perseverance of the saints

Total Depravity
"For the hearts of this people have grown dull. Their ears are hard of hearing and their eyes they have closed..." Matthew 13:15

"For out of the heart proceed evil thoughts, murders, adulteries, fornications, thefts, false witness, blasphemies." Matthew 15:19

"Unless one is born again, he cannot see the Kingdom of God." John 3:3

"No one can come to Me unless the Father who sent Me draws him; and I will raise him up at the last day." John 6:44

Unconditional Election
"Nor does anyone know the Father except the Son and the one to whom the Son wills to reveal Him." Matthew 11:27

"And unless those days were shortened, no flesh would be saved; but for the elect's sake those days will be shortened." Matthew 24:22

"Even so the Son gives life to whom He will." John 5:21

"All that the Father gives Me will come to Me...This is the will of the Father who sent Me, that of all He has given Me I should lose nothing, but should raise them up at the last day." John 6:37-39

"...no one can come to Me unless it has been granted to him by My Father." John 6:65

Limited Atonement
"...just as the Son of Man did not come to be served, but to serve and to give His life a ransom for many." Matthew 20:28

I am the Good Shepherd. The Good Shepherd give His life for the sheep... I lay down My life for the sheep... My sheep hear My voice and I know them and they follow Me. And I give them eternal life and they shall never perish; neither shall anyone snatch them out of My hand." John 10:10-11, 15, 27-28

"I pray for them. I do not pray for the world but for those whom You have given Me, for they are Yours... For those who will believe in Me."
John 17:9, 20

IRRESISTIBLE GRACE
"All that the Father gives Me will come to Me... No, one can come to Me unless the Father who sent Me draws him; and I will raise him up at the last day." John 6:37, 44

"...I have come that they may have life and that they may have it more abundantly... I give them eternal life and they shall never perish; neither shall anyone snatch them out of My hand." John 10:10, 28

PERSEVERANCE OF THE SAINTS
"...whoever believes in Him should not perish but have everlasting life." John 3:16

"He who believes in the Son has everlasting life." John 3:36

"Most assuredly, I say to you, he who believes in Me has everlasting life."
John 6:47

"My sheep hear My voice and I know them and they follow Me. And I give them eternal life and they shall never perish; neither shall anyone snatch them out of My hand." John 10:27-28

POST-MILLENNIALISM IN THE TEACHINGS OF CHRIST
"From that time Jesus began to preach and to say, 'Repent, for the Kingdom of Heaven is at hand." Matthew 4:17

"Blessed are the meek, for they shall inherit the earth." Matthew 5:5

"Your Kingdom com. Your will be done on earth as it is in Heaven."
Matthew 6:10

"But seek first the Kingdom of God and His righteousness and all these things shall be added to you." Matthew 6:33

"...the Kingdom of Heaven suffers violence and the violent take it by force."
Matthew 11:12

"The Kingdom of Heaven is like a mustard seed... which indeed is the least of all the seeds; but when it is grown it is greater than the herbs and becomes a tree... The Kingdom of Heaven is like leaven, which a woman took and hid in three measures of meal till it was all leavened." Matthew 13:31-33

"...I will build My Church and the gates of Hades shall not prevails against it... whatever you bind on earth will be bound in Heaven." Matthew 16:18,19

"...but with God all things are possible." Matthew 19:26

"Sit at My right hand, till I make Your enemies Your footstool."
Matthew 22:44

"All authority has been given to Me in Heaven and on earth. Go therefore and make disciples of all the nations teaching them to observe all things that I commanded you." Matthew 28:18-20

THEONOMY IN THE TEACHING OF CHRIST
"Man shall not live by bread alone, but by every Word that proceeds from the mouth of God." Matthew 4:4

"...Your will be done as it is in Heaven." Matthew 6:10

"Do not think that I came to destroy the Law or the Prophets. I did not come to destroy but to fulfil. For assuredly, I say to you, till Heaven and earth pass away, one jot or one tittle will by no means pass from the Law till all is fulfilled. Whoever therefore breaks one of the least of these commandments and teaches men so, shall be called least in the Kingdom of Heaven; but whoever does and teaches them, he shall be called great in the Kingdom of Heaven." Matthew 5:17-19

"...and the Scripture cannot be broken." John 10:35

"If you love Me, keep My commandments... He who has My commandments and keeps them, it is he who loves Me." John 14:15, 21

"Jesus answered and said to him, 'If anyone love Me, he will keep My Word.'"
John 14:23

APPENDIX 11
THE POWER OF PRINTING

The invention of the printing press played a key role in mobilising the Reformation. Without printing, it is questionable whether there would have been a Protestant Reformation. A century earlier, Wycliffe and Hus had inspired dedicated movements for Bible study and Reform. But the absence of adequate printing technology severely limited the distribution of their writings. As a result, their ideas did not spread as rapidly, or as far, as printing enabled Luther's writings to flourish.

Luther translated the Bible into German. The New Testament was on sale for a week's wages by 1522 and the Old Testament by 1534.

By the end of his life, Martin Luther had written over 60,000 pages of published works. Yet he said that he would rather *"all my books would disappear and the Holy Scriptures alone be read!"*

Martin Luther recognised the power of printing to mobilise grassroots support for Reformation. Luther wrote prolifically – more than 400 titles, including commentaries, sermons and pamphlets that attacked Catholic superstitions and abuses and which promoted Biblical doctrines. In the first three critical years after Luther posted *The 95 Theses* in Wittenberg, from 1517 to 1520, Luther published 30 pamphlets and flooded Germany with 400,000 copies. By 1523, more than half of all the printed works in Germany were Luther's works.

Luther understood that books and pamphlets speak long after the preacher has left the pulpit. Luther described printing as: *"God's highest and extremist act of grace, whereby the business of the Gospel is driven forward."*

John Foxe, the 16th Century author of the *"Book of Martyrs"* wrote: *"Although through might the pope stopped the mouth of Jan Hus, God has appointed the Press to preach, whose voice the pope is never able to stop..."*

In 1517 there were about 24 printing centres in Europe. Wholesale booksellers had also developed distribution centres and hundreds of itinerant book salesmen crisscrossed the continent to make these publications available.

Luther's writings dominated the market and were far and away the most popular. Martin Luther could be described as a pastor, preacher, teacher,

Theologian, professor, composer and Reformer. But perhaps his greatest achievement was the translation of the Bible into German.

When his New Testament in German was published in September 1522, it created a sensation. Five thousand copies were sold in the first 2 months alone! It was the first time a mass medium had ever impacted everyday life. And it was affordable – even to the poor – for but a week's wages! Almost everyone in Germany either read Luther's translation, or listened to it being read. It formed a linguistic rallying point for the formation of the modern German language. Its impact in restructuring literature, arts and culture was so awesome that King Frederick the Great later called Luther *"the personification of the German national spirit."* Even today, nearly half a millennium later, Luther is still considered *"one of the most influential people who ever lived."*

Luther's Bible translation inspired and guided similar translations of the Bible into local languages in Holland, Sweden, Iceland, Denmark and England. One of the many ways Luther left his mark was the order in which he placed the books of the Bible, to which we adhere to this day. Before Luther, there had been no uniform arrangement. Luther's translations particularly guided William Tyndale in his translation of the Bible into English.

Luther has sometimes been described as the world's first great journalist. Why did his writings succeed in changing history? Firstly, he wrote in the common language, instead of in the scholarly Latin – which was only understood by the educated elite of society. Secondly, Luther mastered the use of broadside pamphlets, which were cheap and easy to read and thirdly, he used some of the finest illustrations and woodcuts of the times to make his message understood even to the semi-literate.

Luther showed the way and other Reformers continued his work of using print technology to mass produce Scriptures and Reformation publications. By God's grace, the Printing Press provided the spiritual weaponry needed to make the Reformation succeed.

"If I profess with the loudest voice and clearest exposition every portion of the truth of God except precisely that point which the world and the devil are at that moment attacking, then I am not confessing Christ, however boldly I may be professing Him. Where the battle rages, there the loyalty of the soldier is proved; and to be steady on all the battlefront besides is mere flight and disgrace if he flinches at that point." Martin Luther

APPENDIX 12

25 STEPS YOU CAN TAKE FOR REFORMATION TODAY

INFORMATION
Renew your mind by reading through the whole Bible.
Read more books on the Reformation.
Obtain biographies on each of the Reformers.
Visit the www.reformationSA.org website and related links.
Invest in more resources for Reformation, including CDs, MP3s and DVDs.
Study the *Greatest Century of Reformation.*
Request the Reformation exam paper to test your knowledge.
Subscribe to the *Christian Action* magazine (PO Box 23632, Claremont, 7735, South Africa).

INTERCESSION
Pray for spiritual Revival and Biblical Reformation.
Practice Martin Luther's Practical Programme to Revive Your Prayer Life (Chapter 20).
Incorporate quotes and examples from *The Greatest Century of Reformation* in your prayer meetings.
Restore your devotional life by praying through the Psalms.

INVOLVEMENT
Join The *Reformation Society* (PO Box 74, Newlands, 7725, Cape Town, South Africa, info@reformationsa.org)
Attend *Reformation Society* meetings, *Reformation Conferences* and *Biblical Worldview Summits.*
Participate in a *Great Commission Course* (www.frontlinemissionsa.org).
Organise Reformation Study Groups at your home, school, workplace or church.
Promote a *Reformation Celebration* in your area.
Distribute Christian Action literature and Reformation Society leaflets.
Set up a book table at your church or organise a library.
Present Reformation films, or PowerPoints, to your church or school.
Teach the *"Greatest Century of Reformation"* to your students, mid-week study group or congregation.

Discuss the examples of the Reformers with your children.
Rekindle the fires of spiritual zeal by studying every book of the Bible and by working for Reformation, applying the Lordship of Christ to all areas of life.

INVESTMENT
Support groups working for Biblical Reformation.
Volunteer your time and talents to a ministry dedicated to Reformation Today.

APPENDIX 13
REFORMATION KEY CONTACTS

AFRICA CHRISTIAN ACTION:
P O Box 23632, Claremont, 7735, Cape Town, South Africa.
Email: info@christianaction.org.za; Web: www.christianaction.org.za

ANSWERS IN GENESIS AND THE CREATION MUSEUM
PO Box 510, Hebron, KY 41048, USA
T: (859) 727-2222 Email: info@answersingenesis.org
Web: www.answersingenesis.org; www.creationmuseum.org

ARK ENCOUNTER
P O Box 510, Hebron, KY 41048, USA
T: (855) 284-3275 Web: www.arkencounter.com

BACK TO THE BIBLE MISSION
P O Box 825, Barbeton, 1300, South Africa
T: +27 (0)13 719 8000
Email: shyriesmulder@gmail.com; Web: www.bbmission.org

BANNER OF TRUTH TRUST
3 Murrayfield Road, Edinburgh, EH12 6EL, Scotland.
Email: banneroftruth@btinternet.com; Web: www.banneroftruth.org

BIBLICAL BLUEPRINTS
Email: info@Biblicalblueprints.org; Web: www.Biblicalblueprints.org

CHALCEDON FOUNDATION
P O Box 158, Vallecito, CA 95251-9989, USA.
Email: chaloffi@goldrush.com; Web: www.chalcedon.edu

CHRISTIAN LIBERTY BOOKS
P O Box 358, Howard Place, 7450, Cape Town, South Africa.
Email: admin@christianlibertybooks.co.za;
Web: www.christianlibertybooks.co.za

COALITION ON REVIVAL
P.O. Box 1139, Murphys, California 95247, USA
Email: admin@churchcouncil.org; Web: www.reformation.net

EUROPEAN INSTITUTE OF PROTESTANT STUDIES
Martyrs Memorial, 256 Ravenhill Road, Belfast,
BT6 8GL, Northern Ireland, United Kingdom.
Email: eips@btopenworld.com; Web: www.ianpaisley.org

FRONTLINE FELLOWSHIP
P O Box 74, Newlands, 7725, Cape Town, South Africa.
Email: admin@frontline.org.za; Web:www.frontlinemissionSA.org

JAMES KENNEDY MINISTRIES
P O Box 11184, Fort Lauderdale,FL 33339, USA
T: (866) 534 1294
Email: letters@djameskennedy.org; Web: www.djameskennedy.org

KWASIZABANTU MISSION
Private Bag 252, KwaSizabantu, 3285, South Africa.
E-mail: reception@ksb.org.za; Web: www.kwasizabantu.com

LIGONIER MINISTRIES
P O Box 547500, Orlando, FL 32854-7500, USA.
Web: www.ligonier.org

LIVINGSTONE FELLOWSHIP
Email: mission@frontline.org.za; Web: www.livingstonefellowship.co.za

LIVING WATERS AFRICA
P O Box 948, Howard Place, 7450, Cape Town, South Africa
Email: admin@livingwatersafrica.co.za; Web: www.livingwatersafrica.co.za

LIVING WATERS PUBLICATIONS
9818 Arkansas Street, Bellflower, CA 90706, USA
Email: email@livingwaters.com; Web: www.livingwaters.com

REFORMATION BIBLE COLLEGE
465 Ligonier Court, Sanford, Florida, 32771, USA
Web: www.ReformationBiblecollege.org

REFORMATION HERITAGE BOOKS
2965 Leonard Street, NE, Grand Rapids, Michigan 49525, USA.
Email: orders@heritagebooks.org; Web: www.reformationheritage.org

REFORMATION SOCIETY
P O Box 74, Newlands, 7725, Cape Town, South Africa.
Email: info@ReformationSA.org; Web: www.ReformationSA.org

WILLIAM CAREY BIBLE INSTITUTE
P O Box 74, Newlands, 7725, Cape Town, South Africa
Email: admin@williamcareybi.com; Web: www.williamcareybi.com

WRETCHED RADIO
Email: idea@wretchedradio.com; Web: www.wretchedradio.com

APPENDIX 14
THE GREATEST CENTURY OF REFORMATION
QUESTIONS FOR DISCUSSION

CHAPTER 1: A CENTURY OF REPRESSION, REVOLT AND REFORMATION
1. Describe the situation in Europe at the beginning of the 16th Century.
2. What external military threats were confronting Europe at the beginning of the 16th Century?
3. What internal threats were affecting the moral and spiritual climate of Europe?
4. What were some positive aspects of the Renaissance?
5. What were some of the negative aspects of the Renaissance?
6. What provoked Martin Luther's protest?
7. On what basis did Martin Luther presume to challenge established church tradition?
8. What steps were taken by the Roman Catholic church to silence Luther?
9. Why did the teachings of Martin Luther become a concern for the Emperor of the Holy Roman Empire?
10. How could Martin Luther defy both the political and ecclesiastical authorities?
11. How did Martin Luther escape being burned at the stake, (as John Hus, who had similarly enjoyed an imperial self-conduct guarantee)?
12. Why did the Protestants object to images in church services?
13. What was Luther's emphasis in dealing with idolatry?
14. How did Martin Luther use his time of seclusion at Wartbury Castle?
15. Who was behind the Peasants Revolt of 1524 – 1525?
16. Why did Emperor Charles V, a devout Catholic, send his army to capture and loot Rome and hold the pope for ransom?
17. Why did the people of the Netherlands suffer such intense persecution?
18. In what way was the Reformation launched in Switzerland?
19. How did the Reformation begin in France?
20. How was Geneva won to the Protestant Faith?
21. How did John Calvin come to be called to Geneva?
22. In what way did King Francis I of France disgrace his cause?
23. What key developments in 1547 accelerated the Reformation in England?

251

24. In what ways did Calvin's ministry in Geneva develop international influence?
25. What developments in 1553 undermined the work of the Reformation in England?
26. What developments in 1558 reversed the Catholic cause and advanced Protestant Reformation?
27. How was Scotland won for the Reformation?
28. In what ways did Mary Queen of Scots pose a threat to the Reformation?
29. What methods were used to crush the Protestant Reformation in Holland?
30. Outline the role of William Prince of Orange in the Reformation in the Netherlands.
31. What was the significance of the Battle of Lepanto, 7 October 1571?
32. What were the consequences of the St. Bartholomew's Day Massacre, 24 August 1572?
33. Why was the defeat of the Spanish Armada in 1588 so significant?
34. How did freedom of religion come to be granted in France, in 1598?

CHAPTER 2: PREPARATION FOR REFORMATION

1. Outline some of the influential developments which preceded the Reformation.
2. What invention made possible the rapid dissemination of Reformation doctrines?
3. Which book was placed on The Index of Forbidden Books by the Council of Valencia in 1229?
4. Who were the Waldensians and what did they stand for?
5. Who was John Wycliffe?
6. Mention some of the achievements of John Wycliffe.
7. How did John Wycliffe survive his clashes and controversies with the church leadership of the time?
8. Mention some of the teachings of John Wycliffe.
9. Who were the Lollards and what is their significance to the Reformation?
10. What reasons were given by the church for banning the Bible in English?
11. How did Wycliffe's writings come to Bohemia?
12. Who was John Hus?
13. What were some of the achievements of John Hus?
14. In what ways did the Roman church seek to silence John Hus?
15. For what purpose was the Council convened at Constance, in 1414?
16. What defense was Hus allowed at Constance?

Questions for Discussioin

17. How did Hus die?
18. What was Hus's motto?
19. Mention some of the achievements of Hus's followers.
20. Who was Savanarola and what did he stand for?

CHAPTER 3: MARTIN LUTHER – CAPTIVE TO THE WORD OF GOD
1. Outline the social background of Martin Luther.
2. What education did Martin Luther receive?
3. How did Luther become a monk?
4. What kind of monk was Luther?
5. How did Luther come to be a professor at Wittenberg University?
6. What books of the Bible did Luther lecture on, between 1513-1517?
7. What was the great turning point in Martin Luther's life?
8. In what ways did Luther's visit to Rome affect him?
9. What was the central emphasis of the medieval Roman Catholic church?
10. Explain the Catholic understanding of indulgences.
11. Explain the Catholic doctrine of Purgatory.
12. Explain the Catholic doctrine of Works of Supererogation.
13. Explain the significance of Johann Tetzel.
14. What was the central message of The 95 Theses?
15. What was the response of the church to Luther's protest?
16. In what ways did the Roman Catholic church seek to silence Luther?
17. What was the significance of the Leipzig debate?
18. What was Luther's response to the Papal Bull excommunicating him?
19. Why was Luther summoned before the Emperor and the Princes of Germany?
20. Explain the significance of Luther's "Address to the German Nobility" (August 1520).
21. Outline the central message of Luther's "The Babylonian Captivity of the Church" (October 1520).
22. Outline the central message of Luther's "The Liberty of a Christian Man" (November 1520).
23. What opportunity was Luther granted to defend or debate his teachings at the Diet?
24. When Luther was commanded to recant and retract his writings, on 18 April 1521, what was his response?
25. What is the significance of Luther's stand before Emperor Charles V at Worms?
26. Who protected Luther from the wrath of the Emperor?
27. What did Luther accomplish at Wartberg Castle?

28. The Bondage of the Will was one of Luther's most important books. What is its central message?
29. In response to which important Humanist scholar did Luther write The Bondage of the Will?
30. In what ways did Luther change the church?
31. Name the four basic principles of the Reformation.
32. What were the five battle cries of the Reformation?
33. What were some of the main accomplishments of Martin Luther?

Chapter 4: Ulrich Zwingli – The Reformer of Zürich
1. Who was Ulrich Zwingli?
2. Where did Zwingli study?
3. What led Zwingli to oppose the war economy of mercenary service?
4. In what ways did Erasmus's Greek New Testament influence Zwingli?
5. When Zwingli was appointed pastor at Grossmünster, in Zürich, what bold action did he take that launched the Reformation in Switzerland?
6. What did Zwingli do when Zürich was hit by the plague?
7. Outline some of the aspects of the Revival in Zürich.
8. What was the response of the City Council to Zwingli's teachings?
9. Who was Diethelm Roist and what was his significance to the Reformation in Zürich?
10. What steps were taken to Reform Zürich?
11. What did Zwingli do to reach the surrounding villages with the Gospel?
12. What were the issues at stake at the Marburg Colloquy?
13. Discuss the points of agreement between Martin Luther and Ulrich Zwingli.
14. Discuss the points of disagreement between Luther and Zwingli.
15. What lead to the Battle at Kappel?
16. How did Zwingli die?
17. Discuss some of the legacy of Ulrich Zwingli's Reformation.

Chapter 5: William Tyndale and the Battle for the Bible
1. What is the significance of the Martyrs Memorial in Oxford?
2. For what reasons were Hugh Latimer and Nicholas Ridley burned at the stake?
3. For what reason were seven men and women in Coventry burned alive in 1519?
4. Who was William Tyndale?
5. Where did Tyndale study?
6. Where was the Bible first translated from the original languages?

Questions for Discussioin

7. Where were the first Bibles in English printed?
8. What happened to the first printed copies of the English New Testament?
9. Name two of the titles of books that Tyndale wrote.
10. How did Tyndale come to be betrayed and imprisoned?
11. What were the last reported words of William Tyndale?
12. How was this dying prayer answered?
13. Discuss some of the legacy of William Tyndale.

CHAPTER 6 – HEINRICH BULLINGER – CONSOLIDATING THE REFORMATION

1. Who was Heinrich Bullinger?
2. How was Bullinger converted?
3. How did Bullinger come to be the successor of Ulrich Zwingli?
4. Mention some of the books written by Bullinger.
5. What confessions and agreements did Bullinger author?
6. What are some of the achievements of Heinrich Bullinger?

CHAPTER 7 - MARTIN BUCER - THE REFORMER OF STRAßBURG

1. How was Martin Bucer converted to the Protestant Faith?
2. Which city did Bucer dedicate most of his life to Reforming?
3. Which reformers did Bucer try to reconcile?
4. Which Reformer, when he was exiled, did Bucer welcome and mentor?
5. When he, himself, was exiled, where did Martin Bucer go?
6. Mention some of the achievements of Martin Bucer.

CHAPTER 8: THOMAS CRANMER AND THE ENGLISH REFORMATION

1. Who was Thomas Cranmer?
2. Where did Cranmer study?
3. How did Thomas Cranmer come to be appointed Archbishop of Canterbury?
4. What incidents point to the courage of Cranmer?
5. What event enabled Cranmer to openly advance the Protestant cause?
6. What book did Cranmer write to assist preachers in discipling their congregations?
7. What book did Cranmer write to reform worship in the Church of England?
8. What articles did Cranmer produce to reform the doctrine of the Church of England?
9. What event in 1553 led to the arrest and imprisonment of Thomas Cranmer?

10. What is the significance of the final speech of Thomas Cranmer?
11. What is the legacy of Cranmer's life and work?

Chapter 9 – The Politicians Behind the English Reformation
1. In what ways had King Henry VIII demonstrated his loyalty to Catholicism and the pope?
2. Why was Henry determined to have a male heir to the throne?
3. What role did Thomas Cromwell play in advancing the Reformation in England?
4. In what ways did King Edward VI advance the Reformation?
5. What practical changes could be seen in church buildings and services during the reign of King Edward VI?
6. What developments reversed the progress of the Reformation in 1553?
7. What developments and individuals worked against the Protestant Reformation?
8. What elements were involved in the Catholic Counter Reformation?
9. Discuss the role of the inquisition in opposing the advance of Protestant ideas.
10. What role was played by the Jesuits?
11. Outline some of the sacrifices and sufferings of the Protestants in Holland.
12. How did the Protestants in Europe survive the concerted campaigns to crush them?

Chapter 10 - Anne Askew - A Daughter of the Reformation
1. Who was Anne Askew and why was she put on trial?
2. How did Anne respond to accusations of immorality?
3. How did Anne reply to charges of heresy?
4. How did Anne explain her opposition to transubstantiation?

Chapter 11 – Bloody Mary and the Martyrs of the English Reformation
1. Which prominent Bible translator and Reformer was the first to be martyred under Bloody Mary?
2. What was the relationship of Queen Mary to the king of Spain and the emperor of the Holy Roman Empire?
3. What was Mary's relationship to Lady Jane Grey?
4. What steps were taken by Mary to return England to Catholicism?
5. Name some of the prominent victims of Bloody Mary's campaign to crush the Protestant Faith in England.

Questions for Discussioin

6. Why did Queen Mary send English troop and cavalry to the Netherlands?
7. In what ways did Mary's campaign to crush the Reformation in England fail?

Chapter 12 - Philipp Melanchthon - The Teacher of Germany
1. Who was Philipp Melanchthon?
2. What emphasis in Melanchthon's first lecture so impressed Martin Luther?
3. What were some of the accomplishments of Philipp Melanchthon?

Chapter 13: Guillaume Farel – Fiery Debater and Evangelist
1. Who was Guillaume Farel?
2. What was the ministry of Farel?
3. Mention some of the achievements of Farel.
4. How did Farel come to win Geneva to the Reformation?
5. What was Farel's role in the call of Calvin to Geneva?
6. What was Farel's relationship with Calvin?

Chapter 14: John Calvin – A Heart Aflame and a Mind Renewed
1. Who was John Calvin?
2. Name some of the prominent leaders in history who have described themselves as Calvinists.
3. What is the significance of the Reformation teachings of John Calvin?
4. What countries were particularly influenced by Calvin's teachings?
5. Where did Calvin study?
6. How was Calvin converted?
7. What is the significance of The Institutes of the Christian Religion?
8. What were the six chapters of the first edition of The Institutes?
9. Mention some of the afflictions and problems which Calvin had to cope with?
10. Outline some of the achievements of John Calvin.
11. Explain the significance of predestination in Calvin's teaching.
12. Outline Calvin's position on law and grace.
13. What was the central focus of Calvin's teaching?
14. What was Calvin's motto?
15. Mention some of the achievements of John Calvin in evangelism and missions.

Chapter 15: John Knox and the Reformation in Scotland

1. How did the Reformation teachings come to Scotland?
2. Who was Patrick Hamilton and what was his significance to the Reformation in Scotland?
3. Who was George Wishart and in what way did he advance the cause of the Reformation in Scotland?
4. What was Knox's relationship to Wishart?
5. How was Knox called to the ministry?
6. How did Knox come to be a galley slave in France?
7. What was Knox's response when he was expected to kiss a statue of the Virgin Mary?
8. How did Knox come to be released from slavery in France?
9. How did Knox come to serve in the court of King Edward VI?
10. What did Knox think of Calvin's Geneva?
11. How did Knox come to write The Book of Common Order?
12. Who were The Lords of The Congregation?
13. Discuss Knox's thinking on resistance to tyranny.
14. What did Knox reach about the Catholic mass?
15. What did Knox teach about the responsibility of civil rulers?
16. What is the significance of The Scots Confession?
17. How did Mary Queen of Scots pose a threat to the Reformation?
18. How did Knox deal with Mary Queen of Scots?
19. Discuss some of the achievements of John Knox.

Chapter 16 – Pierre Viret - French Evangelist and Reformer

1. Who was Pierre Viret?
2. How did Viret come to be involved in the work of Reformation?
3. Why were numerous attempts made to kill Viret?
4. What role did Viret have in the winning of Geneva over to the Reformation?
5. In which Swiss city did Viret found an academy?
6. Why did Viret have to return to Geneva?
7. What led Viret to France?
8. Mention some of the accomplishments of Viret in France.
9. What were some of the afflictions and tragedies suffered by Viret?

Chapter 17 - Albrecht Dürer - Evangelist & Reformer in Art

1. How did Albrecht Dürer describe Reformer Martin Luther?
2. How did Dürer explain the motivation of a Christian artist?
3. What are some of the subjects of Dürer's art?

Questions for Discussioin

CHAPTER 18 – HOW THE REFORMATION CHANGED THE CHURCH
1. Describe the situation in the churches of Europe before the time of the Reformation.
2. Give some examples of the type of superstitions that the Reformation delivered the Church from.
3. What was some of the greatest achievements of the Reformation?
4. In what way did the Reformation change the personal devotional lives of believers?
5. In what way did the Reformation change church services?
6. In what ways did the Reformation change the popular understanding of the role of a minister?
7. In what way did the Reformation change the prevalent understanding of holiness?
8. Name some of the benefits we enjoy today which were won for us by the Reformation.

CHAPTER 19 – HOW THE REFORMATION CHANGED THE WORLD
1. In what ways did the Reformation change the concept of marriage and the family?
2. What did Martin Luther teach about marriage?
3. What did Martin Luther teach about women?
4. What did Martin Luther teach about children?
5. Under what circumstances did the Reformers commit divorce and re-marriage?
6. What means did Luther use to disciple his children?
7. In what ways did Luther reform worship?
8. What did Luther teach about music?
9. What famous hymn was authored by Martin Luther?
10. In what ways did the Reformation impact upon science?
11. Name some prominent Protestant scientists.
12. Mention some of the branches of science developed by Bible believing Christians.
13. What are some of the practical benefits that we enjoy today as a result of the Reformation?
14. What was the attitude of the Reformers to education?
15. What were some of the educational innovations and accomplishments of the Reformers?
16. Name some ways in which the Reformation impacted economies.
17. Outline some of the Reformation principles that have impacted on everyday life.

Chapter 20 – Luther's Practical Programme to Revive Your Prayer Life

1. In what words did Luther describe prayer?
2. What was Luther's attitude to prayer?
3. Why did Luther need to reform prayer?
4. What were the prevalent practices and concepts of prayer in the early 16th Century?
5. What tools did Luther recommend to structure and guide our prayer?
6. How did Luther recommend that we could revive our prayer lives?
7. What times did Luther recommend for personal devotions?
8. What spiritual disciplines did Luther recommend?

Schlosskirche, Wittenberg, Germany.

APPENDIX 15
MAP OF THE REFORMATION

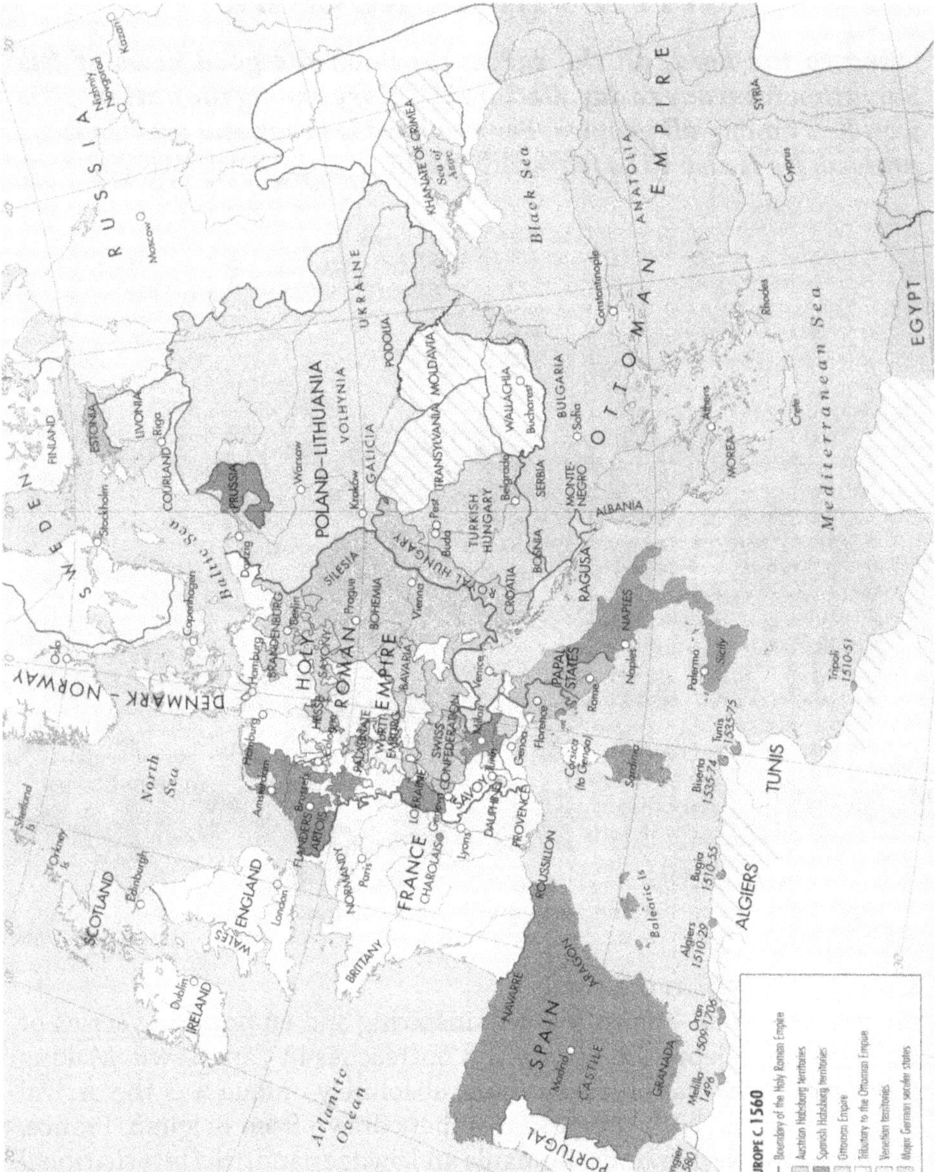

APPENDIX 16
REFORMATION CELEBRATIONS WITH THE EUROCHOR

"Sing to the Lord, all the earth; proclaim the good news of His Salvation from day to day. Declare His glory among the nations, His wonders among all peoples. For the Lord is great and greatly to be praised; He is also to be feared above all..." 1 Chronicles 16:23-25

Rev. Erlo Stegen and the Eurochor at the Waterfront Outreach in Cape Town.

EUROCHOR IN CAPE TOWN
We praise God for a most blessed, inspiring and empowering series of Reformation celebration events and outreaches in Cape Town. Making this year's Reformation celebrations absolutely unique was the arrival of the Eurochor. With over 140 members drawn from Belgium, France, Germany, the Netherlands, Romania and Switzerland, this International Christian Youth Choir has thrilled audiences throughout the world with their multilingual, varied, colourful and captivating concerts.

GUIDANCE AND PLANNING
It was at the Youth Conference at KwaSizabantu Mission, July this year that I learned of the possibility of the Eurochor visiting Cape Town. I immediately issued an invitation and our Mission moved into high gear in seeking out suitable venues. As we prayed for wisdom and guidance, it became immediately clear that the ideal venue for an open-air outreach at a public venue would be the Amphitheatre at the Victoria and Alfred Waterfront, preferably for a Saturday afternoon performance. There was no question that the ideal venue for Reformation Sunday service would be the Strand Street Lutheran church, not only is this the oldest Lutheran church in the Southern hemisphere, but it is also the oldest Protestant house of worship still in operation in Southern Africa. Archival records date back to the 1740s and the present building was constructed in 1771 and officially opened 1780.

ANSWERS TO PRAYER
By God's grace, both of these venues were confirmed with the V & A Waterfront Management willing to make the Amphitheatre available, free of charge, for such a unique International and cultural celebration. The Pastor of the Evangelical Lutheran Church in Strand Street was delighted to hear of the possibility of hosting the Eurochor as an integral part of their 499th Reformation Sunday celebration service. For Reformation Day, Monday, 31 October, we knew that the best venue would have to be the Huguenot Monument, where we have conducted Reformation Day celebration services for two decades and the Dutch Reformed Church in Franschhoek was also willing to have us use their beautiful wood-panelled church for the Eurochor concert on Reformation Day afternoon.

So, by God's grace, not only was the Eurochor available during the last days of October for Reformation celebration events and outreaches in Cape Town, but the ideal venues were also available and open for our programme.

BRILLIANT SUNSHINE, PERFECT WEATHER FOR OUTDOOR EVENTS
We had to pray for good weather as open-air outreaches can be somewhat dampened by rain, which in Cape Town is always possible. However we could not have prayed for better weather. The choir performed in brilliant sunshine at the open-air Amphitheatre at the Waterfront, with seagulls flying overhead. In fact, with the Eurochor coming as they did from Autumn in Europe to Spring in Africa, one of our concerns was the sensitive skins of so many of the choir being afflicted with sunburn, after being hours in the open.

LOGISTICAL CHALLENGES

The logistics of transporting, housing and catering for such a large choir was a challenge, which KwaSizabantu Mission, aQuellé and Frontline worked together to overcome. We praise God for each and every one who had a hand in making this Mission to South Africa and outreaches and ministry in Cape Town such a magnificent and successful time.

A CLASH OF CULTURES

The Word of God declares: *"Wisdom calls aloud outside, she raises her voice in the open squares. She cries out in the chief concourses, at the openings of the gates in the city she speaks her words."* Proverbs 1:20-21. The Waterfront in Cape Town must be one of the busiest thoroughfares and most popular tourist destination in the country. The stands were filling up even as the choir was setting up their equipment and preparing for the performance. Shortly before the 3pm scheduled beginning of the performance, there were the sounds of drums and a Halloween march went past. Several of our Mission workers offered some **Living Waters Africa** Halloween tracts to the participants. Some interesting conversations resulted.

SPIRITUAL WARFARE

We were only a few minutes into the inspiring presentations of the choir and orchestra when Waterfront Management informed us that there had been a complaint about open-air preaching and they would have to close down our performance. Rev. Erlo Stegen has said: *"Where the Spirit*

"Amazing Grace How sweet the sound that saved a wretch like me."

of God is at work then we must expect the spirit of evil to fight back." First Tershia and then I interceded and sought to persuade the Management that the complaint they had received was not justified. Listening to the enthusiastic applause and warm reception, which the Eurochor was receiving from the crowds overflowing the stands and supporting their presentations even from the upper level balconies, it was obvious that most of the shoppers and tourists were very appreciative and supportive. Few of the participants would have been aware of the spiritual warfare going on in the background at this unique event.

Amazing Grace

The choir sang: *"His Name is Wonderful, Let us Praise God Together, Speak to my Soul, O it is Wonderful to be Christian, Make me a Channel of Your Peace, Take my Life and Let it be Consecrated Lord to Thee,* and *I Will Serve Thee."* When the choir began singing *"Amazing Grace, how sweet the sound that saved a wretch like me..."* many in the audience joined in singing.

To the Glory of God Alone

Singing under the intense heat of mid-afternoon sun, we were also well aware of the blessings from Heaven that were accompanying this dynamic public witness to the Glory of God. After the performance, which received a standing ovation from many in the crowds, evangelistic discussions took place. Soon we could see people engrossed in reading Gospel tracts and booklets and engaged in enthusiastic discussions.

REFORMATION SUNDAY IN THE OLDEST LUTHERAN CHURCH IN THE SOUTHERN HEMISPHERE

The Reformation Sunday service at the historic Lutheran church in Cape Town was a never-to-be-forgotten experience. The large Lutheran Church was packed upstairs and downstairs, with over 600 worshippers. The choir began with *Wachet Auf* and *"Surely, surely, He hath born our griefs and carried our sorrows... He was wounded for our transgressions, He was bruised for our iniquities, the chastisement of our peace was upon Him,"* from Handel's *Messiah*.

WHY CELEBRATE THE REFORMATION?

In my address to the congregation, I spoke of 22 years ago, when our Frontline Fellowship Mission team was approaching a remote village in Cuando Cubango province (what the Portuguese referred to as *The Ends of the Earth*) in Angola. The team heard the sound of enthusiastic singing. They immediately recognised the tune, even though they could not understand the words. What they were hearing was: *A Mighty Fortress is our God*, Dr. Martin Luther's great battle hymn of the Reformation, being sung in Ovimbundu. This beloved hymn, based on Psalm 46, is one of the favourite hymns of the persecuted church and one of the most translated hymns in history. A banner was stretched across the road, proclaiming, **31 October 1517**. It was Reformation Day!

CELEBRATING THE 5 SOLAS OF THE REFORMATION

School children had posters and projects with hand drawings of Reformers, Dr. Martin Luther, Ulrich Zwingli, Willian Tyndale and John Calvin. The great battle cries of the Reformation were boldly displayed: *Sola Scriptura! Sola Gratia! Sola Fide! Solus Christus! Soli Deo Gloria*. Christ alone is the Head of the Church. Scripture alone is our authority. Salvation is by the grace of God alone. Justification is received by Faith alone. Everything is to be done for the glory of God alone.

THIS IS THE GREATEST GIFT

These Ovimbundu believers had suffered so much. Their church buildings have been destroyed by communists. They effectively have no Bibles. What was left of the few Bibles and hymn books that they had possessed were now in tatters. When they received Scriptures, they declared: *"This is the greatest Gift anyone could ever ask for! The Word of God in our own language!"*

REBUKED AND INSPIRED

We were inspired and rebuked by the steadfast devotion of these Ovimbundu believers. Here they were, at what had been described as the ends of the earth, and they were celebrating Reformation Day. Since then, we have resolved to celebrate 31 October as the birthday of all Protestant, Evangelical, Bible-believing churches.

SEEKING FIRST THE KINGDOM OF GOD

It was Dr. Martin Luther's earnest quest for peace with God and his intense study of the Scriptures, which led him to challenge the unethical fundraising tactics, superstitions and unbiblical practises of the papacy. This launched the Protestant Reformation. The Lord Jesus Christ taught: *"But seek first the Kingdom of God and His righteousness and all these things shall be added unto you."* Matthew 6:33

THE TRUTH SETS US FREE

It was Martin Luther's love for the Word of God and his dedication to truth that led him to challenge the entire ecclesiastical and political authority of the Roman Catholic papacy and the Holy Roman Empire.

Repentance Not Indulgences

On 31 October 1517, Dr. Martin Luther nailed his **95 Theses** onto the door of the Castle Church in Wittenberg. The 95 Theses begins with repentance: *"Since our Lord and Master, Jesus Christ says: "Repent for the Kingdom of Heaven is near," He wants the whole life of a believer to be a life of Repentance."* Professor Luther maintained that no sacrament can take away our responsibility to respond to Christ's command to true repentance, evidenced by outward change, a transformation and renewal of our entire life. Luther emphasised that it is God alone who can forgive sins and indulgences are a fraud.

Here I Stand

Summoned before the Emperor, Martin Luther declared: *"Unless I am convinced by Scripture, or by clear reasoning, that I am in error - for popes and councils have often erred and contradicted themselves - I cannot recant, for I am subject to the Scriptures I have quoted;* **my conscience is captive to the Word of God**. *It is unsafe and dangerous to do anything against ones conscience.* **Here I stand**, *I cannot do otherwise. So help me God. Amen."*

God is our Ultimate Authority

In this courageous stand Martin Luther argued for freedom of conscience, based upon the authority of Scripture. From these foundational principles flowed constitutional authority. The principle is *Lex Rex* (the Law is King!). No one is above God's Law. Jesus Christ is the King of kings and the Lord of lords. Everyone is under God's Law. *Sola Scriptura* eroded the foundations of political and ecclesiastical totalitarianism.

Foundations for Freedom

The Protestant emphasis on the priesthood of all believers and the supreme authority of Scripture led to the concept of representative governments and constitutional authority as the supreme law of the land. By emphasising the Biblical doctrine of Faith as a gift of God, Dr. Luther undermined the Catholic Inquisition and provided Theological foundations for religious liberty and freedom of conscience. The social and political implications of all this was enormous. The priesthood of all believers and the doctrine of *Sola Scriptura* led to constitutionalism, the concept of representative governments, religious liberty, freedom of conscience, freedom of speech, freedom of the press, freedom of association, checks and balances and all the other out-workings of political and social freedom.

BACK TO THE BIBLE FOR REFORMATION AND REVIVAL

There is no doubt that the Back to the Bible Reformation movement in Europe during the 16th century was one of the most important epochs in history. Today we need a new Back to the Bible Reformation and we need to seek God and earnestly pray for a new Heaven sent Holy Spirit empowered Revival.

REFORMATION CELEBRATION IN FRANSCHHOEK

On Reformation Day, Monday, 31 October, we gathered for a noon day Reformation celebration service at the Huguenot Monument in scenic Franschhoek. Surrounded by spectacular scenery with mountains, vineyards and forests, the Eurochor led us in singing *A Mighty Fortress is our God*. Visitors travelled from as far away as Villiersdorp, Oudtshoorn, Knysna, Alexandria, Port Elizabeth and KwaZulu/Natal to participate in these special Reformation Day events. In the afternoon the Eurochor treated us to a concert in the beautiful, wood-panelled Dutch Reformed Church which had been a site of Revival in the days of Andrew Murray. The galleries and side-wings testify to the tremendous expansion of the original rectangular church that occurred as a result of that Heaven-sent Revival. That was the prayer of our hearts: *"Will You not Revive us again, that Your people may rejoice in You?"* Psalm 85:6

LIVE IN THE LIGHT OF ETERNITY

Here at one of the most historically significant times and places, under brilliant sunshine, at a most spectacular and scenic venue, this International Christian Youth Choir lifted our hearts, souls and minds heavenward as their Scripture songs overflowed our hearts and minds and caused us to focus on what really matters in the light of eternity. Many of their songs became our prayers: *"Take my life and let it be consecrated Lord to Thee, Make me a Channel of Your Peace, I will serve Thee because I love Thee. You have given life to me, I was nothing before You found me, You have given life to me, heartaches, broken pieces, ruined lives are why You died on Calvary. Your touch was what I longed for, You have given life to me."*

WORSHIP IN SPIRIT AND IN TRUTH

"Speak to my soul, dear Jesus, speak now in tenderous tone, whisper in loving kindness, Thou art not left alone. Open my heart to hear Thee, quickly to hear Thou Voice, fill Thou my soul with praises, let me in Thee rejoice." *"Life has purpose now it never had before. There is meaning to each day and even more; for a joy and peace I cannot explain is mine, since I found new life in Christ My Lord Divine. O it is Wonderful to be a Christian; I it is Wonderful to have sins forgiven; O it is wonderful to be redeemed, justified forever, reconciled!"*

LEARNING FROM HISTORY

The Museum could barely accommodate the crowds who came to have a guided tour through the Huguenot Museum. I led a guided tour before the Reformation Day service and one afterwards, just before the afternoon concert.

TO MOVE THE WORLD

At the beginning of the Eurochor Concert in the Dutch Reformed Church, I mentioned the Greek Engineer Archimedes who, referring to the wonders of the lever, declared: *"If I had a place to stand, I could move the world."* In principle, the capacity of a lever is unlimited. An ordinary weakling can move a rock the size of a house. All that he would need would be a fulcrum, a pole strong enough that it would not break and long enough to multiply the force. That and a place to stand. The force multiplying physics of the lever are a function of distance. The heavier the object, or the weaker the person trying to move it, the longer the pole would need to be and the further away from it you would need to stand. However, with the right fulcrum, the right bar and the right distance, all you would need to do would be to push the lever down and the boulder, no matter how heavy it was, would move. So, theoretically, Archimedes famously declared: *"With the right fulcrum, bar and distance, you could put a lever to planet earth and move the world itself, as long as you had a place to stand."*

MARTIN LUTHER CHANGED THE WORLD

Professor Martin Luther moved the world. He changed history because he had a place to stand. Dr. Martin Luther declared: **"My conscience is captive to the Word of God. Here I stand!"** Our Lord Jesus Christ declared that our Faith would be able to move mountains (Matthew 17:20). Martin Luther's Faith moved the world - because he had a place to stand. He stood on the Word of God. The fulcrum he used was the Gospel. This was balanced on the bar of the Law of God. Dr. Martin Luther actually fulfilled what the Greek Engineer, Archimedes, had hypothesised about. Standing on the Word of God, using the bar of the Law of God and the fulcrum of the Gospel, Martin Luther's Faith not only moved mountains, it changed the world. It brought an end to the Middle Ages and ushered in the modern world. The Protestant Reformation and the resultant scientific revolution and industrial revolution produced the most productive, prosperous and free nations in the history of the world. All because Luther had a place to stand and he made his stand on the unchangeable Word of Almighty God.

"Make me a channel of Your peace."

COMMISSIONING SERVICE

One of the many significant events of our Reformation Day celebration service at Franschhoek was setting aside and commissioning the first of our **Africa Reformation Overland Mission** teams who will travel across 14 nations in Southern, Central and East Africa, conducting Soul Winning Seminars, Discipleship Seminars, Evangelism Workshops, Reformation Conferences and establishing Revival Prayer Groups, Bible Studies, Reformation Societies and Christian Action groups that will initiate Back to the Bible movements throughout their countries. *"Do not confirm any longer to the patterns of this world, but be transformed by the renewing of your mind…"* Romans 12:2

CONFRONTING COWARDICE

The sermon at the Reformation celebration service was on **Conviction and Courage.** Dr. Martin Luther's actions were like that of Elijah - confronting the false prophets on Mount Carmel. It was a defining moment when conviction and courage confronted corruption and cowardice. *"And Elijah came to all the people and said, 'How long will you falter between two opinions? If the Lord is God follow Him, but if Baal is god, follow him.' But the people answered him not a word."* 1 Kings 18:21. Sometimes silence is golden. Other times it is just plain yellow.

The Greatest Century of Reformation

"Take my life and let it be consecrated Lord to Thee ..."

WITHOUT A VISION A PEOPLE PERISH

The Reformation was inspired by great vision. Without a vision a people perish. What is your vision? What are you living for? Reformers, like Dr. Martin Luther, were living for a vision far bigger than themselves, far bigger than their times and nations. Their vision continues to impact and bless the world, hundreds of years after their life on earth. The Word of God declares: *"Who will rise up for Me against the evildoers? Who will stand up for Me against the workers of iniquity?"* Psalm 94:16

CAN YOU NOT DO SOMETHING MORE FOR GOD?

The Lord is looking for a man who can stand in the gap and build up the wall on behalf of the land. Are you standing in the gap and interceding on behalf of the land? Are you helping to rebuild the wall? Are you impacting your world for Christ? What does God want you to do?

STAND UP, STEP OUT AND SPEAK UP

When the time comes for you to stand up, **stand up boldly**. When the time comes for you to step out, **step out in Faith**. When the time comes when you must speak up, **speak courageously** and with Christian conviction the truths of the Holy Scriptures. *"Chose for yourselves this day Whom you will serve… but as for me and my house, we will serve the Lord."* Joshua 24:15

LIVESTREAMING AND DVDs

The Frontline Fellowship tech team experimented with our first live streaming of events during this special series of outreaches and services. They have edited DVDs on the various Eurochor performances and outreaches. These DVDs are now available in the *Eurochor in Cape Town* DVD. For more information on the Eurochor, visit www.eurochor.com.

FIELD WORKERS FOR REFORMATION

For more details of the Africa Reformation Overland Missions, we have videos, PowerPoints and audios available on the www.frontlinemissionsa.org website.

RESOURCES FOR REFORMATION

The **95 Theses for Reformation Today** in English, German, French, Dutch and Afrikaans can be downloaded from the www.ReformationSA.org website.

LET THE EARTH HEAR HIS VOICE

As we celebrate the 500th anniversary of the Reformation and seek to educate and evangelise, equip and empower our families, congregations, communities, countries to return back to the Bible, contact us for resources for Reformation and get involved in the Christian Action Network so that we can co-operate together to let the earth hear His voice. *"All the ends of the world shall remember and turn to the Lord, and all the families of the nations shall worship before You. For the Kingdom is the Lord's, and He rules over the nations."* Psalm 22:27-28

Thank you for all your prayers, encouragement and support.
May God continue to be your joy and strength.
Yours for the fulfilment of the Great Commission

Dr. Peter Hammond

"A mighty Fortress is our God ..."

BIBLIOGRAPHY

Bainton, Roland	*Here I Stand: A Life of Martin Luther,* Abingdon, 1950
Boetner, Loraine	*Roman Catholicism,* Banner of Truth, London, 1966.
Brecht, Martin	*Martin Luther: The Preservation of the Church.*
Brown, Ian	*The pope,* Londonderry, 1991.
Calvin, John	*Institutes of the Christian Religion,* Westminster Press
d'Aubigne, J.H. Murle	*The Reformation in England,* Banner of Truth, Edinburgh, 1963
DeKoster, Lester	*Light For the City - Calvin's Preaching, Source of Life and Liberty,* Eerdmans, Grand Rapids, 2004
De Rosa, Father Peter	*Vicars of Christ – the Dark Side of the papacy,* Corgi, Books, London, 1989.
Dickens, A.G	*Reformation and Society in 16th Century Europe,* Thames and Hudson, London, 1966
Edwards, Mark	*Luther and the False Brethren,* Stanford.
Edwards, Mark	*Luther's Last Battles: Politics and Polemics, (1531 – 1546),* Cornwell.
Foxe, John	*The Book of Martyrs,* 1563
Fountain, David	*John Wycliffe, The Dawn of the Reformation,* Mayflower Christian Books, South Hampton, 1984
Gabler, Ulrich	*Huldrych Zwingli – His Life and Work,* T & T Clark, Edinburgh, 1986
Gray, Janet Glenn	*The French Hugenots - Anatomy of Courage*
Haile, H.G.	*Luther: An Experience in Biography,* Princeton.
Harkness, Georgia	*John Calvin, The Man and His Ethics,* Abingdon Press, New York, 1931
Houghton, S.M.	*Sketches From Church History,* Banner of Truth, 1980
Kerry, Douglas	*The Emergence of Liberty in the Modern World,* Presbyterian and Reformed, 1992

Knox, John	*The Reformation in Scotland,* Banner of Truth, Edinburgh, 1982
Kuiper, B.K.	*The Church in History,* Eerdmans, 1964
Lewis, Brenda Ralph	*A Dark History of the Popes,* Amber Books, 2009
Lindsay, Thomas	*A History of the Reformation,* T & T Clark, Edinburgh, 1906
Luther, Martin	*The Bondage of the Will,* Baker, Grand Rapids, 1957
Morrison, J.A	*Martin Luther: The Great Reformer,* Christian Liberty Press.
Ryle, J.C.	*Five English Reformers,* Banner of Truth, 1960
Scott, Otto	*The Great Christian Revolution,* The Reformer Library, Windsor, 1995
Sheats, R.A.	*Pierre Viret - The Angel of the Reformation,* Zürich Publishing, 2012
Stevenson, William	*The Story of the Reformation,* John Knox Press, Richmond, 1959
Stream, Carol	*Christian History,* 465 Gunderson Drive, IL 60188, USA
Van Halsema, Thea B.	*This Was John Calvin,* Baker, 1959
Van Loewenich, Walther	*Martin Luther: The Man and His Work,* Augsburg, 1986
Wilson, Douglas	*For Kirk and Covenant - The Stalwart Courage of John Knox,* Highland Books, Nashville, 2000
Woodbridge, John	*Great Leaders of the Christian Church,* Moody, Chicago, 1988. Updated:

OTHER RESOURCES AVAILABLE

Books
Answering Skeptics ** (Also available in Afrikaans)
Biblical Faith and Modern Counterfeits **
Biblical Principles for Africa (Also available in Afrikaans and French) **
Biblical Worldview Manual
Chaplains' Handbook
Character Assassins - Dealing with Ecclesiastical Tyrants & Terrorists **
Church History Manual **
Discipleship Handbook **
Discipleship Training Manual
Faith Under Fire in Sudan (in both hard cover and soft cover) *
Going On ... With a Nod from God **
Going Through - Even if the Door is Closed **
Great Commission Manual
Greatest Century of Missions **
Holocaust in Rwanda** (Also available in French)
In the Killing Fields of Mozambique
Make a Difference - A Christian Action Handbook for Southern Africa
Old Testament Survey - Exploring the Central Messages of Every Book of the Bible
Porndemic - How the Pornography Plague Affects You and What You Can Do About It
Practical Discipleship ** (Also available in Afrikaans)
Prison Break
Putting Feet to Your Faith **
Reforming our Families **
Rise of the GayGB and the Pink Inquisition **
Security and Survival Handbook **
Slavery, Terrorism and Islam - The Historical Roots and Contemporary Threat **
The Apostles Creed - Firm Foundations for Your Faith **
The Authority of Christ and the First Day Sabbath **
The Christian at War (also available in Afrikaans, German and Spanish)
The Ten Commandments – God's Perfect Law of Liberty ** (Also available in Afrikaans)
The Wonders of Water
    ** Also available as an E-book

DVDs
Reformation 500
Behind Enemy Lines for Christ (107 min)
Sudan the Hidden Holocaust (55 min)
Terrorism and Persecution - Understanding Islamic Jihad (55 min)
Evangelising in the War Zones (35 min)

AUDIO MP3s
Answering Skeptics
Biblical Worldview Summit
Church History Overview
Great Commission Course audio, data and DVD boxset
Heroes of the Faith
Muslim Evangelism Workshop
Old Testament Survey & New Testament Survey
Reformation 500 Audio, Data and DVD boxset
Revival
South African History

www.christianlibertybooks.co.za

About the Author

Peter Hammond is a missionary who has pioneered evangelistic outreaches in the war zones of Mozambique, Angola and Sudan. Since 1982, often travelling by off-road motorbike, Peter has travelled hundreds of thousands of miles to deliver Bibles to persecuted Christians in Africa and Eastern Europe. He has proclaimed the Gospel in 38 countries on four continents. In the course of his missionary activities Peter has been ambushed, come under aerial and artillery bombardments, been stabbed, shot at, beaten by mobs, arrested and imprisoned. On some mission trips he has flown far behind enemy lines to the beleaguered Nuba Mountains in Central Sudan with tonnes of Bibles, books and relief aid. He has then walked throughout the war devastated Nuba Mountains showing the Jesus film in Arabic, proclaiming the Gospel, training pastors and evading enemy patrols.

Dr. Peter Hammond is the Founder and Director of Frontline Fellowship, the Director of the Christian Action Network and the Chairman of The Reformation Society. He is the author of *Faith Under Fire in Sudan*, *Holocaust in Rwanda*, the *Great Commission Manual*, *Putting Feet to Your Faith*, *In the Killing Fields of Mozambique*, *The Greatest Century of Missions*, *Biblical Principles for Africa*, *The Discipleship Handbook*, *Slavery, Terrorism and Islam*, *The Greatest Century of Reformation*, *The Power of Prayer Handbook*, *Sketches from South African History*, *Victorious Christians Who Changed the World*, *The Chaplains Handbook*, *Practical Discipleship*, *Answering Skeptics*, *Security and Survival Handbook*, *Old Testament Survey* and *New Testament Survey*. He has co-authored or contributed to: *Reforming Our Families*, *Fight for Life*, *Make a Difference*, *The Pink Agenda*, *The Rise of the GayGB and the Pink Inquisition*, *Character Assassins* and *South Africa - Renaissance or Reformation?* He is the Editor of both Frontline Fellowship News and the Christian Action magazine.

Peter was born in Cape Town (in 1960) and brought up in Bulawayo (in what was then war-torn Rhodesia - now Zimbabwe). He was converted to Christ in 1977, worked for Scripture Union and Hospital Christian Fellowship, served in the South African Defence Force and studied at Baptist Theological College (now Baptist Theological Seminary), Cape Town. Peter is married to Lenora (whose missionary parents Rev. Bill and Harriett Bathman, pioneered missionary work, mostly into Eastern Europe, for over 67 years). Peter and Lenora have been blessed with four children: Andrea, Daniela, Christopher and Calvin and three grandchildren.

Christian Liberty Books
Resources for Reformation and Revival
PO Box 358 Howard Place 7450 Pinelands Cape Town South Africa
Tel: 021 689 7478
admin@christianlibertybooks.co.za

www.ChristianLibertyBooks.co.za

EXAMPLES OF EXCELLENCE
TO INSPIRE YOU, YOUR FAMILY & CONGREGATION
TO TRANSFORM NATIONS BY CHANGING LIVES

PRINT ON DEMAND WITH lulu

224 pages
& over 200 pictures,
photographs, maps or charts

E-Book

6 Disc Boxset including:
3 Audio MP3 Discs containing
62 Lectures, Devotions & Radio
Interviews 3 Data DVDs containing
24 Video Powerpoints, 74 Powerpoint
Presentations, 81 Lecture Notes,
31 PDF Books & Manuals,
66 PDF Booklets, 39 PDF Tracts,
19 Audio MP3 Lectures & Radio
Interviews, GCC 2019

The Greatest Century of Missions is a **treasure trove** of incredible adventures, inspiring exploits and unbelievable achievements of some of the most extra-ordinary people in the most momentous era of Christian advance.

This book will be **an invaluable resource** for pastors and missionaries and a textbook for senior home-schoolers, Christian schools and Bible colleges. It should be required reading for prospective missionaries.

"This book is at once the most concise and comprehensive testimonial record of pioneer missionaries." Rev. Bill Bathman

EXPLORE THE CENTRAL MESSAGES OF EVERY BOOK OF THE BIBLE

SOLA SCRIPTURA! was the battle cry of the Reformation. Scripture alone is our ultimate authority. However, while Christians claim to believe the Bible few have read the whole Bible. Surprisingly few pastors can articulate the central message and clear distinctives of each Book of the Bible.
288 pages with 32 pictures

"Holding fast the faithful Word… be able, by sound doctrine, both to exhort and convict those who contradict." Titus 1:9

Old Testament Survey Book and MP3 Combo

42 MP3 Audio Sermons (29 Hours) and a PDF book of the *Old Testament Survey*

Buy BOTH Combo packs receive the *Biblical Preaching Handbook*

FREE

May God be pleased to use this *Biblical Preaching Handbook* to challenge, empower and equip Pastors to go back to the Bible, to study, preach and teach through every Book of the Bible and apply the central messages of every Book of the Bible to our daily lives.
112 pages with 24 pictures

The Bible is the greatest Book ever written. It is the most valuable Book in the world. The Bible is the most inspiring Book in all of history and it is the most important Book ever written. There is no question that the Bible is the most life changing Book ever written. *"…But the Word of our God stands forever."* Isaiah 40:8
304 pages with 14 pictures

New Testament Survey Book and MP3 Combo

31 MP3 audio Sermons (25 hours 38 min) and a PDF book of the *New Testament Survey*
* postage not included

Christian Liberty Books
Resources for Reformation and Revival
admin@christianlibertybooks.co.za
www.ChristianLibertyBooks.co.za

www.ingramcontent.com/pod-product-compliance
Lightning Source LLC
Chambersburg PA
CBHW062047080426
42734CB00012B/2571